MAY 2 2 1978

799.17
Orba~~~~~~
Hu~~~~~~
er~~~~~~

D0687693

001275

OCEANSIDE PUBLIC LIBRARY
615 FOURTH STREET
OCEANSIDE, CALIF. 92054

DEMCO

3 1232 00054 0536

Hunters,
Seamen,
and
Entrepreneurs

799.17
O

Hunters, Seamen, and Entrepreneurs;

THE TUNA SEINERMEN OF SAN DIEGO

MICHAEL K. ORBACH

University of California Press · Berkeley · Los Angeles · London

OCEANSIDE PUBLIC LIBRARY
615 FOURTH STREET
OCEANSIDE, CALIF. 92054

1. Fisheries — San Diego, Calif.
2. San Diego Calif. Industries

I. T
II. Tuna Seinermen of San Diego

University of California Press
Berkeley and Los Angeles, California
University of California Press, Ltd.
London, England

Copyright © 1977 by
The Regents of the University of California

ISBN 0-520-03348-5
Library of Congress Catalog Card Number: 76-48361
Printed in the United States of America
Designed by Wolfgang Lederer

1 2 3 4 5 6 7 8 9

12.95

*To my father,
who gave me my love
for the sea*

Contents

List of Illustrations

Plates

Figures

Acknowledgments

I AM INDEBTED beyond description to the men in the tuna fleet who allowed me to share in their experiences and who took the time to tell me about their lives and their occupation. Their cooperation, confidence, and friendship did as much for me personally as they did to contribute to the writing of this book.

Raoul Anderson, Louis Chiaramonte, and Geoffrey Stiles of the Memorial University in Newfoundland; Peter Fricke of the University of Wales Institute of Science and Technology; and Poul Moustgaard of the University of Copenhagen extended hospitality in their homes and departments, and their comments and conversations concerning my research were of great value.

My greatest debts are to Frederick Bailey, under whose guidance the research was performed and whose several readings and consequent substantive and editorial advice improved the end product immeasurably, and to Orvar Löfgren of the University of Lund, Sweden, whose companionship and academic advice during his stay in our home while the manuscript was being transformed from a dissertation into a book kept the spirit of the seaman-ethnographer alive.

The research was made possible by generous support from the Sea Grant Program, and I would like to thank everyone in the Sea Grant Office at Scripps Institution of Oceanography, especially Jim Sullivan, for their kind and invaluable assistance in allowing me the freedom to pursue my interests and the opportunity to exchange ideas with scholars with whom I normally would not have been able to make contact.

Thanks also to Kathy Clark, who typed the final manuscript, and to our old friend Patty Gollong who lent her superior artistic talents to the drawings and figures.

ix

ACKNOWLEDGMENTS

Although these people and many others contributed in some manner to what follows, I alone am responsible for its contents and shortcomings. I wish on all others the good fortune to have a wife, mother, brother, and grandmother like mine to aid them in bearing their responsibilities.

Introduction

Community and Culture

THIS BOOK IS about the men who sail with the high-seas tuna fleet out of San Diego, California, on the West Coast of the United States. It is about their occupation, their lifestyle, and the communities where they and their families, friends, and associates live and work.

It is also a book about cultural systems in a broad sense of that term. When we find a group of individuals who share a physical space or locality, who interact regularly, who share sentiments, perceptions, and understandings about how the world and the people in it are or ought to be, we are encountering a cultural system. With the tuna fishermen we are in fact dealing with two "systems"—one at sea and one ashore—but the behaviors and understandings of both systems are mutually interdependent. The actions of the men at sea reflect the structures and sentiments of their environments ashore, and their actions ashore reflect the events and situations of their careers as distant-water fishermen.

Before the Powerblock

Fishermen have put to sea from San Diego in search of the highly migratory tuna since the 1920s. In the early years of the fleet, the vessels which used San Diego as a base were small craft, owned and manned by men of Chinese, Japanese, Slavic, Portuguese, and Mexican descent. As San Diego grew and changed, so did the fishing fleet. The vessels grew in size and range and the infrastructure of the industry ashore expanded. The Chinese component of the fleet dropped out of the picture very early, the Japanese were forced out by World War II, and the

1

Slavic group gradually diminished in number. Into their places came more Portuguese and a new influx of Italian fishermen.

The Portuguese came from the Azores, a group of islands in the Atlantic, a thousand miles from the coast of Portugal. Although some migrated directly from the Azores to San Diego on whaling ships or following the Gold Rush of the 1850s, most came by way of Portuguese fishing communities in New England or Portuguese farming communities in Northern California. Many of the Italians came from the island of Sicily, and many of those migrated to San Diego from various fisheries on the East coast of the United States and from declining fisheries in other parts of California, notably those in Monterey and San Pedro.

For the first forty years of its existence the tuna fleet fished with what were known as "baitboats." The fishermen stood in special racks outside the rails of the boat while one of the crew threw out "chum"—small baitfish—to draw the tuna close to the boat. Using a bamboo pole with a short line and a barbless hook with a small jig, the fishermen would jerk the tuna over their shoulders and onto the deck behind them. To land the larger tuna, two or three poles would be attached to the same line. Even today, the tuna are described as one-pole, two-pole, or three-pole in size.

Most of these baitboats were built before World War II and were of wooden construction. The trips were often longer than those today, but the style of the endeavor was different. There was a minimum of machinery aboard the boats, they put into port quite frequently to "make bait"—gather the small fish used to chum the tuna—and the level of investment and financial pressure was less than it is in today's fleet.

During World War II most of the vessels in the tuna fleet were either leased or bought outright by the U.S. government for use by the military. The larger of these vessels were from 100 to 150 feet in length and proved excellent for use on patrol and provisioning missions ancillary to the war effort. Men from the tuna fleet manned, and in many cases died aboard these boats.

The immediate postwar period was difficult for the tuna fleet. The boat owners and their crews, by this time almost exclusively Portuguese, Italian, and Slavic, had long been involved in an on-again-off-again relationship with the canneries and other land-based processing facilities. It was not uncommon for a cannery to hold a part interest in a vessel or to have a purchase and unloading agreement with the owner of a boat, but most of the owners were independent and there was no regular system of price-setting and no standard agreement governing the size, amount, and species of tuna the cannery would accept. Sometimes the cannery would not accept fish which were too large; other times they would not accept fish which were too small; other times they would not accept a certain species of tuna; many times they would offer the fishermen less per ton or pound of fish than the latter were willing to accept. With trips lasting upwards of 100 days, many of these preferences changed while the boat was at sea. The fishermen would return to San Diego to find that their fish were not salable.

Added to this was the pressure from foreign imports of tuna, primarily from Japan. Free market agreements between the United States and Japan in the postwar period, coupled with a huge fishing industry operating with low labor and material costs in Japan, produced an influx of Japanese-caught tuna priced below that supplied by the American fishery. The San Diego fleet was trying to rebuild from the loss of its vessels in the war; the new vessels were made of steel and were more expensive, and the competition from the Japanese fishery was pricing them out of existence.

But the postwar period also provided the seeds of a new fishing industry in San Diego, most importantly through technological innovation. The new steel boats had greater capacities and ranges, enabling the fishermen to cover more ground in their search and take better advantage of their sightings. Improved systems of communication and expanded markets led to the establishment of American Tuna Sales, an organization which serves as a bargaining agent between the fishermen and canneries and processors all over the world. Improved systems of manufacturing and transportation facilitated an international system of custom brokers which provides the fleet with parts and supplies in ports in almost any country, most notably those along the Central and South American coastlines. But most important among these developments were the adaptation of nylon as a synthetic for use in seine-net construction and the invention of a hydraulic device called the Puretic powerblock.

The Seining Era

Although fishermen had experimented with nets as an alternative to the difficult and labor-intensive pole-and-line method during the early 1950s, they had neither the material with which to construct nets of sufficient size and weather resistance nor the physical means to haul the heavy nets back aboard. Nylon gave the nets strength and weather resistance, and the Puretic powerblock, a large rubber roller on the end of a long boom, made it possible to bring the larger nets back aboard. Both of these technological innovations were sufficiently developed by the late fifties, and by the early sixties the majority of the tuna fleet had converted to the seine-net method. This innovation brought the San Diego fleet back to its feet by providing a method efficient enough to produce a product competitive with imported tuna. Since that time they have maintained and improved upon that efficiency so that they have been able to operate in a market, as they have always had to do, which offers no special tariff or other protection for their products and in a social and political situation which, as we shall see, puts them at a considerable disadvantage with respect to foreign fleets and fisheries.

The sixties brought a new set of problems. The profit potential of the seining method brought a great influx of capital and thus a greater number of boats into the industry. Partially in response to the increased number of units in the fishery, and partially because of some evidence of decreased yellowfin tuna stocks, the Inter-American Tropical Tuna Commission was established. This international regulatory body marked off a

4

five-million square-mile area of the best fishing grounds in the Eastern Pacific as its Regulatory Area. Limits were set on the amount of yellowfin which could be taken within the Regulatory Area each year. This forced the fishermen either to fish for the less valuable skipjack tuna within the Regulatory Area or to travel 1,000 miles offshore in search of the more valuable yellowfin for the last nine months of each year.

Pressure also appeared from other quarters. The fishermen used some species of porpoise, a marine mammal held in high esteem by the American public, to lead them to the tuna. In the early years of the seining process, before the system was fully worked out, many of these animals would become entangled in the net and some would drown. Various conservation and environmental groups have lobbied vigorously and often emotionally against the seining process, even though the fishermen and gear specialists from the National Marine Fisheries Service have developed techniques which reduce porpoise mortality to a very low level, one fast approaching zero. These groups, and the public in general, have for the most part not realized that ever since they began using the seines the fishermen have gone to considerable personal, physical, and financial risk to return the porpoise to the open ocean from inside the seines. The tuna fishermen, who are participants in one of the only successfully regulated major fisheries in the world, have continuously over the years produced innovations which have contributed to the preservation of the ocean's resources while at the same time supplying a highly demanded foodstuff; it is ironic that they are seeing their industry threatened by the accusation that they are indifferent or even hostile to the environment and its animal populations.

Industry and Community

When fishermen of Portuguese and Italian descent came to San Diego, they settled in two separate areas of the city. The Italians went to the inland side of the bay, near the downtown area, and opened restaurants and grocery stores which catered to their tastes and provided a shore-side economic base for their

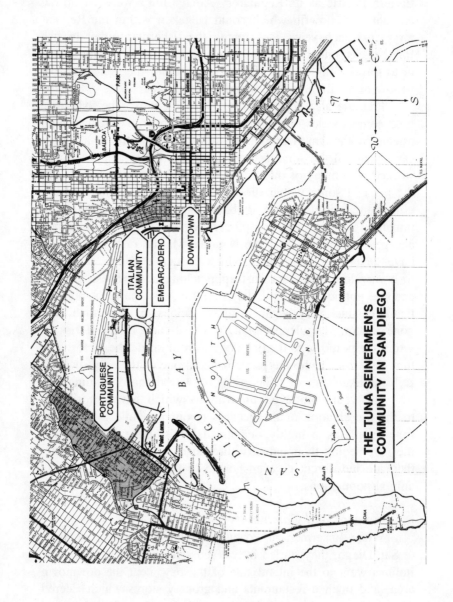

PORTUGUESE COMMUNITY

ITALIAN COMMUNITY

EMBARCADERO

DOWNTOWN

THE TUNA SEINERMEN'S
COMMUNITY IN SAN DIEGO

community. The Portuguese settled on the seaward side of the bay, in an area called Point Loma after the point of land which forms and protects San Diego bay and harbor. There they built a large community center which was nicknamed Portuguese Hall. Each community developed a social life of its own; the Italian centering around the restaurants, shops, and activities connected with one of the large Catholic churches in the downtown area, and the Portuguese centering around Portuguese Hall and the very close-knit residential community which came to be called "tunaville" by many San Diegans.

The Italian community was dispersed somewhat by the construction of a freeway through its midst in the fifties, but many of the restaurants and shops and a small portion of the residences remain. The bulk of the community spread to the outlying residential areas. The Portuguese community is still a cohesive residential community, particularly in the "tunaville" section of Point Loma, and families of Portuguese descent form a high percentage of the residents in several other areas on the Point. The native languages are still spoken quite regularly in these communities. The Portuguese is the larger and stronger of the two communities, owing to its spatial continuity and the continuing influx of young Portuguese men and their families from the Azores. These families are sponsored by their relatives here with promises of jobs aboard the tunaboats.

These men and their families of Italian and Portuguese descent have been the primary driving force behind the development of the tuna industry in San Diego. This will come up again and again throughout the book, and I bring it up here only to emphasize the following point: the success of the industry and the history of its control by men and women of these ethnic groups rest upon a dedication to fishing as an occupation and a lifestyle in combination with prudent and astute investment and business acumen. This dedication and the economic growth and stability of the industry have been the direct result of "community" in three senses: that of an extraordinary occupational community, whose members share experiences much more closely than people in most other occupations; that of a spatially bounded

7

ethnic community, whose members share cultural characteristics and practices; and that of a minority subculture in the midst of a larger complex environment, whose members have been able to counter varied and subtle forms of alienation with financial and social independence.

Performing the Research

I entered into my own relationship with this subculture as a graduate student of anthropology and a rag-sailor of some years experience. Although it was obvious that I was not a fisherman I decided, with the help of advice from people in the University, the National Marine Fisheries Service, and anyone else I could find who knew anything about the tuna fleet, to carry out the study as a working participant in the fleet. Talking to the fishermen and the industry people was enjoyable, informative, and relatively easy. Getting out to sea on a tunaboat was much more difficult.

I was an anthropologist, and I told them so: very few people have much of an idea of what that means. This was especially critical for the tuna fishermen, for they were and are under different kinds of pressure from government, scientific, and environmentalist groups. They feel, in many cases rightly, that they have been deceived and misrepresented by people whom they term "writers," and they were not sure why an anthropologist should be classed as anything other than a "writer." I brought this upon myself, in a way, by firmly prefacing my requests for a job or a trip to sea in any working capacity with a statement that I was an anthropology student who was going to produce a study of tuna fishermen. All were civil, in fact very helpful, but most, even if they had a job available, said that they simply didn't know enough about me to take me to sea for two months.

I spent four months walking the harbor every day before I found a skipper who hired me onboard despite my student status. After that, things changed. Working side by side with them and being together at sea, I found myself having constantly to remind the crew that I was a student. I wrote my notes openly,

8

brought up my student status whenever I had the chance, and otherwise tried hard to avoid leaving the impression that I was trying to hide anything in assuming the role of a fisherman.

This was not made easier by the fact that the fishermen have a sense of deprivation with respect to those whose occupations or skills possess more status ashore than does fishing. They feel this especially about education, and they preferred to treat me as a novice fisherman rather than an M.A. in Anthropology. That was fine with me. I had chosen to do fieldwork in the tuna fleet because I enjoyed being at sea doing the kind of things fishermen do, but I found that unless I actively proclaimed my anthropology student status my intentions were likely to be misconstrued. There are probably still men in the fleet with whom I never had the opportunity to work or talk who are still unsure whether or not "that guy from the University" was a spy for the Tuna Commission or the State Department.

It was a special problem for me, however, because of the complex nature of the environment in San Diego and the nature of the tuna seining occupation. Not only are most of the fishermen at sea most of the year, but their stays in port often did not coincide with each other's or with mine. When they are in port they do not hang around the boats but stay at home with their families or disperse to various bars and other gathering places. These locations are spread over a large area of San Diego. This meant that stories or rumors about my status were hard to catch and rectify, and that even initial contacts were many times hard to make.

Besides making the research more difficult and time-consuming in general, this situation was complicated by the virtually complete absence of demographic data of any kind about the tuna fishermen. Using such sources as the Labor and County Planning departments, union officials and other industry sources, and my own surveys and canvassing of the community, I had to put together my own demography of the fleet, its ancillary commercial and industrial organs, and the fishermen's families and community organizations. This had the virtue of affording me confidence in my own data and necessitated entry

9

into segments of the industry I might not otherwise have had the occasion to investigate; but the process of my fieldwork was slowed and hampered by the fact that I could never contact my informants at regular times or convenient locations. In many ways this was a result of doing fieldwork in a complex urban setting.

Aboard the boats themselves, the situation was the exact opposite. Aside from situations requiring defense of a crewman's "personal space" (which I discuss in Chapter Ten), I had complete access to the rest of the crew virtually 24 hours a day. The access, of course, resulted from the same physical proximity and personal interactional necessity which itself forms a significant feature of the high-seas fishing occupation. My participation in that situation afforded me both unusual access to other crewmen and at the same time enabled me to experience the effects of prolonged close proximity and personal contact. This is the stuff of participant observation.

During the two years which I spent doing this study, my wife and I lived in the "tunaville" section of Point Loma in the midst of the Portuguese community. We, and especially my wife while I was away at sea, experienced the feelings and frustrations inevitable to newcomers in a tightly knit ethnic and occupational community. Her experiences constituted a valuable part of the research.

The other part of the research was the time spent at sea aboard the seiners. After a short stint as an unloader, I made two trips to sea. The first was at the beginning of the 1974 season aboard a 550-ton net capacity seiner. This boat, built in 1966, was one of the smaller and older seiners in the fleet, and we sailed with a predominantly Portuguese crew. This first trip lasted 57 days and we unloaded our catch in San Pedro, 100 miles north of San Diego.

My second trip was aboard a 1100-ton net capacity boat, one of the larger ones in the fleet, on which construction had just been completed for the 1974 season. We sailed with a mixed crew of Italians, Mexicans, and "down-south" crewmen on a trip which lasted 74 days. This second trip was the last of the

10

1974 season. We sailed from the Eastern Pacific through the Panama Canal and unloaded our catch in Puerto Rico, returning to San Diego one week before Christmas. I hired on and worked aboard both of these boats as a deck crewman with the understanding that I was also collecting material for the study.

My own background in boating and aquatic activities helped me to cope with my duties as a fisherman. I hope that I learned enough of what I did not know to have earned my share of the profits—which, befitting my status, was a learner's share. I did perform certain other peripheral tasks aboard the boats; putting high-seas calls through to San Diego for the crewmen who did not speak English, minor medical functions, serving as helmsman at times when we could not use the automatic pilot, and others. The performance of these tasks altered my status somewhat compared with that of a "normal" learner aboard the boats, but it also gave me the opportunity to emphasize my graduate student status more than I might otherwise have felt comfortable doing. The result was that I was treated like a fisherman by the crews, who at the same time realized that fishing was not my intended vocation.

The information on which this book is based was gathered from all parts of the industry and from people in all the various positions in it. While I was ashore I tried to spend my morning at the harbor and aboard the boats and my afternoons in the office of a company executive, cannery representative, or union official. From my position on the boats I viewed the operations of the industry in San Diego, San Pedro, El Salvador, Costa Rica, Panama, Puerto Rico, and Ensenada. Two vessels make a small sample, but they and their crews covered the dimensions of size and ethnicity. I checked and rechecked my data through conversations with crewmen from other boats, both in San Diego and in the various foreign ports which I had occasion to visit, and by talking with various people in all parts of the industry ashore.

What is presented in these chapters is a representation of the understandings and behaviors of individuals in all parts of the industry, with a bias toward those of the men who actually

11

go to sea aboard the seiners. This is the point of view I was the most concerned with capturing and which I spent the most time and effort attempting to understand.

An Ethnography of Tuna Seining

There may be some confusion about the subject of this book, which is understandable. I present some material on the history and development of the tuna fleet, but this is not a history. Diachronic comparisons are made, but, even though the fleet has recently undergone a period of rapid development, this is not a book about change. There are passages where national and international political situations are discussed, but this book is not about politics. There are extensive descriptions of the fishing process itself, the gear the fishermen use, and the biological and behavioral characteristics of the tuna and other marine animals, but my subject is not tuna fish or the seining process.

This is an enthnography of tuna fishermen and tuna fishing in the Eastern Tropical Pacific as I saw them from my role as both participant and observer from June 1973 to June 1975. It is impossible, however, to describe either the fishermen or their highly capitalized, international industry without reference to other subjects. The gear they use and the situations in which they find themselves at sea are an important part of their lives and lifestyles. The intricacies and machinations of governmental agencies and international laws constrain the fishermen's actions in certain ways but each treaty, law, and ruling is perceived, applied, enforced, and observed differently according to the location, the situation, and the relationship between the participants in the event. The biological characteristics of the tuna are known to the fishermen as well as to the marine biologist, and although they are called by different names and organized perhaps less rigorously by the fishermen, these characteristics enter into fishermens' decisions about conservation and resource allocation. For the fishermen, as for us all, history and diachronics are integrated into our lives in the present.

Any study of a community or cultural system must center around the people in whom the sentiments and understandings

12

of that community or system reside. The fishermen share some sentiments, understandings, and experiences with the biologists, some with the politicians, some with the processors and canners, and some with the general public and their neighbors ashore. But they share the largest, most congruent set of understandings and experiences with other fishermen, a somewhat smaller set with their families, and an even smaller set with their non-fishermen friends. The subject of this book is that larger set of understandings, those which the fishermen share with each other and with people in their communities and which I myself either share or have become aware of through my brief participation in the activities of the fleet: understandings about fish, understandings about politics, understandings about past events, understandings about other people and groups of people. These understandings reflect the tuna fishermen's membership in two communities and their participation in two cultural systems— one at sea and the other ashore.

1 The Tunaboats

THE BOATS IN the San Diego high-seas tuna fleet are modern fishing craft. They range from 150 to 250 feet in length, and carry from 200 to 2000 tons of tuna in their holds. Seventy-five percent of the boats are in the 600- to 1200-ton capacity range; 15 percent carry less and 10 percent carry more. All the boats store the tuna in circulating brine and can keep a load of fish frozen in good condition for six months or more.

Even the older boats carry modern radios and other electronic equipment. All have high-seas, VHF, and CB radios; many have several of each in addition to high-power receiving sets, emergency transmitters, and backup and power amplification units. All carry radar and depth sounders. The new boats are variously equipped with directional sonar, weather machines, Loran, Omega, satellite navigational systems, and gyro-compass steering control units. Most are air-conditioned. Many have clothes washers and dryers and other modern conveniences for the crew.

The Layout

The boats have four separate deck levels which altogether contain twelve "spaces." All of the boats have approximately the same arrangement, with minor exceptions which I will point out.

Atop the mast, which serves as both a vantage point and a support for the main boom, is the crow's nest. This is actually a small room which contains a seat or seats, binocular stands, an intercom, a public address system, remote radio units connected to the main systems on the bridge, and various other equipment depending on the particular skipper or mast man who uses the crow's nest. Many of the crow's nests contain remote

14

controls for steering the seiner, a gyro-compass readout unit, and all the other means necessary to control and monitor the boat's travel. Most are enclosed to provide the occupant with shelter from the elements. All have halyards to ferry coffee, food, tools, and other items up and down from the deck.

Many of the boats also have platforms halfway up the mast for the purpose of looking for the tuna. These platforms are usually reserved for the skipper and perhaps one or two members of the crew. Together, the platforms and the crow's nest comprise a single space referred to as *the mast*.

The *upper deck* houses the bridge, a storage area referred to as "the stack," and an open area where the speedboats used in certain kinds of fishing are kept. On many of the newer boats the skipper's cabin is also on this deck, immediately aft of the bridge. This entire deck is referred to as "up above," or "up top," and is subdivided into two spaces, the *bridge* and the *speedboat deck*.

The *middle deck* contains the most square footage of any on the boat and houses the most spaces. Starting from the stern the first space is the *netpile*, the area which contains the seine net with its buoys, rings, and chain, and the skiff. Forward of the netpile is the open *working deck,* where the main winch, deck hatches, shark slides, brailing booms, and other "guts" of the net-setting and retrieving process are located. When someone says "on deck," this is the space to which they are referring.

Forward of this area is the *main deckhouse*, where the galley, cabins, heads, iceboxes, and various small storage areas are located. This deckhouse also contains the rig room where the lines, paint, tools, and small hardware used by the deck crew are kept. This room gives access aft to the working deck, and is considered a part of that "space." The "spaces" inside the structure itself are the *cabin area* where the crew sleeps and the *galley*.

At the bow is another open deck where the anchor winches and a rail-mounted winch used in part of the net-retrieving process are located. Another small enclosed storage area is usually

15

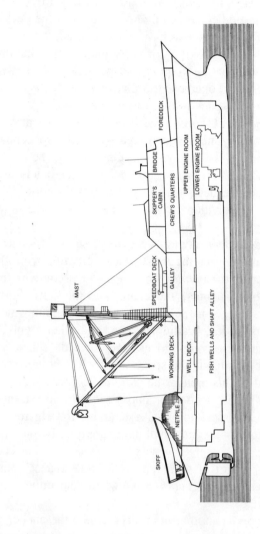

The spaces on a seiner.

found at the very bow of the boat. This entire space is referred to as *the bow*.

The lower deck is divided into two spaces; the well deck and the upper engine room. The well deck with its 12 to 16 well hatches is the area where the fish are actually funneled into the wells, the chutes which accomplish this process are stored, and the salt for mixing the brine used in the wells is kept. This space, being aft, is directly beneath the working deck. In its center, between the well tops, stand the engine and the machinery for all the hydraulic equipment onboard the boat. The ammonia condensers for the refrigeration system are also in this space.

Forward of the well deck is the upper engine room, where one or two of the auxiliary generators, the refrigeration compressors, and the monitoring and control panels for all the mechanical, hydraulic, electronic, and refrigeration systems are located. This entire lower deck is referred to as *below*. On some of the older boats the galley and main iceboxes for the crew's food were located on this deck. Some boats also have storage areas either aft, forward, or both on this deck. A few boats have wells forward of the upper engine room as well as aft, and on some boats all the wells are forward and the upper engine room is aft. Those boats with flume tank stabilizers have them on this deck beneath the netpile at the stern. In all of these cases, the two main spaces on this deck are the *well deck* and the *upper engine room*.

At the very bottom of the boat are two spaces which are not generally referred to as forming a "deck." These are the *lower* or *main engine room*, and the *shaft alley*. The lower engine room houses the main engine, reduction gears, one or more auxiliary generators, the ammonia accumulators, and various other machinery. The shaft alley runs from the lower engine room aft and provides access to the main propeller shaft from the reduction gears at the main engine to the stuffing box where it goes through the hull. It also houses all the controls for the brine circulation and ammonia cooling systems for the fish wells. At the aft end of the shaft alley is a small room (called the "tiller

17

flats") which contains the steering ramps and rudder mechanism. This room is considered part of the shaft alley.

The "spaces" on the boat, then, are as follows: (1) the *mast;* (2) the *bridge;* (3) the *speedboat deck;* (4) the *netpile;* (5) the *main working deck;* (6) the *galley;* (7) the *cabins;* (8) the *bow;* (9) the *well deck;* (10) the *upper engine room;* (11) the *lower engine room;* and (12) the *shaft alley.* The importance of these areas as separate behavioral "spaces" will be discussed in later chapters. Here they are set out only to describe the physical layout of the boats.

The Crew

The boats carry a crew of from fourteen to eighteen men. The distance which must be traveled to the fishing grounds, the nature of the search procedure, and the behavior and migration patterns of the tuna themselves—which make it necessary to cover large areas of ocean each day—tend to put a lower limit on the size of the boats in the fleet. Costs, crew recruitment problems, and the highly mobile and sometimes evasive nature of the tuna themselves tend to put an upper limit on the size of the boats. Current thinking in the fleet is that the "optimum" boat size is between 1000 and 1200 tons capacity. The mechanics of the seining method itself and the nature of the equipment on board the boats make it possible to run a 1600-ton boat with 17 men, but difficult and dangerous, if not impossible, to run even a 400-ton boat with less than 14 men. Thus all the boats in the fleet, regardless of size, fish with an average crew of about 15 men.

Almost all of the boats in the fleet are of sufficient size to be required by the U.S. Coast Guard to carry three certificated men: a Master, a Mate, and a Chief Engineer. Some are also required to carry a licensed Assistant Engineer. The boats are officially classed as "uninspected vessels," a category used by the Coast Guard for fishing vessels and other craft for whom the licensing and other requirements are not as stringent as those applied to cargo and passenger vessels.

Each boat is run by a skipper. In the past, because the fleet evolved from smaller boats to the present "superseiners" in a relatively short time, and because of the nature of the process by which one became a skipper, many of these men did not have the necessary Coast Guard licenses. This situation was remedied by hiring a "paper Master" or "paper Mate" who received a full share although often he performed only minor tasks aboard the boat. The skipper retained complete control of the boat and all its functions while the paper Master satisfied the Coast Guard requirements, signed the boat in and out of port, and perhaps did the navigating. On those boats where the paper Master navigated, the paper Mate simply worked as a deck crewman. This situation still exists today aboard many boats.[1]

Besides these "officers"—the skipper, Master, Mate, and Chief Engineer—each boat carries a cook, a deckboss, four or five speedboat drivers, three or four general deck crew, a skiff driver, and sometimes a mast man. Each of these men's tasks in the fishing process will be described in the next chapter.

When the boat is not fishing—that is, not actually making a set—approximately half of the crew work on deck and take deck watches under the direction of the deckboss. The other half work below under the direction of the Chief or Assistant and take engine room watches.

Accommodations

The accommodations aboard the boats are very comfortable. Most are air-conditioned throughout the main deckhouse and bridge. All have hot showers and nice, even fancy, head (toilet) facilities. The galleys are modern and well-equipped. Many boats have a crew lounge with a card table, color television, and stereo system.

All of the interiors are wood paneled. All parts of the main deckhouse except the galley and heads are carpeted. All the boats have either a separate cabin or a large alcove which serves as a chapel and houses beautifully carved statues, figurines, and other religious ornaments and implements.

---

1. An official of a large British steamship company told me in the course of my study that this situation also exists in Britain's shipping industry.

The cabins themselves reflect the formal division of statuses aboard the boat. In the forward portion of the deckhouse is what could be called a fo'c'sle—a large cabin with six or eight bunks. Each bunk is large—approximately 4' × 7'—and has a reading and a night light, extra space for books, and a curtain which closes it off from the rest of the cabin. The bunks are in two tiers. This fo'c'sle has its own head.

Besides the fo'c'sle there are usually one four-man and two or three two-man rooms. These are furnished in the same style and quality as the fo'c'sle, except that the two-man rooms have a writing table. The four-man room will share a head with one of the two-man rooms, or two two-man rooms will share one. Although there are no strict rules the cook, deckboss, mastmen, senior crewmen, and sometimes paper Mates and paper Masters usually occupy these smaller cabins in various mixes. The speed-boat drivers and regular crew generally sleep in the fo'c'sle.

The fo'c'sle and the two- and four-man rooms all have identical drawer and hanging-locker facilities. They are all furnished alike with such niceties as matching bunk covers which the men are careful to put on their bunks before making port. The only difference between them is the number of occupants.

The Mate or Master, Chief Engineer, and sometimes the Assistant Engineer or the deckboss have their own rooms. These are large cabins with double beds instead of bunks, refrigerators, desks, and large closets and sets of drawers. Usually two of the single cabins share a head. These single cabins are upholstered differently from the rest of the crew's quarters although only the color, not the quality, is different. The carpet, curtains, and wall paneling are of the same kind as in the crew's quarters. Their size, privacy, and room for personal belongings distinguish them from the rest of the crew's quarters.

The skipper's cabin is in a class by itself. These cabins have thick carpeting, higher quality paneling, wet bars enclosed in antiqued-mirror alcoves, walk-in closets, leather couches, king-size beds, large private heads, and fancy wall ornaments and artwork. They have their own television and stereo systems

20

and remote units connected to the ship's radio and intercom systems. On most of the boats built in the seventies the skipper's cabin is on the bridge deck. Some boats have another cabin on the upper deck for the Mate or Master, but these are of the same caliber as the Chief's on the lower deck. The skipper's cabins are truly luxurious, and are always a step above the other single cabins.

These accommodations are designed by naval architects in consultation with the owners or skippers of the boats. They tend to reflect some of the patterns and styles of accommodation aboard merchant vessels, which generally have the reputation of being more plush than those aboard fishing boats because merchant seamen as a whole spend more time at sea than fishermen. The tuna fleet is an exception to this, and the men who design the interiors of tunaboats give considerable thought to tailoring the quality of the interiors to the requirements of long periods at sea.

All the accommodations in the main deckhouse are for the most part quiet and comfortable. They are acoustically insulated from the noise and vibration of the engines on the decks below. The lighting is fluorescent and plentiful. If the main deckhouse were not on a boat, it would be a place few people would mind living.

Time Away From Home

The fishermen's year is divided into "trips," and the trips take place in two different "seasons." Because they fall under the resource conservation agreements administered by the IATTC (The Inter-American Tropical Tuna Commission), the first one, two, or sometimes three fishing trips of the year are called "quota trips." These trips are shorter, easier, and much less dangerous than the trips made later in the year. The fishing is done relatively close to shore where the fish are more often plentiful, the weather is better, and repair facilities are close at hand. After this "season" (which concerns only yellowfin tuna) closes, many of the boats fish "outside the line"—beyond

21

the regulatory area which extends approximately 1,000 miles offshore in the best fishing areas—rather than fish selectively inside the line for the less valuable skipjack tuna, which is harder to find and preserve. For the past few years this "season" has closed sometime in March.

The average trip length is from 40 to 60 days. This figure fluctuates considerably over the years. In the days when the tuna were caught primarily with a pole and line, the trips were often 80 or 100 days. The advent of seining, with its improved efficiency, shortened the average trip length. The increase in the size and capacity of the seiners since that time, however, has enabled the boats to stay out longer and longer. Since the middle sixties the introduction of the quota, the rapid increase in the number of new units in the fishery, and an indeterminate amount of resource depletion have made longer trips more commonplace. Forty to sixty days is approximately the amount of time the boats can spend at sea fishing normally with the amount of fuel and provisions they carry. It is the amount of time on which both the crews and the owner-managers ashore base their plans and their expectations.

Most of the boats unload their catches in San Pedro, California, while others travel through the Panama Canal and unload in Puerto Rico. It is cheaper to unload and process the tuna in Puerto Rico and ship it by sea back to the mainland United States than it is to unload and process in Southern California and ship by rail. The trip from the prime fishing grounds in the Eastern Pacific to Puerto Rico takes approximately the same time as the trip back to California. With increasing costs in California and greater competitive pressure on the fishing grounds, more and more boats are taking their catches to Puerto Rico.

If the boat is one which usually unloads its catch at a Southern California cannery, the crewmen can expect about two weeks at home—sometimes longer during the "season," when the boats tend to arrive in port at the same time and must wait their turn to unload at the canneries—before they leave on their next trip. During the season major repairs and maintenance items which require time to perform are put off, the fishermen preferring to maximize their time at sea under the quota. Later in the year, when time is taken for these repairs and maintenance, the periods in port lengthen slightly on the average.

Most of the maintenance and repair work is left until the end of the year—between Thanksgiving and New Year's—when the weather is rough on the fishing grounds. By this time the boats have presumably made an acceptable amount of money for the year, the crews are ready to enjoy the holiday season, and the work on the boats has to be done to prepare them for the opening of the new quota season on the first of January.

Three trips in a year is generally considered minimally acceptable. Four is considered good, and the average is probably around three-and-a-half. Five trips in a year is considered excellent. The crews expect to spend the last month or two of the year at home, and the boats make as many trips as they can in the first ten or eleven months. This schedule results in the men being at sea for eight or nine months each year. They are home two or three times for two- or three-week periods, and at the end of the year for about a month.

Those boats which unload at the canneries in Puerto Rico, a growing portion of the fleet, work on a slightly different schedule. They return to San Diego only once a year for maintenance, usually over the Christmas holidays, and sometimes not even then unless they need repairs or maintenance which cannot be done elsewhere. When they have a full load the Puerto Rico boats go through the Panama Canal and on to either Ponce or Mayaguez, Puerto Rico, to unload at the U.S.-owned canneries there. Generally, on these boats half the crew flies home from Panama when the boat begins its passage through the canal. The skipper calls them on high-seas radios the night before the boat gets into Colon on the east side of the canal on the way back from Puerto Rico, and the men fly back down to meet the boat as it completes its return transit on the west side. They go from there back to the fishing grounds. On the next trip, the other half of the crew flies home. The half that remains on board helps with the unloading in Puerto Rico.

The round trip by sea to Puerto Rico is about six days. The

boats usually stay about a week to unload. For the men who fly home this results in approximately the same time at home between trips as the men on boats that unload in San Diego have. For the others who stay aboard to unload, the time is cut in half, and they do not get to see their families unless they fly them down to Puerto Rico. This is a common practice in the ranks of the skippers and Chiefs, but is much less common among the regular crewmen.

This system results in the men on "down-south" boats going "home" only once every other trip. These boats which unload in Puerto Rico are generally those which are owned by large corporations. This has advantages and disadvantages for the crewmen. The company usually pays the crewmen's flights home every other trip and at Christmas if the boat does not return to San Diego. These company boats are, however, likely to stay at sea fishing longer at the end of the year. The company boat I was aboard returned to San Diego just one week before Christmas. Men on these "down-south" boats can generally expect to spend roughly half as much time at home as their counterparts on boats that unload in Southern California.

During the course of a trip equipment may break down or provisions will be needed which will occasion a visit to one of the ports on the Central or South American coast. Puntarenas, Costa Rica, and the Canal Zone at Panama are most frequently used for this purpose. Only as much time is spent in port as is needed to make the necessary repairs or take on the necessary supplies, and the visits rarely extend beyond two or three days. These visits are extremely welcome to the crew. They are, however, infrequent. On my first trip we made two such visits and everyone commented on how lucky I was to see port twice on my first trip. One can normally expect these visits two or three times in a year. While they are welcome, like the week unloading in Puerto Rico, they are not considered the same as time at home in San Diego.

Thus each man may reasonably expect to spend eight or nine months of the year at sea. He can expect to be home for two or three two-week periods during that time, and in port "down south" for another four or five days. He is usually home the last month of the year. As important as the amount of time he spends away from home, however, is the nature of his environment while he is at sea.

Being at Sea

The environment at sea is limited in many ways. It is limited in space, it is limited in interactional alternatives, and it is limited in sources of relaxation or amusement. It is also limited, if consistent, in the kind of sensory stimulation it provides.

One of the first things that one notices is that one is completely surrounded by an impenetrable barrier—water. You are dependent on the boat to keep you from being soaked by it, smashed by it, and from sinking into it. The boat's movement is a constant reminder of this fact.

The second thing you notice is that it is impossible to get more than about 50 feet from any of the other 15 men with whom you are going to spend the next two months. You can draw curtains or close doors and remain out of sight a good part of the time, but you can never get *away* from them, and the nature of the fishing process forces you into regular interaction with them.

A third fact is that most of the men you are with are men with backgrounds, experience, and most often with attitudes and interests very much like your own. There is a difference between choosing to be with people much like yourself and *having* to spend *all* of your time, day and night, with people much like yourself—and no one else.

The constant quality of the environment is also striking. Continually, even when drifting at night, there is the clatter and whine of the diesel auxiliaries which make much more noise than the main engine. Their noise and vibration along with the motion of the boat produce a condition much like the proverbial "sea legs," but much more pervasive. Many crewmen cannot sleep for days when they return home; it takes that long to condition themselves to the different quality of the environment

25

ashore. The sea and sky usually assume the colors of only half of the spectrum; greys, blues, greens, silvers, and whites. The occasional colorful sunset does very little to break this monotony, and even it is regular; it occurs only at the end of the day. Pattern and rhythms are much more regular. At home you have blinking signs, television interrupted for commercials, traffic which stops at stoplights and then starts up again, dogs which bark and then stop, and the occasional phone ringing. At sea you have the regular sound and vibration of the engines, the regular roll of the ship, the regular drum of the waves on the side of the boat, the continual roar of the bow and stern wakes, and the constant whistle and touch of the wind created by the forward motion of the boat itself.

There are not only constant realizations of where you *are,* but also of where you are not and how very far away you are from anything but your boat and your fellow crewmen. You have no access to or control over events ashore, events which you know are somehow affecting your friends and family. You are, for eight or nine months of the year, a resident of a different community, one far removed in many ways from your community ashore.

The effects of these conditions will be discussed in detail in subsequent chapters. Here I would emphasize four points: the environment at sea is very different from that ashore; it is a physically isolated and confining environment; it contains a very limited number of social alternatives; and it is an environment which provides limited, constant sensory input.

Spending the Time

The time onboard the boats is divided into two segments. From sunup to sundown is the "workday." No fishing is done at night aside from the completion of the occasional set made late in the afternoon. Besides a two-hour watch which rotates each night, the time after the evening meal, taken approximately at sunset, is each man's own.

Daylight is the time to look for fish. Only a few of the crew can perform this function effectively at a given time, but all are expected to maintain at least the pretense that they are somehow helping with the process throughout the day.

For those who are not looking for fish, there are the chores of routine maintenance: painting, light carpentry, splicing, sewing net, salting the wells, cleaning, and many others. The crewmen are divided into two groups: deck crew, who work under the direction of the deckboss and are generally responsible for the maintenance of all running rigging—nets, ropes, cables, and chains; and engine room crew, who work under the Chief or Assistant and are responsible for all the machinery. The deck crew generally work on the upper decks and have bridge watches at night; the engine room crew usually work "below" and have engine room watches at night. Most of the work of the general maintenance kind which these two segments of the crew perform is done before lunch. The afternoons are less busy and are spent going on and off of the glasses and generally trying to keep occupied without exerting oneself too much.

It is a common understanding aboard the boats that no one should sleep, or even be in his bunk, during daylight hours. In fact, there are certain places aboard each boat where it is common knowledge that people go to sleep during the day—the rig room, or perhaps the crew's lounge—and people, the skipper included, stay away from these places as much as they can in order to avoid a confrontation with someone who is "breaking the rules." Reading, card-playing, and similar pastimes are also frowned upon during the day although almost everyone indulges in them from time to time. Men slip into their cabins for a few minutes of reading, take a quick nap sitting up next to their bunks, or play a game of cards or two in the galley. They always look slightly guilty, however, if someone comes upon them in the middle of one of these activities. It is understood that during the day, except for mealtimes, one ought to be out of the cabin and galley area, somehow working on an activity which contributes to the fishing process.

The breaks in this routine, and they are mostly viewed as

27

such, come when the boat makes a "set"—lays out the net in an attempt to encircle the tuna. A set always means at least three hours of work and more if it is a "big jag"—a lot of fish—or if there is trouble in the set. Some particularly troublesome problems can literally take days to correct. It is not uncommon to make a set in the afternoon, experience one of these problems, and then not finish—that is, be ready to set again—until the next morning. When problems of this kind arise the crew works non-stop until the problem is corrected and the boat is once again ready to set.

No one knows when fish will be spotted and a set made. On my first trip we set on only 27 of the 57 days we were at sea. Twelve times there were intervals of from two days to a week between sets. The rest of the time—from sunup to sundown—was spent searching.

On the other hand, if you find a good "area" of fish you may work around the clock. I once made five sets in a day. By the time we finished, that particular workday was 18 hours long, and we set again at dawn the next morning. One boat I was aboard had earlier in the year caught 1100 tons of fish in one week in a particularly troublesome kind of fishing. They were on a 24-hour schedule for that entire week, sleeping only when they became too drowsy to perform their jobs safely.

That brings up another factor which is integral to an understanding of how these fishermen spend their time at sea, and that is danger. Almost everything about tuna fishing is dangerous.

Simply being at sea is dangerous. Three boats in the fleet— big boats—have sunk in the last year and a half. Anyone with even a passing knowledge of the sea knows, or ought to know, the surprises it holds for the seaman who doesn't have the skills or doesn't use them, and the blows it can deal to even those who do.

Working around heavy equipment, especially heavy running rigging, is also dangerous. Working with a seine net the size of those on the tunaboats differs from fishing methods employed in other fisheries on boats of approximately the same size as the tunaboats. The methods employed in the other fisheries actually "grab" the fish in one way or another with equipment designed to be relatively controllable from the boat. The seine net on the tunaboats, however, is primarily simply a way of putting up a "corral" around the tuna, and then slowly tightening the boundaries until the fish are swimming in the net right next to the boat. Only at the very end of the process are the fish in any way touching or suspended by the net itself, and the skippers are very careful to keep that suspension time to a minimum. The net is simply too large (three-quarters of a mile long, 350 feet deep, weighing by itself seven tons) to be controllable after it has been set, and the fish weight contained in a good set (50 to 100 tons) is too great for one to depend on even the strongest of equipment to hold it in the kind of weather in which the boats often have to set. This lack of control and consequent dependence on precise timing make the entire process more dangerous for all those involved in it.

The actual injury rate resulting from these conditions is hard to pin down. The industry keeps only sketchy figures on accidents and injuries. I personally know of at least ten major accidents requiring hospitalization which occurred in the year I was aboard the boats. I am sure there were more, besides those lesser injuries which did not require hospitalization. In a population of approximately 2,000 workers, that adds up to a relatively high injury rate.

Even if the rate itself were not high, it is obvious to everyone on board that the *potential* for serious injury is always present. This knowledge is in itself a factor in being at sea with the fleet.

Food, Drink, and Recreation
The food on the boats is, to say the least, spectacular. Because of the routine nature of the time at sea, most of which is spent searching, meals are important events, not mere occasions for taking sustenance. The cooks understand this and act accordingly.

All breakfasts are cooked to order; eggs, bacon, sausage,

29

pancakes, toast, cereal, milk, french toast, juices, and jams and jellies are standard. Other items vary depending on the tastes of the cook and the crew; on one of my boats, machaca burritos, spanish omelets, and turtle or chorizo instead of bacon were favorites.

The lunches and dinners are always full-course meals. Steak and prime rib are served often, and the meal always includes a substantial meat dish. Fresh salads and three or four varieties of cooked vegetables are always offered. Dessert is always available—ice cream is the favorite. Wine is served on most boats with lunch and dinner. Most of the crews are Catholic and fish is served on Friday—shrimp dishes are common—although a meat dish is usually present for those who want it. Each table in the galley has a box containing ten or twelve condiments and dressings.

The cook often makes fresh doughnuts or churos and will leave various snacks out or in the galley refrigerators for the crew to munch on during the day or while they are on watch at night. Fresh coffee is brewing twenty-four hours a day, and tea, cocoa, and other drinks are always available.

Before dinner there is always an appetizer—cheese, marinated sashimi, squid, olives, crackers, tuna with salsa, or some other goodie. The food is made to be fancy, not just adequate; butterflied shrimp, parsley garnish, pimiento strips for color are common. Barbeques on deck are frequent and very much enjoyed by the crew. Skippers will brag about the cooks and their meals to other skippers over the radio, and the best cooks are known around the fleet.

The crews like to be fed in style and in overabundance. The cook on one of my boats was once out-of-sorts for a couple of days, and prepared more than adequate but not fancy food during that period. The crew began complaining among themselves, eventually even to the skipper. They didn't complain about the quality of the food, they complained instead that there wasn't *enough*. This was in itself a ludicrous complaint in view of the amount of food left on the table at the end of the meals, but it illustrated how touchy the crew was about getting meals of the highest quality.

Most of the boats carry hard liquor for cocktails, and many carry beer for general consumption. Cocktails are drunk before dinner with the appetizers, and two or three per person is common. Only the best brands of scotch, gin, vodka, whiskey, and rum are carried, and they are supplemented by an adequate array of mixers. There is very little drinking done after dinner. Perhaps an occasional beer or glass of wine, but never any hard liquor. Everyone has night watches, and most will tell you that it just isn't a good idea to drink too much onboard. They cite tensions within the crew and memories of home as two major reasons for this, besides the effect that liquor has on one's general safety at sea. While extraordinarily good food is common aboard many kinds of ships which are at sea for long periods, it is rare to find liquor as available as it is on the tunaboats. This reflects the more egalitarian and self-determined atmosphere among the seiner crews compared with other seafaring populations.

The recreational alternatives at sea are very limited. Television reception fades relatively close to shore, as does most commercial radio. Many of the boats have film projectors or videotape machines which plug into the television, and they carry eight or ten feature length movies for viewing during the trip. Some boats rent video "packages" from a San Diego establishment which contain prime-time television, newscasts, movies, and television specials. The cost of these is borne by the crew and they usually total anywhere from ten to fifty hours of entertainment. Boats meeting at sea often exchange movies, thereby expanding each other's selections.

Card-playing is a favorite activity, although games with no betting or standard bets per hand are the rule. A few skippers don't allow any card-playing at all on the theory that it only causes arguments or increases existing tension aboard the boat. Poker is the biggest offender, and on many of the boats poker-playing is left for the trip home when the fishing is completed and the tension is usually at an ebb.

Some crewmen read, although the general level of education aboard the boats is fairly low and reading is not a very popular activity. If the boat is drifting at night, many men fish or target shoot at the sharks which gather under the deck lights. Some bring guitars and other musical instruments, although the constant noise of the engines makes it less than pleasant or practical to play any but the loudest instruments. All of the cabins and bunks have electrical outlets and many crewmen bring their own stereo systems to sea with them. These must of necessity run off of tapes, and it is difficult to bring enough tapes for a two-month trip.

Not many practice the "traditional arts of the seaman." Some of the older crewmen carve or do fancy ropework, and various people will work at polishing a swordfish bill or turtle shell they have picked up on the trip. As in many other populations, however, these traditional activities and arts are dying out.

A Typical Day

The day starts at dawn. The crew is awakened by the cook or the man on the four-to-six watch who traverses the passageways ringing a bell. The exact times for calling the cook, general wake-up, and breakfast are written on a chalkboard in the galley the night before. Cooks are called at four or four-thirty, the rest of the crew at five-thirty or six. Breakfast is usually half an hour after that.

After breakfast people wander back to their cabins or out on deck. Within the next hour or so they settle into whatever job they have to do that day. Some go onto the glasses, some do maintenance. The work schedule is very informal and the work itself very loosely organized. The men take a break whenever they want, usually going into the galley for coffee.

About an hour before the noon meal, which is at the same time every day, the men try to complete whatever job they have been doing that morning. There is a strong feeling that the morning and afternoon are different kinds of time segments, and they don't like to leave work to carry on into the afternoon. Some jobs, of course, demand this but most may be planned in order to perform them in morning segments on successive days.

At eleven-thirty or twelve, depending on the pleasure of the cook or the skipper, the crew is summoned, again by the bell, to lunch. This meal usually takes about half an hour.

After lunch there is a sort of institutionalized lounging period after which "work" resumes again. Work in the afternoon consists of once again manning the glasses and pursuing a less demanding, more puttering-around type of activity than was performed in the morning. Part of the reason for this is the weather. Most of the fishing is done in what could be considered the tropics. The tuna are found most often in water between 70 and 80 degrees and the weather is correspondingly warm and in many cases very hot. When the boat is moving it creates its own wind, and of course the interior of the boat is air-conditioned. When the boat is in a set and stopped, or when the weather is unusually hot, afternoons are not a pleasant time to be doing heavy work.

Because of these weather conditions the tunaman's dress while at sea would probably not fit the average person's picture of a high-seas fisherman. The most common dress consists of swimming trunks, shorts, or thin nylon underwear; t-shirts or tank tops or no shirts at all; and tennis shoes. This is true day and night, because the weather does not cool off very much when the sun goes down. When stacking net the men sometimes don nylon jackets or slickers, but for the most part their dress is casual, light, and skimpy. There is no dress differential by "rank."

Shortly before sunset the skipper gives the men on the glasses the okay to cover them for the night. This is the signal for showers or cocktails or both. The cook again gives the bell a short ring to indicate that the appetizers are ready and it is officially cocktail time. After about a half hour or whenever the cook is ready, the bell is given a longer ringing which indicates that dinner is served.

On most boats washing the dishes and keeping the living quarters clean are chores split among the crewmen on a rotating

33

basis. Most gladly do their share, and these chores take up only a small amount of their leisure time. Some are even performed in slack periods during the day.

After dinner the crew drift off to whatever recreation is their pleasure. Most gather in the galley, which because of its good lighting, tables, and comfortable seats—and on many boats, its windows opening to the aft deck and to the side—is one of the more pleasant places onboard. Some regularly gather around a particular crewman's bunk to talk. Others meet in one of the smaller cabins of a friend to talk or listen to music. Each man with the exception of the skipper, cook, and sometimes the Chief has a two-hour night watch which rotates each night and may be anywhere from six to eight o'clock at night until two to four o'clock in the morning. Most of the crew is in bed by nine or ten.

Sets, when they occur, break up this routine. Meals are missed, watches skipped, and the day's schedule thrown off considerably. The cook may have to alter the mealtimes, but no watches are changed. It is common to come off of eight hours of exhausting work from two or more sets at ten o'clock at night, eat, go to sleep at eleven, have the two-to-four in the morning watch, and be expected to be up and ready to set again at six the next morning.

Not all of the time on a trip is spent in sets or looking for fish. The four days or a week each way it takes to get to and from the fishing grounds is spent either readying the boat for fishing or cleaning and putting away equipment and getting ready to unload. These are time-consuming processes, but they fit well into the same temporal routine as the activities of actual search days.

Conclusion

The main points of this chapter are these. The men are at sea for long periods of time—most of the year—in an environment very different from their environments at home. The work at most times is either difficult and dangerous or boring and nerve-wracking. Although they have many comforts—the weather, accommodations, and food are notable—the relative values of these comforts are deceptive to one not involved in the occupation. Much of what follows will be a discussion of how these men use these comforts and the other resources available to them to deal with their obligations to themselves, to their families and community, and to the fishing process itself.

2   The Seining Process

Setting the Net

THERE ARE three major components to the seining process: the seiner, the skiff, and the seine net itself. The seine nets are anywhere from 200 to 800 fathoms in length (1200 to 4800 feet) and are from 100 to 400 feet deep at their maximum. They are made of heavy nylon twine. When stacked on the net deck they occupy an area approximately 25' by 25' and six or seven feet high and weigh seven tons. At each end of the seine is a fitting called the "oertza" (pronounced "ortsa"). It is a thick stainless steel ring usually shaped like a triangle or a capital D, and to it are bound the bitter ends of the seine. One of these is called the bow oertza, and the other simply the oertza. The net is asymmetrical, the maximum depth being slightly off center toward the bow oertza. The bow oertza is the last part of the net to be taken back aboard after the set, and the portion of the net immediately adjacent to it is used to contain the fish while they are actually being "brailed"— taken aboard the seiner.

The nylon twine itself is of approximately neutral buoyancy so the upper edge of the seine must be held on the surface by some flotation device and the bottom edge must be weighted down. To accomplish these purposes a series of corks are strung onto the heavy braided nylon line which runs along the top of the net, hence the name "corkline," and a series of chains and iron rings are attached to the bottom. The chains and rings serve two additional purposes besides weighting the net down. The rings are the leads through which the purse cable is led. The "chains," which may actually be heavy braided line with a lead core, also separate the bottom of the net from the purse cable which runs through the rings. This purse cable is used to draw

36

the bottom of the net closed after the fish have been encircled by it. It is important that the webbing does not get caught in the rings and purse cable.

Somewhere near the middle of the net, laced into the top strip, is what is called the "Medina panel." This is a section of net which protects the porpoise which may be involved in certain portions of the set.

The second major component of the setting process is the skiff. The skiff is a wide, flat boat up to 40 feet in length with a powerful diesel engine. It has three "skids" on the bottom to enable it to be pulled up onto the stern of the seiner, which is specially angled and constructed for this purpose. Its propeller and rudder are enclosed in caging to prevent their fouling in the net, lines, or cables. It has a large king post for the purpose of securing lines and cables, and a thick rubber guard rail to prevent as much damage as possible from the inevitable bumping between the skiff and the seiner. It is difficult to appreciate the size and bulk of this "skiff."

The important items on the seiner itself, in terms of their use in the set, are the mast, the boom, the main winch, the bow winch, the ring stripper, and the powerblock. The mast serves as a resting place for the crow's nest and as support for the cables holding the main boom. At the end of the main boom is the powerblock, a hydraulically operated bobbinlike hard rubber wheel with which the net is brought back aboard. The main winch controls the major cables used in the set, while the bow winch is used primarily to control the corkline during the net-retrieval process. The ring stripper is used to hold the rings after the bottom of the net has been pursed closed.

These are the major mechanical components of the process. The net gets from the boat into the water in the following manner. The equipment and the setting process are shown in Plates 1–9. Before a set, the net is on the net deck of the seiner, carefully stacked so that the oertza is at the lower front of the netpile and the bow oertza is on top of the aft part of the netpile. The corks, and thus the top of the seine are all stacked to starboard

PLATE 1. *The Working deck before a set.*

The corkline is stacked to starboard and the rings, behind the man seated in the picture, to port. At the lower right is the main winch, and at the far right the long white object on the rail is the ring stripper where the rings are stacked after the net is pursed closed. In the middle of the deck is the hatch where the fish are funnelled below using the hopper, which is sitting on top of the netpile.

PLATE 2. *The Skiff.*
One can see why lifting the skiff
in a heavy sea causes quite a
strain on the equipment. The
caging around the rudder and
propeller prevents them from
damaging the net. The brailer
scoop is lying in the skiff on
the right.

PLATE 3. *Making the set.*
The seiner has dropped the skiff
and is proceeding to attempt
to encircle the tuna and the
porpoise. The skiff, at the upper
left, has started its engine and
is pulling opposite the direction
of the seiner's motion. The
porpoise can barely be seen
just ahead and to the left of the
seiner. National Marine
Fisheries Service Photo; Eric
Barham.

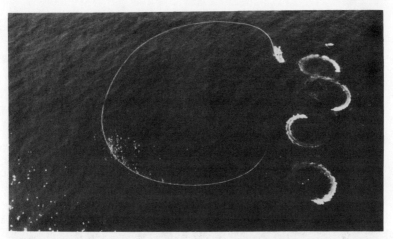

PLATE 4. *Bringing in the towline.*
The seiner has let out quite a
bit of towline on this set and is
starting to winch the oertsa
back to the stern of the boat.
The circular wakes are the
speedboats "working" to keep
the porpoise inside the net.
Note the size of the seine.
National Marine Fisheries
Service Photo, Eric Barham.

PLATE 5. *Lifting the rings.*
The rings have been lifted out of
the water and stacked on the
ring stripper in the center of
the seiner. The net is just
beginning to be rolled back
aboard. Official U.S. Navy
photo; Bill Evans.

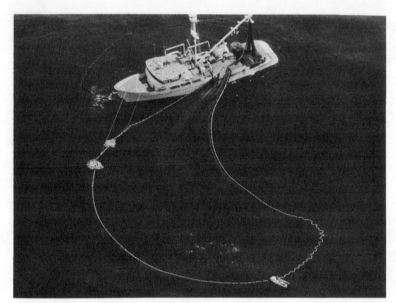

PLATE 6. *Starting the back-down*
Part of the net is now stacked
on the net deck, and the webbing
and corkline have been secured
to the port rail. Two of the
crew are in the speedboat ready
to help the porpoise, which
are gathered at the edge of the
seine over into the open sea.
The seiner has just started
to move backwards. Official
U.S. Navy Photo; Bill Evans.

PLATE 7. *Over they go!*
The seiner's motion has
elongated the net and is pulling
it out from under the porpoise.
The splashes at the bottom of
the picture are porpoise which
have just swum free of the seine.
U.S. Navy Photo, Bill Evans.

PLATE 8. *Stacking the net.*
This seiner has just overhauled
its net and is stacking it for
its next set. The men on the
right are stacking corks, the men
on the left the "chain." Note
the three grooves for the skiff
slides, and the steps down
which the deckboss must climb
to attach the double block to
the bridle on the skiff. It's a long
way up to the powerblock.

PLATE 9. *Stacking the rings
and "chain"*
The crewman with the hard-hat
is pulling the "chain," in this
case the lead-core line, over to
the side of the netpile, and
the other man is threading the
rings onto the tagline. The man
at the upper left is operating
the console which controls
the powerblock. Imagine
performing the work pictured in
these two plates when the seiner
is rolling from side to side and
the wind is blowing 25 miles
per hour.

and the rings and chains, the bottom of the seine, are all stacked to port. The net is stacked so that it will run off of the stern smoothly, the bow oertza first and the oertza last. The skiff is resting on the slanted stern of the seiner, held there by a cable which is fitted at one end or the other with a quick-release fitting. The end of the cable opposite the skiff is shackled either to the middle of the working deck or to the mast. The bow oertza and one end of the purse cable are both connected to the skiff. What we have, then, is one end of the net connected to the seiner and the other end to the skiff.

When the skipper thinks that he is in proper position relative to the fish, the wind, and the seas he gives an order for the skiff to be released. This is accomplished either from the deck by one of the deck crew or from the skiff itself by the assistant skiff driver, depending on where the release fitting is located. The skiff then slides into the water amidst a flurry of rattling chains and flying netting and corks.

As soon as the skiff hits the water the cables, which have been led around its starboard side, spin it around so that the skiff and the seiner are stern to stern. The skiff in the water provides some resistance so that the seine begins paying off of the stern of the seiner into the water. The skiff driver then starts his engine and begins towing in the direction opposite the net in an effort to keep the bow oertza end of the net as stationary as possible.

Sets are usually made at least at cruising speed, from twelve to sixteen knots. The seiner circles the school, always with the fish on the port side of the boat. When the school has been completely surrounded, the circle is closed by the seiner slowly approaching the skiff which is still at the point where the set was begun. The skiff must always be on the seiner's port side during this approach. A line is tossed from the skiff to two men on the foredeck of the seiner who are positioned by the bow winch. This line is connected to the bow oertza and to the other end of the purse cable, the ends of which are still in the skiff. The men on the bow haul in this line and the items connected to it using the bow winch if necessary. They then connect the bow oertza and

45

the purse cable to a line or cable leading aft to a block on the block arm and into the main winch.

The bow oertza and purse cable are winched aft to the block arm. The bow oertza is connected to a fitting on the rail there where it will usually stay for the rest of the set. It is called the bow oertza because in this position it is more toward the bow of the seiner than the oertza, which remains on the stern. The purse cable is led through a block and into the main winch.

All of the net must run off the boat for the normal procedures used in the retrieval of the net to work. Because of the size of the seine and the sea conditions, however, it is difficult to gauge the seiner's progress so that the oertza runs off of the stern at the exact moment the seiner reaches the skiff, which is the ideal situation. Instead, the skippers usually plan for the oertza to run off a little before the seiner meets the skiff. This is where the towline, the cable connected to the oertza comes in. When the oertza, and thus the end of the net, runs off the stern, the towline starts paying out off of its drum in the main winch. As soon as the bow oertza is secured the skipper gives the order for the towline to be brought in bringing the oertza back to the seiner.

The skiff, now free of all cables and lines, then motors around the stern of the seiner (passing over the net and corkline, a feat made possible by its skids and the cage around its rudder and propeller) and drops the assistant skiff driver off on a ladder built into the starboard side of the seiner. A heavy line is thrown to the skiff, and he proceeds to motor straight away from the seiner to starboard. When the line comes taut, the skiff continues to pull under the supervision of the skipper in order to keep the seiner off of the net and conversely, the net out from under the seiner.

At this point the net is "set." Both of the oertzas are on board, the purse cable is attached at both ends, and the skiff is keeping the seiner away from the underwater portion of the net.

Retrieving the Net

The setting of the net may sound simple, but it is not. Besides the fact that the skipper is having to deal with a body of fish or porpoise who move quickly and unpredictably—even in some cases with strategies of their own—many parts of the process allow only one attempt to perform them correctly. If the skipper comes back to the skiff too soon, if the men on the bow of the seiner miss the throw from the skiff or if the throw is short, or if a cable slips while it is being hooked up, the result is likely to be costly. "Losing the oertza," most often meaning the bow oertza, may mean losing the whole net, a $150,000 mistake.

That a "simple" mistake like losing an oertza may mean the loss of the whole net points out a fact which is difficult to grasp for anyone who has not had to deal with the equipment and forces involved: once the net is set, it is virtually out of anyone's control until some of it has been rolled back aboard. The seine is so large, and the forces of the ocean so great, that more than once I was reminded of trying to catch a 2000-pound fish with 10-pound test line. You have to work with the ocean, not against it. Part of working with the ocean is setting the net correctly, and it takes years of experience to be able to do this consistently under all conditions.

While it requires high levels of skill and competence, however, putting the net into the water is not likely to be particularly hazardous. Getting it back out again is another matter.

As soon as the oertzas are secured, the pursing process begins. The winch man, on instructions from the skipper or deckboss, starts the main winch purse drums rolling, which begins drawing the bottom of the net closed. From his vantage point atop the mast, the skipper keeps a close eye on the configuration of the net under the water. If a portion of the net is collapsing—drifting toward the center—or if the corkline at the "half-net buoy" at the far side of the net is sinking, he may order one or both of the purse drums stopped or slowed to help keep the net afloat and in its proper shape. Pulling that tremendous amount of netting through the water and lifting the chains and rings at the same time puts a huge amount of strain on the purse cable. The strain is aggravated by the friction of the cable against the rings. The lay of the cable tends to make it into a saw which cuts into the rings as it passes through them and at the same time wears

47

the strands in the cable itself. The cable is replaced often to avoid breakage induced by these factors.

The purse cable is made of several different diameters of cable spliced together. These lengths increase in diameter towards the center section of the cable. The speed of the two winch drums, each with one end of the purse cable, must be gauged so that when the rings finally all come together at the side of the seiner they are supported by this heavy center section of the cable. It is the only section strong enough to hold the weight of the rings and chain as they are lifted aboard the boat.

One of the worst of the tuna fishermen's nightmares—when it occurs—happens during this pursing process. It is called a roll-up. A roll-up is what the name implies, a portion of the webbing getting rolled up in the rings or around one of the cables. Sometimes a splintered strand on the cable will catch in a netting mesh and pull it through the ring. Sometimes an underwater current will wrap the net around a portion of the cable. Sometimes a portion of the net will turn itself inside out, forcing the purse cable to drag a dense blob of net instead of a relatively sparse sieve of mesh through the water.

A roll-up creates at least three potential problems. First, the tangle itself must be undone, a process which may take hours or even days to perform. Second, each portion of the seine is constructed so as to be able to bear the *normal* stresses which are placed upon it. To overstress the entire seine would be to make it too large and unwieldy. A roll-up creates uneven stress distribution throughout the seine, placing greater than normal stresses on certain portions. This often results in large rips and tears in the net which are costly, time-consuming, and difficult to repair. Roll-ups and their attendant effects on the seine often necessitate a seiner putting into port, where the crew has more space to get the seine sorted out and repaired. Third, you cannot leave the net in the water indefinitely. A roll-up often means that you cannot use your powerblock to roll the net aboard. However, because the seiners usually have the powerblock to assist them, the seines have grown so large and cumbersome that it is difficult or impossible to get them back aboard in heavy or even medium weather *without* the powerblock. The whole process is dependent upon setting the net and then getting most of it out of the water again in a relatively short amount of time. Left to the effects of wind, swell, and currents, the seine will in time become an even less controllable mass than it is under the best conditions.

Assuming, however, that there is no roll-up, the purse cable goes through the rings smoothly and the rings are eventually drawn up to the side of the seiner free of the net, which hangs below them. To have the "rings up" is a tremendous relief for the crew, not only because it means that there is no longer any chance of a roll-up but also because it means that the fish now have no escape from the net. Until the rings are up there is a big gap right under the seiner through which the fish may escape as the net is being pursed. The next step, lifting the rings aboard the boat, puts more strain on the equipment than any other.

When the rings are out of the water hanging from the block arm by the purse cable, two cable clamps are attached to the cable. One clamp goes on each end of the purse cable where they come out of the rings. These cable clamps are devices which grab the cable. They have an eye into which a lifting hook may be fitted. When the hook is pulled taut, the weight of the rings is transferred to the lifting hook and off of the main winch, although the stress is still born by the section of the purse cable which goes through the rings.

Putting the cable clamps on is the deckboss's job, and it is very dangerous. Like so many of the other jobs aboard the boats, it is not dangerous because it is tricky or difficult. It is dangerous because it is necessary in most cases to get out and stand on the rings to perform this task, and there is always the chance that the purse cable will break. I was once standing about 20 feet away from a purse cable that broke under these circumstances; the deckboss was going to get the cable clamps and preparing to go out onto the rings. Three-quarter-inch cables slashing through the air and tons of rings thundering into the water amid a shower of steel splinters creates a lasting impression, one which the average tuna fisherman has refreshed all too often in one form or another. The cable in question had been replaced a few days

49

before and had no visible signs of wear. No matter how well one has cared for the equipment, things like this will happen from time to time. It is the physical risk which makes jobs like this dangerous, and the weight of the uncertainty of equipment failures and many other hazardous occurrences equals the weight of the risk itself.

Once the cable clamps are put on they are hooked to the "double," the largest of the two or more lifting hooks which are electrically or hydraulically operated and hang from the underside of the main boom. The main boom is swung outboard so that when tension is taken up on the double, the rings swing aft to a position right beside the rail and directly under the place where the double's upper block is attached to the main boom. At this point the rings are hanging immediately aft of the ring stripper.

The forward end of the purse cable, now slack because the tension has been taken up on the cable clamps, is led through a groove in the end of the ring stripper, through an open check block at the base of the ring stripper where it meets the rail, and pulled taut by the main winch. The double is then lowered, putting the weight of the rings onto the ring stripper via the forward end of the purse cable and onto the cable clamp on the aft end of the purse cable. This frees the forward cable clamp, which is then taken off the cable and left to hang.

The rings are now hanging on the purse cable, which runs from the cable clamp on its aft end through the rings, onto the end of the ring stripper, and down into the main winch. The double is slowly raised, and as the sag in the purse cable straightens out the rings slide onto the ring stripper. Often one of the rings catches on the end of the ring stripper and the double must be lowered to clear the offender with help from the deckboss's sledgehammer. The rest of the crew "takes cover" during this process because of the tremendous strain on the rigging and the chance of equipment failure. As soon as the rings are securely on the ring stripper the seine is ready to be brought back aboard.

"Rolling net" is one of the most time-consuming parts of the process, and often one of the most miserable and dangerous.

50

The whole crew—with the exception of the skipper, Chief, Mate, Assistant, and sometimes the cook—are involved in the stacking of the net.

As soon as the order to "roll it" is given, the powerblock starts to pull the seine, oertza first, up out of the water. The main boom has been moved back inboard, and from the powerblock the net falls directly onto the net deck. Some boats stack the net in a continuous manner, moving the powerblock toward the stern by lowering the main boom as the netpile approaches the proper height in the front. Others stack the net in two segments, making one netpile on the forward half of the net deck and another on the aft portion. There are many variations on these two methods.

There are certain requirements which must be met no matter which stacking configuration is used. The net must be stacked so that all of its parts run off of the seiner smoothly and in the proper order when the skiff is next released. There are three separate jobs associated with the stacking of the net which serve this purpose.

First, the rings and chains must be stacked in the proper order along a low rail on the port side of the netpile. This is done to keep them separate from the webbing in which they may become entangled during the set, and to enable the crew to run the purse cable through the rings in preparation for the next set. There are two men whose job it is to stack the rings as they come down through the powerblock. One man pulls the chains and rings over to the port side of the netpile while the other strings a tagline through the rings which will be used later to thread the purse cable through. It is important that the rings do not get placed on this tagline out of order. Twisted rings on the purse cable will almost certainly cause a roll-up. On many boats "threading" the rings is the cook's job.

Second, the webbing itself must be spread out evenly and in the proper order over the net deck. This takes at least four men. The webbing is heavy, and there are sometimes sections of it up to four hundred feet wide coming through the powerblock. Often there are men both forward and aft of the net pulling

51

it into its proper place. The men performing this task must work together. Because of the shape of the net it is necessary to continually pass webbing to the man on one side of you and take up webbing from the man on the other side. All this is done with a clump of webbing up to a foot or a foot-and-a-half in diameter in your hands at any one moment. Although an attempt is made to move the main boom and the powerblock around to help distribute the net evenly, the powerblock can only be over one spot at a time, and to stack the net properly you are continually pulling webbing five to ten feet from where it wants to fall naturally.

Third, the corkline must be stacked properly on the starboard side of the net deck. This is considered the most physically tiring job in the set, although it is also one which becomes exponentially easier with experience. This task is considered something of a privilege. Many times the older crewmen or crewmen with high status of one sort or another are found stacking the corks. Styles differ, but normally the corks are stacked in a six- to eight-foot strip along the starboard side of the netpile. They are stacked from side to side and from fore to aft, generally staying abreast of where the webbing is being stacked at the time. With the rings and the webbing it is possible to simply ''hang on'' much of the time, while with the corks one must be continually struggling to twist the corkline into the proper configuration. While a bit of webbing can go astray here and there, the corks must all be in the proper place.

All the men on the netpile are subject to several sets of conditions which range from mildly annoying to potentially very dangerous. The powerblock is always from 40 to 50 feet or more above the deck, and the wind often turns the falling net into a huge sail which the crew must fight into place. On many of the boats built before about 1970, those without stabilizers, the seiner rocks considerably from side to side due to the waves and the swell. This often makes the falling net start swaying in period with the boat's roll, a condition especially dangerous for the men stacking the chain and rings. Sometimes the deckboss orders everyone off the netpile because the swinging chains, net, and corks make it too dangerous to try to stack until the rolling has settled down. It is not unusual to find crews stacking net on their knees because they are not stable enough against the wind and motion of the boat if they stand up.

All of the men on the netpile wear steel, aluminum, or shatter-proof plastic construction workers' helmets, because a lot of things come through the powerblock besides the seine itself. Even the parts of the seine do not go through the power-block smoothly. Because of its shape the seine is distorted going through the block, and this causes a condition called "slack chain" when a tangle or a bunch of chain comes through the block all at one time. When it clears the block it falls in a heap on a large area of the netpile below and it is no fun to be under that heap. This is particularly dangerous for the men stacking rings and for the two or three men on the port side of the netpile stacking webbing.

All kinds of sealife also come through the block and shower down on the heads of the crewmen below. Crabs, small fish, bits of tar, and other flotsam splat regularly onto the netpile and the men stacking net. The worst of these small objects in terms of their annoyance value are the jellyfish.

Those fortunate enough to be unfamiliar with jellyfish or their relative the Portuguese Man O'War should be told that the jellyfish are sea creatures with a round, umbrella-like body which they open and close to give themselves mobility. Underneath their umbrella they trail long strands containing a stinging poison. Their entire being is of a jelly-like substance which varies in color from clear to red or purple to, in the case of the Portuguese Man O'War, many colors. The strength of their sting varies with the temperature and salinity of the water. Their sting is at least annoying and at worst very painful, producing large red welts on the skin. Any part of the jellyfish containing the stinging cell, no matter how dismembered the jellyfish may be, is capable of producing the sting hours and even days after dismemberment.

There are many, many jellyfish in the warm waters where the tuna are found. The seine with its huge frontal area as it is pursed through the water is a perfect jellyfish-catcher. It picks them up, shreds them as the net goes through the powerblock, and deposits them in a fine rain or in small clumps on the fishermen stacking net below. Most of the men wear nylon windbreakers to ward off the effects of the jellyfish, but when the jellyfish are "hot" they go right through all but the most nonporous material. Even with the right material they fall on your hands and slip down your sleeves. They occasionally find their way down your neck, and even after your hands have grown numb to their sting the constant sound of small pieces plopping onto your helmet reminds you of their presence.

Jellyfish are not, however, the most dangerous of the things which come through the block. Many times sharks and tuna are caught in the net by their fins or tails and there are often more than one of these on their way up to the powerblock. Every attempt is made to grab the webbing and to "shake 'em down" as they pass the rail on the way up, but it is often either impossible or impractical to shake them out of the net and they go on up to the powerblock. Because most of the fins and tails are swept back toward a fish or shark's tail, as soon as they go over the powerblock and head down they often fall free of the net. The result is a 100 to 200 pound tuna or shark falling 50 or more feet to the netpile below.

Both the men on the netpile and the man running the console from which the powerblock is controlled are aware of this problem and keep a sharp eye out for things "going up" in the net. The man at the console, who is usually the Mate or Master, will often reverse the powerblock and then quickly roll it forward again thus shaking the net in an attempt to get the fish to fall back into the water. This has the effect of jerking the net on the netpile out of the hands and from under the feet of the men stacking net, and is almost as annoying as fish coming through the block are dangerous. The calls of "fish going up," or "shark in the block," or with the Spanish-speaking crewmen, "ojos arriba" (eyes up), are heard frequently and always capture everyone's attention.

After dark when the net is being rolled, or even in the daylight when the fish are deep in the folds of the webbing, a fish

54

may go up to the block unnoticed. A sound like that of a huge zipper is heard as the fish slides down the webbing accompanied by the cry "coming down" from the crewmen as they jump out of the way and the fish lands with a thud on the netpile. A crewman on one of my boats had a fresh three-inch scar on his arm where a 100-pound tuna falling unseen one night had grazed him and laid his arm open with its fin. Falling fish are, to say the least, dangerous.

Everything which falls from the block except very small marine life must also be carried from the netpile before the stacking can be resumed. Besides smelling extremely unpleasant after a few hours, fish left in the net may possibly create snags in the webbing in the next set and in any case will attract unwanted sharks by their smell in the water. Carrying a 150-pound tuna which is flapping furiously or a six-foot shark with its jaws gaping from the netpile in a hurry gets to be very annoying when you are tired and have other things to do.

As more and more net is rolled aboard, the "bowl" of the seine in the water gets smaller and smaller. For most of the set the seine is nothing more than a corral. Not until the very end of the process are the fish suspended in any way or even touching the net. Even then, when the "sacking up" begins, care is taken to cluster the fish only close enough together that they can be "scooped" out with the brailing net in reasonable quantities. If the fish are crowded and die from asphyxiation, they become dead weight. None of the cables designed to attach the net to the seiner could hold the large weights obtained in some sets, and the danger of equipment failure grows as the time the fish are left in the sack increases.

If the set has been on yellowfin tuna who were traveling with porpoise, a procedure called "backing down" must be performed to get the porpoise out of the seine before the fish are brought aboard. Nothing but tuna may be put into the wells, and anything else which is brailed aboard must be hand-carried to the rail and thrown back into the sea. No one wants to do this because it simply adds more work and more potential danger to the set. The backing down procedure is an attempt to avoid this problem. The fishermen also realize that the porpoise are a great help to them in finding the fish, and they want to free the porpoise without any harm so that they can eventually lead them to more tuna.

At some point in the stacking of the net, usually when a bit more than half of the seine has been rolled aboard, the skipper gives the order to "back 'er down." The crew comes off of the netpile and stands along the port rail or on the bridge or speedboat deck to watch. Some of them secure the net hanging into the water from the powerblock to the port side of the seiner.

The seiner is then put into reverse and its motion elongates the net. The porpoise, who are milling around in a bunch in the center of the net, in effect have the net pulled out from under them. As the seiner pulls the net they move toward the end of the seine away from the seiner. This is the section of the net where the Medina panel is installed. This is the only place where the porpoise usually have contact with the net, and the small mesh in the Medina panel prevents the porpoise from catching their snouts in the webbing below the waterline where they would die from lack of oxygen.

The movement of the net also makes the corkline at the far end of the seine dip under water, much as hauling in the purse cable too fast makes the corkline at the half-net buoy submerge. Since the porpoise are at the surface and the tuna are deeper in the net, this usually allows the porpoise to escape while keeping the tuna in the net. The speed of the seiner must be gauged very carefully, however, to prevent the corkline sinking far enough to allow the fish to escape also. A certain number of tuna usually go over the corkline no matter how careful or skillful the skipper is at regulating the speed of the seiner.

There is also one and sometimes two speedboats tied with long bowlines to the corkline above the Medina panel. The crewmen in these speedboats help the porpoise over the corkline if it is not quite low enough for them to swim over by themselves. The men sometimes have to jump into the water themselves to accomplish this. The ever-present sharks are a worry in this case, but the men try to keep the net between themselves and any shark

56

they see. If the shark is on the inside of the net, they climb out-side. If the shark is on the outside, they climb inside. If there are sharks on both sides they either straddle the corkline and pull their feet up or climb back into the speedboats.

In high winds or heavy weather this backing-down proce-dure is time-consuming and puts a heavy strain on the equipment. Fish tend to get caught in the net which is pulled closer to the sur-face by the process, and this creates more danger for the men on the netpile. Even under the best conditions this procedure takes twenty to forty minutes, and if many fish are trapped in the net they become dead weight besides being more susceptible to spoilage. The length of the interval from the time the fish dies until it is put into the wells and frozen is very critical in terms of its condition when thawed out at the cannery, sometimes months later. The backing-down process is costly in terms of time, money, and potential danger to the crew, but it is necessary to get the porpoise out of the net.

When the backing-down is complete and the porpoises are out of the net, the powerblock starts rolling again and almost all of the rest of the net is stacked. When the space inside the seine is reduced to the point where the fish are beginning to school together closely, the skipper gives the order to "sack up."

Brailing

At this point the skiff line is released and the skiff returns to the seiner and picks up two more crewmen, who will assist the skiff driver in the brailing operation from the skiff. Getting to and from the skiff from the seiner is a tricky business. The skiff is bulky and hard to control. The seiner is often rolling, and the skiff is pitching with the waves. The skiff driver noses the bow of the skiff up to the seiner and the crewmen have to jump from the seiner to the skiff, as the assistant skiff driver had to jump from the skiff to the seiner earlier. I know of at least one man who was lost when he misjudged the motion of the skiff as he jumped.

The skiff then motors around to the port side of the seiner, pulling up on the side of the net opposite the larger boat. The

57

skiff is made fast to the seiner at the skiff's bow and stern, often a difficult operation because the skiffs are hard to steer and have little power in reverse. The corkline on the side of the "sack," that portion of seine still in the water opposite the seiner, is tied securely with the help of the winch on the skiff to a bar and a series of cletes on the skiff's starboard side.

At this point the net still extends far below the surface of the water, up to a hundred feet. The webbing on the seiner's side of the sack must be "sacked up" (pulled aboard the seiner) to bring the fish to the surface. To accomplish this, the whole crew stands at the port rail of the seiner and gathers up the loose webbing as the deckboss threads a rope sling through the webbing in approximately the middle of the sack. The sling is then hoisted with one of the single block lifts attached to the main boom. When the sling is 20 or 30 feet above the deck, a thick line called the "choker" is thrown around the section of net which has been lifted out of the water. The choker is then tightened in order to prevent the net from slipping back into the water. The single block lift with the sling is then lowered to the deck and another "bight" taken through the webbing at the deck level. This process is repeated, the deckboss placing the sling and directing the gathering of the loose net so as to draw the sack out of the water in a uniform manner. The powerblock cannot be used to sack up because the sack must be made abeam of the working deck, where the fish can be brailed directly onto the deck at the hatch openings which lead below to the wells. It must be made forward of the netpile and away from the webbing, which is hanging down from the powerblock itself. Sacking up must be done with the hydraulic assistance of the single block lift and the choker because the seine, even with only a small load of fish, is far too heavy to pull out of the water by hand.

When the net is being sacked up the crew find out for the first time how well their efforts have been rewarded. Sometimes, during the backing down operation, the yellowfin tuna will panic when they realize that the porpoise are no longer in the net with them. Their frantic movement creates a turmoil inside the net itself thereby giving the crew a brief glimpse of their catch, but

58

it is not until the seine is actually sacked up that the men know the true extent of their "jag." The deckboss can usually tell by the strain on the webbing at this point how much fish is in the net.

Occasionally a couple of porpoise will end up in the sack, having been missed by the backing-down operation. If this happens some of the crew again jump into the net to guide the porpoise to the corkline and lift them over into the open sea. This is more dangerous and certainly more unnerving than being in the water during the backing-down operation. There are usually sharks in the sack also, and the webbing scrapes the scales off of the fish around the edges of the sack sufficiently so that there is some blood in the water. When you are in the sack with the tuna and other sea-life swimming around you things which you cannot see are continually bumping into your legs, arms, and body underneath the water. The fish are often so dense that you have to wade through them on your way to a porpoise. A hundred-pound tuna has a big mouth and small but sharp teeth. They are generally swimming around in the sack with their mouths open and always give you a few scrapes and scratches even though they don't actually bite.

The porpoise, for their part, usually become completely docile when you take hold of them and are easily led to the edge of the sack. They are heavy, however, and often a man in the skiff or one straddling the corkline has to help the man in the sack to lift the porpoise out. This is tricky because even with a moderate wind and swell, the rail of the skiff is constantly being thrown against the side of the seiner immediately above the sack, and you have to pay attention and remember to stay low lest you become caught between the two boats. While men are in the sack getting the porpoise out, the other crewmen on the deck of the seiner are on the lookout for sharks. The procedure for avoiding them is the same as that employed during the backing-down; keep the net between you and the shark.

When the deckboss is satisfied that the fish in the sack are sufficiently dense to be brailed, the choker is put on the last bunch of netting to have been pulled from the water and secured. The deck is then rigged for brailing. A large aluminum slide with a door on one end called the hopper is carried to the rail of the seiner by the sack. The middle deck hatch is then taken off, exposing another slide below decks which funnels the fish to the waiting wells. The hopper extends from the rail all the way to the deck opening.

Each load of fish which is brailed aboard is dumped into the hopper for sorting. Nothing but tuna of the proper size and species can go into the wells. There are often other species of fish—mahi-mahi, wahoo, triggerfish—and even other species of tuna such as "blackies"—black skipjack tuna—mixed in with the "good" fish. The cannery will pay the fishermen nothing for these other species, although they take whatever is missed by the sorting and use it as catfood, fish meal, fertilizer, and other products. Thus everything but acceptable tuna is sorted out and thrown back into the sea. When the hopper is "clean" the door at the end by the deck hatch is opened and the tuna slide below.

Sorting can be quite a job. The sharks are a particular problem. They are heavy, and their skin is too thick to be pierced by the gaffs used to move the tuna about. Since their skin texture makes sliding them across the wooden deck almost impossible, another aluminum slide called the "shark slide" is hooked to the edge of the hopper. It leads to a door in the railing of the starboard side of the seiner, and is used to slide the sharks back into the sea with a minimum of effort. The sharks do not slide very well even on this smooth surface, however, so water must be continually run down the slide and a man usually has to push them along to the rail and over the side.

Sometimes there are just too many sharks for the shark slide to accommodate, and the crew ends up having to carry or drag the sharks to the rail and throw them over. In one set we brailed 15 tons of skipjack tuna aboard and 30 tons of big hammerhead sharks. It took us three hours to get those sharks off the deck. They had to be brailed aboard with the rest of the fish because, unlike the porpoise, there is no other way to get them out. A crewman once walked up to me after an episode such as this and said, "You tell them when you write your book; big, rich fisherman—sure! You walk like an old whore from the work when

60

you're 40!'' He walked away in his very best imitation of an old whore—with a smile on his face. I didn't have to try very hard to imitate that stance on that particular day.

The fish are brought aboard with a device which resembles a large tropical fish scoop. This device, the brailer, holds anywhere from one to two tons of fish at a time depending on the size of the seiner. It is made of very small mesh webbing lashed to a steel hoop approximately five feet in diameter. Attached to this hoop is a steel and aluminum handle approximately twenty to twenty-five feet long. On the end of the handle is a rope ten or fifteen feet long. The bottom of the netting is open and may be drawn closed by a small chain or cable threaded through the bottom of the net opposite the hoop.

There is a bridle attached to the hoop in three or four places. Attached to this bridle are two cables. One runs up to a special boom called the brailing boom which is swung out directly over the sack. This cable is for lifting the brailer out of the water. The other cable runs either to the main boom or to the main winch and is used to pull the brailer in over the hopper. One of these two cables is controlled by alternately tightening and slipping it over a continuously revolving winch. The other is usually hydraulically or electrically controlled.

The brailer is kept in the skiff. When the sack is ready to brail, the cables are swung out to the men in the skiff and connected to the brailer. The brailer is then lifted to the starboard side of the skiff with the hoop extending out over the sack and the handle lying athwartships. The skiff driver has a whistle with which he signals his needs to the men on the seiner who control the lifting cables.

Two of the men in the skiff stand at its starboard side holding the brailer handle immediately adjacent to the hoop. The third man stands at the end of the handle on the port side of the skiff. When the skiff driver signals with his whistle the men on the seiner slack the cables and the man in the skiff at the end of the handle boosts it into the air as high and as hard as he can. These actions tip the brailer into the vertical position and it slides down the side of the skiff into the sack.

61

The man who threw the handle into the air then crosses over to the starboard side of the skiff and the three men together put all their weight onto the brailer handle and drive it down into the sack. At the skiff driver's whistle signal the cable directly above the sack is pulled taut, raising the brailer. If the skiff driver thinks that the brailer is not full enough he signals for the cable to be slacked again. The men in the skiff once again thrust the brailer deep into the sack until the skiff driver whistles again. This process is repeated until the skiff driver is satisfied that the brailer is full enough to be taken aboard the seiner. He then blows the whistle several times in quick succession, he and the other men in the skiff back away from the rail, and the brailer is lifted clear of the sack.

As the brailer is lifted up to the level of the seiner's rail, one of the men in the skiff must keep the brailer handle under control. If left unattended this heavy piece of steel and aluminum swings around considerably, posing a danger to the men in the skiff. Controlling the handle is a difficult and dangerous job because both the seiner and the skiff are moving, but with different motions. The seiner is rolling with the swell from side to side, while the skiff is both rolling and pitching in the chop besides surging fore-and-aft along the side of the seiner. If the man holding the handle loses his grip everybody in the skiff heads for cover. Holding onto the handle often means being lifted off of the deck of the skiff when the seiner rolls away from the skiff, or when the skiff pitches down in the trough of a wave. Holding the handle became my job for a while on one boat; the regular man had been lifted off the deck in this manner and had smashed his foot when the skiff abruptly rode the next wave up to meet him again. The best method is to try to control the handle with the line attached to its end when it pitches up out of reach, but it is difficult to catch the handle again when it comes down.

When the brailer is lifted too high for the man in the skiff to reach, he must rely on the control line. This is the most dangerous part of the lifting process for him; he could be clubbed by the handle, if the seiner should roll or the skiff ride high on a wave, or he could be skewered on the end of it. He must keep control

62

of the handle until the brailer is actually over the working deck. Brailing in the skiff is considered the most strenuous job on the boat.

When the brailer is high enough to clear the rail of the seiner, the cable which leads to either the winch or the main boom is drawn taut, pulling the brailer inboard. The crew on the working deck must pay close attention when the brailer swings over the deck because the only way to stop it from swinging clear to the starboard rail is to slack the lifting cable and drop it either in the hopper or onto the deck, and there is absolutely nothing to prevent it from swinging fore-and-aft. The men controlling the cables must be very skilled and very attentive, gauging their manipulations of the cable controls to allow for the effects of the wind, the boat's motion, and the "bounce" in the rigging. It is imperative that their actions be coordinated. Once the brailer has started swinging in the wrong direction there is virtually nothing anyone can do to stop it. Even with the best men at the cable controls the two-ton mass of the brailer coming aboard always manages to smash a few plates and bend or break a few pipes and fittings on every trip.

When the brailer is finally dropped into the hopper the chain or cable which has been holding the bottom of its webbing shut is released. There is one man whose job it is to control the purse line for the brailer, and he may perform this function either from the skiff or from the seiner. Some purse lines have fittings which lock them shut when they are pulled tight, while others are simply hand-held. I fished with both kinds, and the frequency of slips with the hand-held type and improper locking with the other type seem to be about the same. If the purse line does release prematurely, thousands of pounds of fish cascade back into the net, onto the rail, or over the working deck—wherever the brailer happens to be at the time. Assuming that it is released at the proper time the brailer is then lifted, leaving its load in the hopper, and swung back over the rail and onto the skiff to begin the procedure again.

When the fish pass below decks they are in the hands of the Chief and his Assistant. The Chiefs carefully plan the order in which the wells will be filled. For reasons of stability no more than one pair of wells may be "slack" (empty) at any one time. When they are not being used they are kept filled with either salt water or fresh water as a supplement to the boat's regular water supply.

The wells on an average size seiner range from 35 or 40 to 60 tons capacity each. They are each the size of a large room, and are lined with thick pipe through which runs the ammonia used in the refrigeration system. Each is equipped with its own filler tube and drain, so that the rates of circulation of the brine in each may be controlled individually.

It is the Chief's responsibility to keep the fish in good condition until they reach the cannery. When they slide down the chutes they plunge into a heavily salted brine which has been cooled to anywhere from zero to 15 degrees Fahrenheit. This subfreezing temperature is made possible by the increased salinity and the fact that the brine is kept circulating. Once in the brine, the fish freeze in minutes.

A lot of planning goes into how each well is filled, and in which order. A jag of large fish, for example, should not be put into a well on top of a jag of small fish. The smaller fish are more easily damaged, and the weight and individual density of the large fish may crush the smaller fish into useless waste (to the fishermen, not to the cannery) before the boat ever reaches the dock. Often a Chief has two wells partially filled at the same time to avoid this problem.

The temperature in the wells is critical. A constant watch must be kept over the rate of the brine circulation, the state of the ammonia in the refrigeration system, and the salinity in the well, all of which affect the temperature. Letting the temperature go too high may allow the fish to spoil or become loose enough to move around too much and damage each other. Letting it go too low (which is easier than one might think to let happen) may overfreeze the fish and make them impossible to get out, besides hindering the brine circulation. All of these factors must be monitored constantly by the Chief, and he is often called in the middle of the night by one of the engine room watch who has detected an abnormality in one of these several systems.

While the Chief is busy with preparing and filling the wells, back on deck the brailing is bringing more fish aboard. An average set will take from half an hour to 45 minutes to brail. As the sack empties more and more of the webbing is sacked up out of the water in order to keep the fish concentrated.

When the brailing is finished one of the men in the skiff climbs up the webbing onto the seiner. The lifting cables are unhooked from the brailer and taken back aboard the seiner. The skiff is cast off from the seiner and motors a short distance away where the skiff driver and the other man left in the skiff lash down the brailer and generally clear the skiff to get ready to lift it back aboard the seiner.

The crewmen on the seiner clear away the hopper, replace the deck hatches, and clear off the working deck. Then they go back onto the netpile and the rest of the net is rolled aboard. When all the net is stacked they prepare to lift the skiff aboard.

Picking Up the Skiff

Getting the skiff back aboard is often a difficult task. The skiffs are big and heavy and generally sluggish, slow, and hard to maneuver. The procedure for getting them back aboard is as follows. The double block, the largest one on the main boom, is taken around to the aft side of the netpile. This is normally accomplished by dropping the hook to the working deck and pulling several fathoms of cable off of the double's reel in the main winch, stacking it neatly on the deck. Two of the crew then grab the hook and take a running start around the port side of the netpile where the rings are stacked. The four or six strand purchase on the double block makes the cable run out slowly enough so that the men's momentum from their run and their body weight just overcome the resistance on the double. The two are often air-borne on their way around the netpile. As they progress toward the stern the cable which was pulled out onto the deck runs out, hopefully freely. Once the hook is on the aft side of the netpile,

65

it is held there by one of the crew just at the top edge of the slanted portion of the seiner's stern.

The skiff has by this time circled around and is following the seiner. The seiner, dead in the water during the entire brailing operation, has started up and is moving slowly forward. There are various theories concerning in which direction it is best for the seiner and skiff to be heading at this time with respect to the wind and swell. Some say it is best to be going upwind and swell, others say downwind and swell. Most seem to prefer going upwind, although I have seen it done both ways. It must be done without a cross-swell, however, which would make it impossible for the skiff to stay lined up properly on the seiner's centerline. The skiff driver's assistant has by this time brought the bridle and a short cable with an eye in its end which is attached to the bridle up out of the water and onto the bow of the skiff, ready to pass to the men on the seiner to hook onto the double.

The deckboss then climbs down a set of steps on the seiner's stern. From there he directs the skiff driver and the man at the console who has control of the double. The skiff driver comes slowly up to the stern of the seiner, attempting to put the middle runner of the skiff into the wedge-shaped end of the recessed center guide on the seiner's stern. This often takes several attempts. In any but the smoothest weather the skiff is rolling and pitching against the stern of the seiner as the driver attempts to place the skid in the guide. Directing the operation is another job the deckboss inherits partially because of the danger involved.

When the skid is finally in the groove, the deckboss gives the skiff driver a signal by waving his hand in a circular motion above his head which means "full speed." The skiff has enough power to drive itself a foot or two up on the seiner's stern. The deckboss then reaches down and hooks the bridle cable onto the double hook, which often means getting between the skiff and the seiner. When the bridle is hooked up, he signals the man at the console to take up on the double.

It is important not to hook the double to the skiff until the skiff is firmly pressed against the seiner. Even after the skiff is partially up onto the seiner's stern, a wave may come and lift the skiff out of its guides. This is extremely dangerous because the skiff is then unable to motor free of the seiner, being restrained by the double which is difficult to slack quickly. The skiff then slides and bumps along the stern of the seiner with every roll and pitch. The deckboss makes sure that the skiff is in good position before he hooks up the double.

Assuming that all goes well, the skiff is drawn up with the double until it is high enough to reach the cable from which it was released at the beginning of the set. This cable is attached to the bridle, and the double is slacked until the release cable is drawn taut.

Sometimes a set is made in bad weather, or the weather worsens during the set, so that it is too dangerous to attempt to "pick up" the skiff. When this occurs the skiff simply motors alongside the seiner until the weather calms down, sometimes a matter of days. Attempting to pick the skiff up in weather which was too rough has over the years resulted in several skiffs battering themselves to pieces against the stern of the seiner and sinking.

Once the skiff is up the set is essentially complete. The cables must be trailed over the side of the seiner to eliminate any kinks or twists, rewound onto their drums, and then led once again to their various positions. The deck must be hosed down, various equipment put away, and the skiff and speedboats re-fueled. Once the skiff is up, a good crew can be ready to set again in ten to fifteen minutes. No one relaxes until the boat is completely ready to set again.

3 Decision-Making in the Search and Set

WHEN A SEINER leaves San Diego for the fishing grounds the skipper must begin to assess his alternatives. He weighs these alternatives and comes up with a plan designed to bring in a full load of fish with the minimum amount of expense in the shortest possible time.

At the outset the skipper knows he has certain physical constraints. He has approximately 40 days worth of fuel, which he may stretch by drifting at night or running below cruising speed. Drifting at night is a common practice, but running below speed is done only when the fuel situation is extremely critical. To run half speed is to give up the search potential of quite a few square miles of ocean per day. On the other hand, the skipper knows that if he runs too far and too fast too early he may give up the chance to seize opportunities late in the trip.

He knows that he has a limited amount of provisions and other necessary supplies for the crew's sustenance and comfort. Although fuel is the major expense and generally the most difficult and time-consuming item to obtain, the skipper must also satisfy the needs of his crew as well as the needs of his ship. To ignore or stretch either to their limits are courses most skippers avoid.

The Starting Point

As he heads toward the fishing grounds the skipper considers three general factors: the time of year; his knowledge of others' progress in various areas at that time; and his own past experience. These factors determine the place where his search will begin.

68

The time of year is important partly because the tuna are migratory; they come in from the west and travel south to north along the coast. The skippers know that the southern grounds are better early in the year and that the northern ones have more fish late in the year. On the first trip of the season, a skipper may put off initiating a search pattern until he is in the better fishing areas off Central America. Later in the year the same skipper might begin searching off the tip of Baja California, several hundred miles north of where his search on the earlier trip began.

The time of year is also important because of the "quota," the IATTC regulatory agreement which provides for the conservation of yellowfin tuna within the regulatory area, a 5,000,000 square-mile portion of the best tuna-fishing grounds in the Eastern Pacific. (See map, Chapter Five.) Before the season closes—usually around March—the boats may fish any species of tuna and may do so almost anywhere they wish. After the season, however, they have to go "outside the line"—beyond the limits of the regulatory area—if they wish to fish for yellowfin, the prime resource.

The San Diego seiners fish principally for two species of tuna, yellowfin and skipjack. If a skipper decides to fish inside the Regulatory Area after the closing of the season he must take only skipjack tuna, a species which brings approximately $30 per ton less than yellowfin at the cannery and is more difficult to locate. Fishing for yellowfin, even though it must be done "outside the line" after the closing of the season, is an attractive alternative. On the other hand, fishing "inside" is considerably safer and more convenient. The "outside" is much rougher and farther from repair, supply, and medical facilities.

The extent to which a skipper "decides" to fish for either yellowfin or skipjack is unclear. After the season has closed a decision to fish inside the line is necessarily a decision to fish skipjack. If a skipper heads outside the line, that action is usually sufficient evidence to assume he is going to fish yellowfin. If a skipper is outside looking for yellowfin and comes across a school of skipjack, he certainly will not pass it up. If a skipper is inside looking for skipjack and comes across a school of yellowfin: (1) it is against the rules to fish for yellowfin within the regulatory area after the closing of the season; (2) there is in the regulations provision for an "incidental catch" ratio which allows for the facts that the two species are sometimes found together and that it is sometimes impossible to take skipjack without getting some yellowfin; and (3) fish is money. Different skippers handle this situation in different ways.

Before the season closes the options are not so clear. There are areas which are known to be good for yellowfin at certain times of the year; likewise for skipjack. While skipjack bring less per ton at the cannery, they average only approximately one-quarter the size and weight of the yellowfin and many more skipjack can be much more densely packed into a fish well. Boats with full loads of skipjack often reach the cannery over their rated capacity, while boats with yellowfin loads often come in under.

Besides the relative economies of the two species, there are many differences in the expertise required and danger and trouble involved in capturing each. The general rule is that the skippers go where there are the most fish of either kind, but these considerations are only a small part of each skipper's total set of decision parameters.

The closing of the season itself is a constraint on the skipper's choices. The boats must clear into port by a certain date to qualify for one more trip "inside" before the season closes for the year. This date varies, and while the skipper is second-guessing its exact time he must make sure he conducts his search close enough to port to allow himself time to clear should his guessing prove wrong.

Before he ever reaches the fishing grounds or starts actively searching, the skipper has a certain amount of information about the fishing success of those already on the grounds. While he is in port he has access to information networks which give him some idea of where fish are being found and caught. Once he is at sea he begins to communicate with other boats in the fleet and gains additional information of this nature. This information turns into inputs into his decisions about where to head as he travels south from San Diego.

In the absence of any good information, and sometimes even in spite of it, the skippers many times simply use their own past experience in determining their starting points in the search. Favorite reefs, current areas, coastlines, and other locations often lead to strategies independent of the successes of others. It is important to note that it is not uncommon for a seiner to travel 15,000 miles in a single trip.

Finding a Good Area

It is implicit in the thinking of all skippers that there are certain areas of the ocean in which they are more likely to find fish. Some of these areas—banks, river mouths, and the like— are permanent. But the concept of "area" also implies that portions of otherwise indistinguishable ocean are at certain times more likely to have tuna in them than others, portions whose locations change over time. This area concept is one of the prime arguments in favor of larger boats. While many of the fishermen do not like bigger boats, almost all of them believe that if you find an area of fish there is a good chance you can fill up as many wells as you have empty at the time. At 50 tons per well— $28,000 worth at 1974 prices, or between $500 and $800 to each man—the more wells you have the better.

Once the boat has reached the grounds where the skipper has decided to begin his search, there are several criteria applied to determine if one is in a good area.

The Role of the Weather

The first of these parameters is weather. If the swell is large, the wind high, and the sky cloudy or rainy it is not only physically dangerous and potentially costly to set on a school, but the schools themselves are much harder to find. Even schools of porpoise are hard to spot with whitecaps and a moderate swell. The setting process is dangerous enough in calm weather because of the size of the equipment and the strain on it, and the danger of

71

breakage or injury grows exponentially with the deterioration of the weather. A crewman requiring immediate hospitalization when you are five days from the nearest port is a responsibility skippers wish to avoid. Setting in weather which is too rough may also result in a lost net, and with nets costing $150,000 apiece, a skipper soon learns to avoid rough weather if he can.

To enable them to use weather conditions in their decision-making process, the skippers have three avenues of information. They have their own experience and knowledge of wind patterns, currents, swell directions, cloud formations, and weather fronts. This they can combine with their own observation to make weather predictions. Second, they have weather information they receive from skippers on other boats in other areas. Third, they have government weather information broadcast over high-seas radio. Some boats have a "weather machine," a teleprinter which receives detailed weather maps from National Marine Fisheries Service stations in the United States. It is generally the experience of those who have these machines that they are a tremendous asset, but the machines are expensive and many of the fishermen who have never used them are still distrustful of the information they carry. Also, the machines themselves are not known for their reliability.

Using these resources the skipper can both choose the areas with the best weather to begin his search and determine the best direction to move if he finds himself in bad weather. The boats have the speed to move 300 to 400 miles in a 24-hour period. This gives the skipper the power to "select" his weather conditions.

Signs

Assuming that they have acceptable weather conditions, the skippers look for what they call "signs"—indications that fish are likely to be in the vicinity. Several factors may contribute to an area having "good signs."

One of these is the presence of marine life other than porpoise or tuna themselves. The fishermen know about the food chains in the ocean, and the presence of "tuna crabs," squid, flying fish, and other small marine life on which the tuna feed are taken as good signs that they are searching in an area with potential. Phosphorescence in the water created by microscopic animals and plants is also sometimes interpreted in this manner. There is a feeling that where there is a lot of marine life, food for the tuna or not, there is likely to be a lot of tuna. While there are exceptions—certain types of porpoises or whales are believed by some fishermen to scare tuna-carrying porpoise or the tuna themselves away—this feeling is fairly general. Sharks, turtle, and dolphin-fish (mahi-mahi) are all considered good signs.

Another factor is based on the fact that when tuna are not actively migrating they seem to need an object with which to orient themselves in all that ocean. This is the basis for what is called "logfishing." Skipjack tuna will often be found gathered around floating logs, a resting turtle, milk cartons, or anything that floats on or near the surface. Even when they are traveling they will often link up with whales, remaining with them even if the whale dies or stops for long periods of time. Because of this behavior, areas with lots of flotsam are considered potentially good for tuna.

Temperature, color, clarity, thermocline depth, and "condition" of the water are also significant factors in the search. Tuna have a condition akin to warm-bloodedness—that is, they have a body temperature—and they are found in warm water, generally 70 to 80 degrees Fahrenheit. All the boats have instruments with which to gauge sea surface temperature. The fishermen know the general areas where they can expect water of the correct temperature, and they are aware of the major currents and other factors which determine changes in the movements of bodies of water of different temperatures.

The color and clarity of the water are important because the seining process is without a doubt hunting in every sense of the word. A hunter whose trap is invisible to his prey stands a much better chance of capturing it than a hunter whose trap is obvious. Skippers who are school fishing, generally for skipjack, will avoid clear, blue water which is deeper and makes it more likely that the fish will see the net and move to avoid it.

The thermocline depth is the point at which the ocean's top "layer" ends and there is a drastic change in the temperature of the water. The tuna will usually not dive into this colder water, even if it is deep and clear. The thermocline acts as a "bottom" to the net until it is pursed up and the fish are completely trapped within it. The skippers look for areas with shallow thermoclines, preferably shallower than the depth of their net. If you can find one of these areas you are virtually assured that if you can encircle the school with your net the fish won't dive out the bottom.

Measuring the thermocline depth is more difficult than measuring surface temperature. It takes special instruments, some of which may be obtained from the NMFS (National Marine Fisheries Service) on an experimental basis. Only a small portion of the fleet as of 1974 was equipped with these instruments. An alternative to carrying the equipment oneself is getting the information on the thermocline depth from another boat who does have the instruments. This is fairly easily done, though not to very great advantage if the other boat is not very close by.

Besides color, clarity, and temperature there are notions held by some fishermen concerning the "condition" of the water. One man told me that the area where we were at one point during our trip was not good because the water was not "fast." This phenomenon was later explained to me as one which occurs with changes in tides caused by the pull of the moon, usually around the spring and neap tides. The explanation was that the tides stir up the nutrients in the ocean and start a reaction throughout the food chain which makes the tuna more abundant and easier to catch. The teller may have been trying to rationalize scientifically a folk myth. There are many such notions as this, although as far as I could tell most were held by older fishermen and did not contribute significantly to skippers' decisions.

Perhaps the most important "sign" is the presence of bird life. Birds have the best vantage point of all from which to view objects under the surface, and they depend on the same small marine life on which the tuna feed for their own subsistence. Birds will often travel with tuna or porpoise schools even if those schools do not at the moment contain any fish on which the birds themselves could prey. They seem to know that they are both looking for the same thing.

These parameters—weather; water temperature, thermocline depth, clarity, and color; and "signs" such as marine life, flotsam, and the birds—are the major first-hand inputs a skipper would combine with his knowledge of international regulations, past experience, and pre-trip information if he were compelled to conduct the search entirely on his own. It has been suggested that these inputs into fishermen's decision-making processes are too complex to deal with in themselves, and that discussion ought to center around the *processes* used in the decision-making rather than the inputs and outcomes (Quinn, 1971). The inputs, as we have seen, are certainly numerous and complex. But it is the nature of the decision-making process—specifically the weights assigned to the various inputs—rather than the definition of the inputs which makes analysis difficult. It is not as hard to discover what information a skipper possesses as it is to discover what he does with that information.

There are, for example, approximately 150 other seiners from the San Diego fleet alone out there searching for the tuna. The presence of these other boats—most of whom are manned by relatives, friends, and acquaintances—both adds to and alters the inputs and processes a skipper uses to make his decisions. The mechanics of the system of communication between the boats will be described in the next chapter. What follows here is a description of some of the styles which the various skippers use to integrate information from other boats into their own decision-making processes.

Individual Differences and Information From Others

Each skipper has a different set of responsibilities, resources, abilities, and preferences from every other skipper. Some differences between skippers are small in any one or in all of these areas, while in others they are very great. One skipper may have an old, slow, small boat which is paid off and is carrying a crew of his relatives out of San Diego. He himself may be known for his ability to corral the porpoise when yellowfin fishing. He may be the owner or part owner of the boat and involved in the fishing venture with only a relatively small amount of private capital behind him.

Another skipper may have a new, fast, big boat with three times the capacity of the first skipper's. He may be working "for" the large corporation which financed and built the boat and may share the responsibility of meeting the sizable mortgage payments. He may be carrying a crew composed mostly of men from Costa Rica or Panama and be known for his ability to set successfully on school fish.

These differences may lead to different decisions and decision-making strategies. The skipper with the slow boat may not bother to head toward a bank where good catches are reported; he knows that bank fishing is usually crowded, and with his slow boat he would simply be outrun to the schools. The skipper with the new boat may take more chances—setting in rougher weather or setting on doubtful signs of a school under the water (called "setting on bubbles" by the crews)—because his equipment is stronger, or because he is "hungrier"—under more pressure from his financial and other obligations. The skipper with his relatives on board may cut a trip short, especially after an inordinate amount of time at sea or around Christmas, under pressure from the crew; whereas a skipper with a foreign crew will stick it out to get a full load. A skipper of a large boat may leave an area where only small schools are being caught because he believes it would be too much work, time, and risk to fill his boat in small increments; he will seek an area with larger schools. The skipper with the small boat may be very content to stay and load up on the smaller schools.

Partly because of their different sets of constraints and resources and partly because of their personalities and other individual differences, the skippers tend to develop different strategic characteristics in their search procedures. Prominent examples are what are called in the fleet the "hunter" and "chaser" strategies.

76

Some skippers are known as hunters: that is, they rely on their own experience, observations, and hunches to find fish. Others are known as chasers; they rely mostly on information coming over the radio about where other boats are catching fish to make their decisions. Some skippers are hunters solely by virtue of their personalities—they just don't like to depend on information from others and have confidence in their ability to find fish without that information. Some have more of a "chaser" personality not only because it may not bother them to depend on others for their information, but because they have social stock in belonging to the networks through which the information is passed. On the other hand, some skippers are chasers because they have a slow boat, and it is obvious to them that having access to information from faster boats which can cover more ground in their search is extremely useful. Others, especially newer boats, some of which are equipped with helicopters, can afford to be hunters by virtue of their equipment advantage.

The fact that the categories of hunter and chaser with their attendant strategies exist within the fleet brings up a very important point: everyone in the fleet, crewmen and shore-side managers included, has his own perception of the alternatives available to him. These perceptions may or may not coincide with each's "actual" alternatives—those which each could select and take advantage of if he was willing to make the attempt. Some skippers use the hunter strategy because they feel at the time they have the "luck" to find fish without gathering information from others. Other skippers use the hunter strategy because they don't believe they will be able to get useful information from other boats. Some use the chaser strategy because they feel they have obligations to their relatives among the ranks of the skippers to participate in the information network and are hesitant to strike out on their own. Some use it because they believe they are maximizing their alternatives by maximizing their number of information inputs. The same hunter—or chaser—type behaviors can result from radically different perceptions and motives.

Hunters and chasers are of course ideal types. Most skippers possess characteristics of both and use the strategies of each in different mixes. There are skippers in the fleet who are known widely as one or the other, and such a reputation can make big differences in the kind or volume of information one skipper gets from others.

All of these differences will be dealt with systematically in later chapters, but given that each skipper has different resources and constraints and different information sources, he also weighs the information he has differently. Some of these differences stem from differences in preference: a skipper may simply prefer school fishing to yellowfin-porpoise fishing; another may prefer to rely on water temperature more than on the presence of certain "signs." Others' differences stem from attributes of the boat or the crew; the skipper of an old boat may weigh weather conditions particularly heavily because of the age of his equipment; a skipper with a particularly good set of speed-boat drivers will weigh good yellowfin-porpoise information more heavily.

Still other differences in weighings stem from the source of the information: each skipper has his own impressions of how trustworthy each of the other skippers is, and how good the information he passes on is likely to be. While the weights of certain factors, particularly when they occur in combination with one another, are generally agreed upon, there is always room for considerable differences in evaluation and strategy—which can be seen partly from the wide dispersal of boats on the fishing grounds at any point in time.

Short-circuiting the Search Procedure

Most of the time the skippers seem to proceed on what might be termed a "rational" course in terms of the decision processes they normally employ; receiving inputs, evaluating them, acting and generally behaving in a regular and predictable manner. Sometimes, however, this search procedure seems to be interrupted.

For example, I was off the coast of Colombia where we were seeing good signs, the water temperature was right, and it was the crew's general impression that we were in a good "area" when our skipper heard over the radio that one boat had made a fairly good set some 500 miles to the north. To the surprise of the crew we immediately headed north at full speed with the understanding which sometimes accompanies such moves that we didn't have to overexert ourselves on the glasses because we were "in transit." We arrived a day-and-a-half later to find that only one boat had made only one good set, and we were forced to begin a new search in our new—and as it turned out, less desirable—location. In the meantime the boats that had been with us in our former location to the south had hit on an area of school fish soon after we left.

Actions like this are not uncommon, especially among the ranks of the chasers. Although it could be argued that it was simply a case of weighting—the expected value of the new location as evidenced by the one other boat's success outweighed the present value of the signs we were encountering in our former location—the skippers who exhibit these actions will seldom try to defend them as such. They will make comments like, "We didn't have any fish down there. I was just taking a chance." There does not seem to be evidence of any "rational" calculation.

What the skippers often say when asked about actions such as these is that they were acting on a hunch. The word "hunch" can mean many things. It could mean what the standard definition of the word implies—that the skipper had an intuitive feeling about a particular area or course of action. Not only the skipper, but everyone on board gets these "feelings," especially after a long time in the search and more especially after a search without fish.

An interpretation less charitable to the skippers themselves is the sense of "hunch" which is synonymous with whim or fancy. Besides obvious economic decisions and decisions which are determined by complex social factors, many decisions do indeed seem to be made simply at the skipper's pleasure. Every crewman can cite examples of decisions of this sort, and although the kind of incomplete information to which most crewmen are privy makes their opinions on these matters somewhat less than

79

fully informed, even those close to the skippers concede that decisions of this type occur fairly often.

Another interpretation of decisions of this sort is that they are made when all the alternatives have equal value or weight. This may sometimes happen, but it is rarely put in these terms. The skippers hold their position by virtue of their control over the process and their ability to make decisions. To admit that all alternatives have equal weight would be to admit that their particular contribution to the decision-making process, in this case at least, has no value. If there is no basis for a skipper's decision between alternatives, they will not usually let that fact be known.

There are circumstances, however, where skippers will admit that there is no "rational" basis for their decisions. When a boat has good weather, good signs, and all the indications that they should be "on fish" yet does not succeed in bringing a catch aboard, the skipper will often pick up and steam off to another area or instigate a new search pattern solely for the purpose of "changing his luck." In most of these cases the crew is in agreement that "there's no reason there shouldn't be fish here," and often the skipper's decision to move on is determined as much by the crew's state of mind as by the lack of fish.

The Visual Search
The tuna schools are found almost entirely by sight alone. The directional sonars with the capability to "see" underwater found in other fisheries do not enjoy very much popularity in the tuna fleet, largely because it is possible to spot tuna with binoculars at distances of 5 to 11 or 12 miles, while the best sonar sets have a range of only a mile or so. It is true that sonar sets can pick up a school running deep which would be missed by a man with binoculars, and some boats keep their vertical depth sounders running just in case they "run over" a school which is too deep for the men on the glasses to have spotted.

The directional sonar units are expensive, and in the year I fished with the fleet only six boats out of over a hundred were equipped with them. I fished aboard a boat which had one, with a man very skilled in its use. He could use the equipment with a fair amount of success in determining the size of the school, its density, direction of movement, and even to some extent the size and species of fish. The skipper used this information where it supplemented his own observations and judgment, but in most cases these alone were sufficient to capture the school. Few people in the fleet have access to an experienced sonar man such as the one with whom I fished, and at least up until now the general success of the fleet with its present methods has been good enough to allow them to ignore this bit of technology.

Besides this, it is generally true that most skippers are not willing to wait around for a deep school to "show"—to come close enough to the surface to be accessible to the seining process—because this may take hours or even days. Setting on a school which is not "showing" can create problems. Even if the net will reach deep enough, deep objects create an identification problem. Skippers who have set on a "school" which was not "showing" well have often come up with a few tons of squid. A good visual sighting is assurance that at least a portion of the school is at a shallow depth, and since a good portion of the search is for porpoise, which the tuna follow and which are on the surface anyway, most skippers do not bother with the depth sounders.

The binoculars used in the visual search are a very specialized piece of equipment. They are from two to three feet long and usually have 20 power magnification and a three degree field. If you join your thumb and your forefinger in a circle and hold it at arm's length and look through the circle, that is approximately as much area as you see through the glasses. Most men say that this is about as much as one can practically "scan" at one time. Some also say that 20 power is the greatest magnification that is practical with the movement and vibration of the boat at sea, but larger glasses with different fields and greater magnification are being tried all the time.

The glasses are mounted in supports which allow them to be moved up and down and from side to side. Some are hung on shock cord to take up the vibration of the boat. Half an hour

81

of looking through glasses of that power is tiring, but if they are vibrating the least bit they can also cause severe headaches.

What one is searching for through the glasses is anything which may indicate the presence of tuna: porpoise, jumping fish, birds, floating objects, whales, any other form of flotsam or marine life, or changes in the "condition" of the sea surface. This is where what the fishermen call "good eyes" become important. Often the clues one has to recognize are infinitesimal compared to the total scene observed through the glasses. A porpoise or a fish jumping twelve miles away and making a small splash when it lands, a piece of plywood bobbing in a rough sea, or tiny flashes of white indicating birds diving and exposing their light-colored undersides to the sun are often the only things with which one has to work.

This problem is most pronounced in what is called "school fishing," where the tuna are neither gathered around a piece of flotsam nor following porpoise. Often the only indication of their presence is what is called a "breezer." If you have ever seen a still body of water swept by the first bit of wind in the morning or seen fish swim close to the surface in a tank or pond, the ripples and scallops which appear on the surface of the water are what forms a "breezer." At sea, breezers are caused by some form of marine life swimming in a group close to the surface. They often take the form of a calming of a rougher surface or some other slight alteration in the wave pattern and action. They are made more difficult to spot by the motion of the surrounding sea.

Some but not all of the fishermen have incredibly "good eyes." Many times other crewmen and I took turns looking through the glasses for what one of these hawkeyes told us was a big school of porpoise, a flock of birds "working," or a big breezer. From the minutest visual clues, ones often not even visible to other men, they can tell you amazing things about the size of the school, the type and size of the fish, their behavior, and the likelihood that you will be able to catch them. Those with "good eyes" are the men who are used as mast men, or on boats where only a portion of the crew uses the glasses, as "glasses men."

On boats where everyone "looks" there is a hierarchy involved in using the glasses, and this varies from boat to boat. In general, the men with more success at finding signs and the older men in the crew use the glasses most, the former because they produce results and the latter because their seniority has earned them the right to be on the glasses, a less physically demanding job than repair or maintenance work.

Each man picks one particular set of glasses which suits him best (the glasses have large eye-pieces which are meant to conform to facial features in order to shut out outside light), and he usually only relieves men using that set of glasses.

At the beginning of the trip everyone wants to look for fish. The ones with the "good eyes" generally spend more time on the glasses, partly because everyone is anxious to catch fish and partly because the "glasses men" want to prove their abilities and exert their status. As the trip wears on, more regular glasses watches are set up. People become more insistent that someone relieve them after their half-hour interval, the normal duration of a "glasses watch."

As certain "threshold figures" are approached, in terms of catch and length of time at sea (see Chapter Seven), the glasses schedule gets more lax. Often one pair will be left empty for various periods of time, until someone feels like looking, or the man who left to take a break returns, or the skipper comes on the bridge and notices they are empty. This is the point at which neither the fish nor the status derived from spotting a school can override the fact that the men are just plain tired of being out on the ocean looking for fish.

Within the watch schedule itself, younger or more inexperienced men tend to fill in the gaps which the men with good eyes leave open, always yielding to the latter if they wish to "look."

The Sightings

When something is sighted which a man thinks bears investigation, the skipper is called immediately. He will usually want to look for himself, but sometimes he will take the word of an experienced man with good eyes that whatever the latter

83

sees is something for which it is worth altering course. Likewise, an inexperienced man will often call a more experienced one to confirm his sightings before he calls the skipper. At this point the skipper's set-making decision process begins.

The skipper's decision to turn toward signs of the presence of tuna is determined by a hierarchy of understandings about the "goodness" of various kinds of signs. One of the most commonly sighted signs is a flock of birds. The birds are evaluated as to their individual size, their species, the size of the flock, and their behavior. Large birds are considered better than small birds. Large flocks are considered better than small ones. Man-'o-War birds—large black birds with a long split tail, which tend to fly at higher altitudes and only congregate where "something is cooking"—are considered the best ornithological sign of fish. There is a saying that there will be 10 tons of tuna for every Man o' War. Birds which are "working"—diving, swooping, generally moving in vertical patterns—are considered better than birds which are "moving"—simply flying across the water.

The other category of sightings where there is no direct visual contact with any submarine creatures is that of the "breezers" mentioned earlier. These are evaluated according to their size—large surface areas affected are better than small ones—and their "strength"—they vary from light to medium to heavy depending on the texture of their imprint on the sea surface. Two other conditions which could also be included under this category are "boilers" and "foamers." The "boiler" occurs when the school's underwater activity intensifies and gives the sea surface the appearance of boiling water. The "foamer" occurs when the fish's activity increases to the point where the sea surface is churned into a froth or foam. Boilers and foamers are not really classified as kinds of breezers by the fishermen, although many times they share the breezers' attribute of concealing from sight what is creating the surface condition. Heavy breezers are considered better than light ones, and boilers and foamers are considered better than "regular" breezers in ascending order. Like "working" birds, these latter two sightings more often indicate that the fish are concentrated, close to the surface, and occupied in feeding or some other activity which will make them less likely to react to the presence of the boat or the net.

A third category of sightings are those where the tuna themselves are actually visible. These range from "shiners," where the reflections of the sun off of the shining silver and gold sides of the tuna can be seen clearly from above the surface; to "finners," where all that is visible is the dorsal and possibly the tail fins of the tuna breaking the surface; to "jumpers," where the tuna break the surface with most of their bodies, often leaping high in the air.

Within this last category, it is less clear which condition is preferable. For example, while jumpers make it more certain that it is tuna which are present and not some other species of fish of their size and type, it also often means that the fish are "on the move" and will be hard to work and to "wrap" with the net.

A fourth and very important category of sightings is "log" sightings. Any piece of flotsam which has attracted tuna is termed a "log." With log sightings the size of the object is important— bigger objects being preferable—but the size is not as important as the amount and species of marine life in the water around the log. Skippers will sometimes tie the log to the seiner with a long line and simply drift along with it. "Log fish" are known to exhibit a ranging behavior back and forth about their log, sometimes going more than a mile in each direction before returning to it. The skippers, realizing this, are often willing to wait and see if tuna will collect around the log even if there are none in sight when they first approach it.

The last category of sightings is porpoise. There are three species of porpoise which "carry"—are followed by—tuna in the Eastern Pacific; the fishermen call these "spotters," "spinners," and "white-bellies." These species are differentiated by their color and body type. Spotters are grey spotted porpoise with curving, swept-back dorsal fins; spinners are darker in color and

85

have more triangular dorsal fins; white-bellies have clearly de-marcated white undersides. They are also differentiated by their behavior.[1]

The spotters are generally considered the best species be-cause they carry tuna and are reasonably workable a good per-centage of the time. They are calm and group together when they are inside the net, which makes them easy to get out again before the fish are brailed aboard the boat. The spinners are the least preferable because they often carry little or no tuna and because they are spooky and tend to scatter more than the other species when they are inside the net, thus making them harder to get out. They are easily recognizable by the spins they perform when they leap clear of the water. The white-bellies often carry large numbers of tuna but they have the reputation of being the hard-est species to herd with the speedboats and keep inside the net until the bottom is "pursed" shut. For these reasons many skip-pers will never set on white-bellies, considering it a waste of time. The behavior which the porpoise exhibit is a very important input into the process, and it will be explained in more detail presently.

These categories of sightings occur often in combination with one another and their values are additive. Birds and porpoise together are considered preferable, for example, to either por-poise or birds alone. One could probably elicit an inter-category value hierarchy also, such as big birds working being preferable to spinner porpoise alone, but the comparisons would have little meaning. It is very rare that signs from two different categories are sighted at the same time but separated enough in space to require a decision between the two.

There are also other factors which enter into a skipper's decision to investigate a sighting of good signs. Most sightings are of birds and are ambiguous enough in their expected value to allow the skipper considerable leeway in his decisions. If he is anxious to get to another area where he thinks the chances are better of "making a trip"—filling the boat—he may choose to

1. See Perrin (1968, 1969) for more on the porpoise-tuna relationship.

ignore even relatively promising signs. If the crew is tired from a continuous period of activity or if it is late in the trip, the weather is rough, and he is aware that the boat is over the crew's general "threshold" level in terms of an acceptable load (see Chapter Seven), he may also choose to simply continue on course. If the signs appear directly on his course, however, or if they are in the form of a heavy breezer, boiler, or spotters with big birds working, he may have no choice but to investigate and move into the next portion of his decision-making process; that of whether or not to actually make a set.

To Set or Not?

As soon as the skipper makes the decision to investigate the signs further, one of several things may happen. If the signs are good and it is porpoise fish, he may order the "rig"—the speedboats used to herd the porpoise—into the water immediately. If he does this, he himself climbs immediately to the crow's nest at the top of the mast to get a better view of the school and eventually to direct the speedboats by radio in their herding of the porpoise and the setting of the net.

If the signs are of school or log fish and are good, he will order the crew to get ready for a school fish set and also climb up the mast. Often, though, the signs in these cases will be inconclusive until the seiner gets closer to them, and the whole crew including the skipper will gather on the bridge to inspect the situation. If the signs look promising the skipper will then go up the mast for a better view; if not, the seiner will turn and continue on whatever course is the skipper's pleasure.

Several things enter into a skipper's decision to actually set the net. Often he must weigh all of them in a matter of seconds in order to avoid letting the school get away from him. He knows that anytime he gives the order to "let 'er go" he is committing the boat and crew to anywhere from one and a half to three hours work. Under normal conditions it takes almost the same amount of time to make a "skunk" set—one with no fish at all—as it does to make a set and haul 20 or 25 tons of tuna aboard. Since the tuna are not cleaned or processed in any way, the only added time is that taken sacking up and brailing the fish, which is small compared to the time it takes to simply get the net back aboard. Each set also puts a tremendous strain on the equipment. Cables and other running equipment are replaced often, and skippers do not usually want to subject the equipment to the wear and the men to the danger inherent in even a skunk set unless they are fairly sure of getting a "jag"—a haul of fish—out of it.

The skipper must also decide if the weather conditions will permit a set. He must take into account the wind, swell, sea surface chop, the presence of any tide rips or other strong underwater currents which might play havoc with his net, and the chance of rain or fog which may impair vision and cause his speedboats to get lost (a situation which many, unfortunately, have encountered) or hinder his ability to direct the set. In this regard he must also take the time of day into account. Several times we were out in the speedboats and the skipper ordered us back to the seiner because it was getting too dark for him to see either us or the porpoise. Generally, if a skipper can be assured of surrounding the school and hooking both ends of the net up to the seiner before it gets dark, he will go ahead and set. This is the portion of the set which requires visual contact. There is a form of night fishing done for bluefin tuna in certain parts of the Pacific where there is a sufficient level of phosphorescence in the water. This enables the skipper to monitor the behavior of the fish by watching the "fireball," as they call it, created by the school's movement. This is not done very much, and is very unpopular with the crews because of the danger involved.

He must take into account the behavior of the porpoise and the tuna themselves. Often, either of them will exhibit behavior patterns which make them "unworkable"—spookiness, not bunching together properly, the entire school making sudden changes of direction or diving too deep for the seine to reach them.

Finally, he must take into account the condition of the crewmen themselves. If it is the fourth or fifth set of the day or the end of a long trip with a comfortable load on board, and if the crew is tired and missing cues, lacking the alertness necessary to the process, or otherwise exhibiting signs of mental or physical fatigue, a skipper may pass up a school on which he might otherwise have attempted to set.

All these factors will be tempered by the skipper's "hunger" and his perception of his opportunity costs—what he thinks he may be able to find given an equivalent amount of time continuing the search or traveling to another location or area. At the end of a long trip with only a small load, after a period of more than a couple of days without bringing any fish aboard, or after a series of frustrating near-misses a skipper may be willing to set where he otherwise might not. This can also mean, however, that they will be willing to set in weather which is too rough thus subjecting the equipment to more strain and the crew to more danger. Some skippers are reputed to be like this all the time. The action orientation inherent in "hunger" is admired in skippers by many men, but their accompanying willingness to take chances is considerably less popular.

Stalking the Tuna

Once the decision to attempt a set has been made, the skipper begins to stalk his quarry. Although the term "industrial hunting" (Anderson and Wadel, 1972) is sometimes used to characterize fisheries which use modern machinery yet must contend with an evasive quarry and an unpredictable environment, I use the term "stalking" here rather than hunting or simply "fishing." The portion of the process I am about to describe is neither groping nor looking for anything; it is employing strategy to capture a quarry once it has been located, a quarry which has considerable evasive capabilities and, in the case of porpoise, evasive strategies.

While the deckboss has the major responsibility for the retrieval of the net and for the brailing, skiff-lifting, and re-rigging operations, the skipper has the sole responsibility for the decision-making in the stalking and encircling of the tuna. All commands and directions during this period come from the skipper's position in the crow's nest.

There are three different stalking procedures: one for porpoise fish, one for school fish, and one for log fish. I will describe them each in turn.

Porpoise

An obvious question is why fishermen looking for tuna pay any attention to porpoise. The answer is that one species of tuna, the yellowfin, travel with certain species of porpoise. No one knows exactly why the yellowfin follow the porpoise, although the best theories to date are that the tuna and the porpoise feed on the same kinds of smaller marine life and that they share some of the same natural predators. Sharks, for example, for whom the tuna have no love, seem to shy away from contact with certain kinds of porpoise. It may even be that the porpoise follow the tuna, but observation seems to indicate otherwise. None of the present theories explain why only the yellowfin tuna follow the porpoise, or why they only follow certain species of porpoise.

The tuna "follow" the porpoise in the sense that they swim under or just behind the porpoise. The porpoise are mammals and must surface to breathe, so they tend to do most of their swimming at shallow depths. The depth at which the tuna swim varies from immediately under the surface, in among the porpoise themselves, to several hundred feet. The general idea in "porpoise fishing" is that if one can surround the porpoise school with the seine, the tuna underneath them will be surrounded also. This may or may not actually happen. Assuming that the porpoise in question are carrying tuna, the tuna will often suddenly stop following the porpoise, apparently deciding to go off in their own direction.

The species of porpoise which carry the tuna are very frolicsome. They leap out of the water as they swim, and can often be seen "riding" steep swells or the bow wake of a ship. They are famous for swimming along diving and darting about under the bows of ships, sometimes for hours on end. This behavior, particularly the leaping out of the water, makes their school visible for quite a distance. They travel in schools of anywhere

90

from a few porpoise to thousands. They are capable of swimming very fast and are extremely agile under the water. They are also one of the most intelligent mammals.

The general procedure for stalking the porpoise is this. When the school is spotted and tuna are seen jumping around the school or there are other indications that the school is carrying fish, the skipper orders the "rig" into the water. The rig consists of the four or five speedboats stored either on the bridge deck or the working deck of the seiner.

The speedboats are approximately 15 feet long. They are made of fiberglass or aluminum and are relatively light for their size. They have a single seat directly on the centerline of the boat. Immediately behind the seat is a twelve-gallon gas tank. The speedboats are powered by outboard motors, usually from 60 to 80 horsepower.

There are various mechanical devices for lifting the speedboats over the side of the seiner into the water. Some boats lift them with the brailing and unloading booms, some with extendable hydraulic booms called "cherry-pickers," and some with an apparatus designed especially for the speedboats. It is usual on most seiners to make what are called "full-speed launches" of the speedboats. When the skipper gives the order to launch the rig, the driver of the speedboat nearest the rail (they are stored abreast of one another across the seiner) climbs into his boat and makes ready to be launched. Each man's seat is equipped with a four- or five-inch thick foam or pneumatic pad to absorb the impact of his ride. The speedboat drivers wear a headset through which they receive the skipper's instructions via the boat's "Mickey Mouse" radio, and if the weather is rough, lifejackets. Around his midsection the driver wears a "kidney belt"—a wide, heavy elastic belt—to protect his internal organs and back from the jarring he will encounter.

The boats have a sling attached at the bow and at each corner of the stern. This sling has a lifting ring in the center over the driver's seat, at the balance point. When the driver gets into his boat he hooks the lifting cable into the lifting ring, checks to see that the drain plug in the bottom of the boat has been replaced, that his radio is working, and that his gas cap vent is properly adjusted. He then signals the lift operator to take him over the side. The procedure is called a full-speed launch because the seiner does not slow down as the speedboat is put into the water. It maintains its full speed of from 12 to 17 knots.

An outrigger has been set up which extends ten or twelve feet out at right angles to the side of the seiner. A line is led through a block on the end of the outrigger and from there to the bow fitting on the speedboat. This line is attached to the speedboat with a quick-release fitting. The line which releases the fitting from the bow of the speedboat is led back to the rail of the seiner. When the speedboat is lowered over the side of the seiner, sliding down padded rails which prevent either from damaging the other, it is halted two or three feet from the water. The driver then starts his engine and revs it up to match the speed of the seiner. He then signals the lift operator to lower him the rest of the way into the water. Once in the water the line on his bow which runs up to the block on the outrigger tows the boat and helps keep it under control.

At this point the speedboat is in the water beside the seiner, still attached to the outrigger by its bowline. In front of the speedboat is the bow wake of the seiner, usually two or three feet high, and behind it is the quarter wake, usually three or four feet high but breaking as a wave breaks on the beach. As soon as the driver feels that he is under control he signals the man with the release line to pull his bow fitting loose. He then must jump the bow wake and get clear of the seiner before the quarter wake catches up to him, in which case his boat would be flooded. If the skipper should subsequently decide not to set and the speedboats must be picked up again at full speed, the drivers must perform this procedure in reverse; jump back over the wake to get alongside the seiner, inch up to a ring which is dangling from the block at the end of the outrigger, let go of the controls with both hands, attach the bow line to the ring, and catch the lifting hook and attach it to their lifting sling.

This process is certainly not without its dangers. Occasionally, lifting slings break or hooks and lines slip, and in rough weather the seiner is rolling and the drivers must contend with the swell and the cross-chop on the sea surface. Accidents, however, are relatively infrequent.

When all the speedboats have been launched they line up in order—the number one speedboat is the leader and is generally the fastest boat, the number two man the second fastest, and so on—with the number one boat next to the seiner and each of the others to the right and slightly behind the boat to its left. When the skipper decides to start working the school, he tells the speedboats to "take off" and sends them out one at a time starting with the number one boat. The interval between them is determined by whether the porpoise are concentrated or spread out. Each boat falls in line and follows the one in front of it, with the skipper directing the number one boat. The boats are often sent out to start working the school when the seiner is five or six and sometimes up to ten miles away from the school; this distance is limited only by the skipper's ability to see the school and the gas in the speedboats' tanks, which at full speed will last about 45 minutes. When the skipper gives the order to go, the drivers put their boats at full throttle and usually leave it there until the net has been set. In a calm sea the speedboats can make about 30 knots.

One of the ways that the skipper can tell if it is too rough to set is by observing the action of the speedboats. Porpoise sets can be and are made in up to about ten-foot seas and 30 knots of wind, and in anything over three or four feet of sea and 15 knots of wind the going begins to get rough for the speedboats.They fly from the crest of one wave to another, slamming into the water just long enough for their propellers to get a bite and thrust them out of the water again. Certain parts on the outboard motors must be replaced often because they are simply beaten apart by the slamming of the seas. Back and kidney injuries to the drivers themselves are another all-too-frequent consequence of manning the speedboats under these conditions. If it is rough enough so that the speedboats simply fly out of the water, the wind catching their undersides and lifting their bows so that they head almost straight out of the water and bounce back down again on

93

their sterns unable to make headway, the skipper calls off the set.

If the weather permits the speedboats to work, the general procedure they follow is fairly standard. The seiner approaches the school with the porpoise on its port side and the speedboats in line on its bow. The speedboats then gradually turn in towards the school, attempting to drive it to the left. As the school's direction is altered, the seiner bears to port to follow it. This tends to have the effect of bunching the school together from its right side.

As the school bunches closer together the skipper directs the speedboats to start out around the school, which they do in the form of a semicircle, always pushing the porpoise to the left. This constant pushing to the left, with the seiner bearing left to follow, results in the seiner eventually coming full circle. If they started to work with the seiner headed in a northerly direction they swing toward the west, then the south, then the east, and eventually back to the north again. As this is going on the skipper must keep a constant watch on the wind and swell direction, because it is important that he be downwind of the school, "in position" when he lets the skiff go.

The circling movements and the constant push from the speedboats eventually close the porpoise into a tight group. The ideal is to bunch the porpoise closely enough together that the speedboats will be able to almost surround them. In this situation the porpoise will often stop moving and start to mill around in a group, which is perfect for the skipper. He can then round into position and make a smooth circle around the school.

All of this is, of course, wishful thinking most of the time. The speedboat driver has to keep one eye on the waves so he does not beat his brains out, listen to the often excited directions from the skipper which may be coming alternately in English and in Spanish, Italian, or Portuguese, and at the same time keep track of the porpoise, which often disappear behind swells or into the glare of the sun and who are invisible under the water most of the time anyway. If you have ever watched a cowboy herd cattle on a horse, that is approximately the way the speedboat drivers herd the porpoise—zig-zagging back and forth amid sprints to get ahead of a renegade section of the school or to keep up with the whole school itself. The porpoise can swim as fast as the speedboats can motor and they have the frustrating ability to simply dive under the speedboats—analogous to a cow having the ability to jump over the cowboy and his horse. If a speedboat driver gets too close to the porpoise in his "pushing," they will dive out to the right under his boat every time. Once porpoise break out to the right of the semicircle made by the speedboats and the seiner, they are virtually impossible to herd back to the main part of the school.

The reason that the porpoise can be herded at all seems to be that they are afraid of the noise of the propellers and engines and the general commotion of the speedboats. The behavior of the porpoise in response to the speedboats has changed, however, since the advent of tuna seining in the nineteen sixties.

When seining was first introduced into the tuna fleet, it was possible to round up a school of porpoise easily with the seiner and one or two speedboats. As the porpoise came into contact with more and more seiners, however, they became harder and harder to work. Now it takes five speedboats to work most schools, and even then it is impossible to get many of them to bunch together, much less to stop and mill around in one spot. Instead they wander off in small groups, seemingly impervious to the antics of the speedboats, often even playing under the speedboat much the same as they do under the bows of larger ships. The whole school may shift direction rather than allowing itself to be "pushed" together. Often they will dive and remain submerged for long periods of time to avoid the nuisance of the speedboats. Even more frustrating, different species of porpoise and porpoise in different areas of the Pacific seem to have consistent strategies for dealing with the seiners.

The spotted porpoise off the coast of Nicaragua, for example, will consistently let themselves be worked smoothly into a tight school. But when the skiff is released and the chains and rings start rattling down the stern of the seiner, a sound easily perceived by the porpoise, they explode in all different directions, as if someone had put a bomb in their midst, and the seiner ends up with an empty net.

The white-belly porpoise off the coast of Costa Rica are the worst offenders in this regard. White-belly porpoise in other parts of the Pacific do not seem to "carry" tuna as much as the ones off Costa Rica, which are often spotted carrying large schools. The white-bellies are harder to work than the other species, but they can sometimes be "wrapped" with the seine. Consistently, however, they will mill in the center of the seine, sometimes until the net is more than half pursed, and then suddenly dive out the open bottom, often taking the tuna with them. This particular behavior causes many skippers to refuse to make a set on white-bellies, considering it a waste of time and effort. This is the kind of thing to which I have been referring when I have spoken of the "behavior" of the porpoise. They are fast-swimming, intelligent mammals capable of adapting to situations and their "skills" are becoming more and more a match for those of the tuna fishermen.

To further complicate things, the movements of the porpoise are sometimes independent of those of the tuna. If the white-bellies dive out of the seine—which, by the way, any of the species of porpoise or even the fish themselves may do on occasion—sometimes the tuna will *not* follow them. Sometimes, on the other hand, you may wrap the porpoise only to find that the tuna were swimming too deep for the seine to reach or simply "decided" to keep swimming when the porpoise slowed down and started milling. Whether the porpoise are wrapped with the seine, or whether they proceed to dive out the bottom, it is often no better than an even bet that you will end up with a "jag."

Setting on porpoise is a prime example of what makes the particular brand of uncertainty involved in tuna fishing bear harder on the fishermen than the uncertainties in many other fisheries: it is uncertainty that must be borne in the face of expectations raised by the presence of the porpoise, or by the knowledge that there *was* a school there when the seiner started the chase. It is almost always the case that the men have actually seen the

96

fish they expect to catch. Even after the men know that they have successfully circled the school, they must wait until the rings are up to be sure of their catch. In the time that must pass until then—usually at least half an hour—they have little control over whether or not the fish stay in the net.

Even if the porpoise do not "misbehave" the school is often too big or too spread out for the skipper to hope to get all of the porpoise inside of the seine. In this case he has to "cut" the school, going for the part for which he is in the best position or which are bunched the most closely together. Although good speedboat drivers can anticipate decisions such as this, only the skipper has the vantage point to make the decision properly. The crewmen on the deck below sometimes exhibit considerable bravado in disagreeing with the skipper's opinion in this matter, although never in his presence. Everyone can see the porpoise, and comments as to where the skipper went wrong in his decision to cut or to go for the whole school are voiced vigorously until the latter climbs down from the mast.

To get all of the porpoise he desires inside the net, the skipper often has to let out a considerable length of towline. This leaves an even bigger gap in the seine, often extending a hundred or more yards off the stern of the seiner. As soon as the seiner begins to approach the skiff and the totally unobstructed outlet to the surrounding sea is closed off, the skipper orders all of the speedboats but one to the towline. They proceed to race up and down the towline at full speed in an attempt, usually successful, to keep the porpoise away from the still-open portion of the seine under the towline. The other speedboat is kept in reserve, in case the porpoise break toward the net in another place or an extra hand is needed for some other purpose. When the oertza is finally drawn to the stern of the seiner, thus closing the circle completely, the speedboats come back to the seiner and are lifted aboard. The exception to this occurs during a set made on white-bellies. In a white-belly set, the speedboats are left in the water and spaced out around the net until the rings are almost up, in an effort to prevent the white-bellies from diving out of the seine. Often, however, the white-bellies simply ignore the

97

speedboats and perform their usual routine, swimming out under various parts of the seine at their pleasure.

These are the usual procedures used in a set on tuna-carrying porpoise, although my description certainly does not cover all of the possibilities nor does it address itself to the many, many subtleties of the process. The procedure is somewhat different for a set on school fish, which are tuna traveling or found in an area by themselves without accompanying porpoise.

School Fish

School fish are most often skipjack tuna.[2] Some yellowfin are sometimes mixed in with a school of skipjack, but in most school fish sets, one is dealing with skipjack. More care must be taken in determining exactly what species of fish it is that you are dealing with when contemplating a set on school fish. Black skipjack tuna and a small mackerel-like fish called "bullets" closely resemble "good" skipjack (acceptable to the cannery), but neither are of any value to the fishermen. Skipjack tuna are smaller than the yellowfin, rarely averaging over 40 pounds, while the yellowfin often average over a hundred. If the water is murky or if the school is not "showing" properly, lines with jigs are trailed off the stern of the seiner to catch a sample of the school to determine their species and size.

Stalking school fish in many ways demands more subtlety than stalking the porpoise. The porpoise lend a certain consistency to the behavior of the tuna, a consistency noticeably lacking in school fish. School fish are much spookier, and they change

2. In talking to fisheries biologists since this chapter was written, I have discovered that a great many of the school-fish sets recorded during the 1975 season, the year after I fished with the fleet, were made on yellowfin traveling without porpoise. This is discrepant with my experience and the information I obtained through conversations with the fishermen during my year with the fleet. Further research into the fishermen's perceptions of the resource, more biological research on the tuna populations themselves, and refinements in both of these systems of data collection will help to reduce discrepancies such as this. For further information concerning the tuna populations, see the "Publications Issued by the Inter-American Tropical Tuna Commission," listed in the References.

direction more often and in a more erratic fashion. Whereas you actually confront the porpoise and actively manipulate them, you more or less have to sneak up on school fish.

The breezer-finner-jumper-boiler-foamer taxonomy is very important with school fish. If a school is "traveling"—moving in one direction at a good rate of speed and exhibiting none of these characteristics save perhaps a light breezer—it will be almost impossible to catch. There are other conditions, such as schools feeding on flying fish (in which case they tend to scatter in all different directions rather than bunch together as they do on a school of submarine feed), that also make it very difficult to wrap the fish.

Once the determination is made that the school is of the proper species and size and that their behavior is satisfactory, the set goes much the same as described earlier. Speedboats are rarely used because they simply spook the fish and make them scatter rather than pushing them together as they do the porpoise.

The fishermen would like the net itself to be practically invisible to the fish, and skippers prefer to set on school fish in murky water. An expedition to the southwest Pacific to explore new tuna resources there failed because, among other things, the water was too clear and the fish always scattered away from the net. Most of the school fishing is done inshore partly for this reason, because the inshore coastal waters are generally more disturbed and cloudy than those far out at sea.

Once the net has been set around the school, the big problem is to keep the fish from swimming out of the seine through the large opening under the seiner. This is more of a problem with school fish than with porpoise fish, because with the former the fish are often far under water where it is both difficult to monitor their behavior and to have any effect on it. There are four general means the fishermen use to control the fish once the net has been set and the towline and purse cable are being drawn in.

One is what are called "seal bombs." These are firecracker-like explosives with a sand or metal weight built into the body of the charge just below the powder. They are not very powerful but make a good-sized "pop" when they go off. When the net is being closed, two or three men stand at the port rail of the seiner and light these seal bombs with cigarettes which they carry for that purpose and throw them into the water around the seiner. The seal bombs sink a few fathoms because of the weight inside and then explode, scaring the fish away from the open portion of the net. They are not powerful enough to damage the tuna.

A second means of control is dye or dye-covered rocks. The dye with which the rocks are covered is phosphorescent green and it colors the water as the rocks sink. The use to which the dye is put is slightly ambiguous. Sometimes the rocks are thrown into the water from the time the skiff is let go, coloring the water along the entire length of the net, and sometimes they are used only next to the seiner after the school has been encircled. Some say the purpose of the dye is to hide the net, while others say it is to scare the fish from the area which is being dyed. It seems to serve both purposes.

A third method employed to keep the fish in the net is an air hammer. This is a device which emits a powerful burst of compressed air at short intervals. It is lowered on a long hose into the water directly beneath the seiner, and to the fish it probably has the same quality as a large seal bomb.

The fourth and simplest method of control, but often the most effective, is simply pounding on anything metal connected directly to the hull of the seiner or to the seine itself. On some boats there is a special metal plate welded into the deck on the port side on which one or more crewmen pound with sledgehammers while the net is being pursed. The hull transmits the sound and vibration of the pounding to the water, hopefully scaring the fish away. In a like manner, some crewmen pound on the metal purse cable with crowbars. While this looks rather comical at the time and the men joke about it, it seems to work.

If all of these methods fail, which they sometimes do, an exasperated crewman or two may jump into the water and frantically splash and kick. This seems to do nothing more than attract sharks and is not done too often. It does, however, illustrate how frustrating it can be to watch $50,000 worth of fish suddenly turn, ignoring all of your best efforts, and dart en masse under the seiner and out of the seine.

Log Fish

Log fish are essentially a special case of school fish. They are almost always skipjack and exhibit many of the same behavioral characteristics as school fish without a log. The main advantage of log fish is that the schools generally stay fairly close to the log and are considerably less spooky than free school fish. The fishermen look on log fish as a picnic in terms of the difficulty of stalking them, although log fish have one major disadvantage. That disadvantage is that the log is often surrounded by other species of fish also, notably the infamous "bullets." It is very common to wrap a large number of bullets along with the good tuna in sets on log fish.

The problem with bullets is that they are on the average about a foot long and three inches in diameter, which is exactly the right size to enable them to swim half way through the mesh in the seine. There they stick, their size not allowing them to go through and their fins not allowing them to back out even if they had much mobility in that direction, which they do not. As the net is rolled and the bowl in the water gets smaller and smaller, more of these fish try to swim through the net and get stuck. Sometimes you get what the fishermen call a "Christmas tree." In a Christmas tree, every mesh in the triangle of the net—from the apex where it meets the powerblock to its base where it meets the water—has a fish stuck in it. Sometimes the entire seine, from the half-net buoy to the bow oertza, is filled with bullets.

This creates several problems, the most urgent of which is that the fish being smashed in the powerblock cause the net to slip and the powerblock to lose traction. This means that you cannot get the net out of the water. To remedy this, the bullets have to be extricated from the net as it passes the rail of the seiner, a slow process at best. The problem is made worse by the fact that the bullets are stuck tightly in the meshes. It is necessary

101

much of the time to twist them in half to get them out of the net. Even if the crew can clear enough of the bullets out of the net to permit the powerblock to gain traction the net must later be "rolled back" onto the working deck and the rest of the net cleaned. Bullets stink if left in the net, and sharks will literally devour the seine itself if the bullets are left in the mesh until the next set.

In sets where the boat is "killed with bullets" the deck becomes ankle-deep in extricated fish parts. The pieces which are missed go up to the block and rain down on the men stacking net. The deck and netpile reek for days, no matter how thorough the cleaning is, and it is not until several sets later that the seine is back in its original condition.

"Bullet sets" also create other problems. Because the sacking up goes so much more slowly than normal, many more tuna die in the sack. This creates more strain on the equipment and increases the possibility of spoilage in the fish. The brailing, sorting, and re-rigging all go more slowly in a bullet set. In one 30-ton set which should have taken three hours, we set at ten in the morning, got "killed with bullets," and didn't pull the skiff aboard until two o'clock the next morning.

For all the trouble that bullets and other small marine life are likely to cause, however, log fish are still considered prime targets. The fishermen's thinking regarding log fish is parallel to their thinking about "areas" of fish in general. Finding a log with tuna is liable to mean a good number of full wells, more than could be gotten "scratching." A good log is analogous to a good area—both are prized objects of the fishermen's search.

Conclusion

A tremendous number of factors enter into a skipper's decisions about where to search for and how to locate the tuna. These include the time of the year; the point in time with respect to the "season"; past experience; knowledge of others' successes and circumstances; weather; signs; water conditions; international regulations; his own personality and personal preferences; his perceptions of his responsibilities, resources, and abilities; his confidence in the information he receives from others; and his whims, intuitive feelings, and estimation of those of his crew members.

Other factors influence his decision to actually set the seine. Among these are the quality of the sightings; his perception of his opportunity costs; the physical and mental condition of his crew; the time at sea and the catch record on that particular trip; his "hunger"; the behavior of the quarry; the species of porpoise or tuna with which he is dealing; and once again, the weather.

This chapter and the preceding one have focused on the decisions which must be taken and the actions which must be performed to find and catch the tuna. The ability to find the fish requires a considerable amount of experience; and the ability to surround them with the seine, bring them aboard, and store them in the wells requires a high degree of knowledge and skill, particularly on the part of the key men, and also requires skill, strength, and a willingness to take chances and bear risks on the part of the entire crew.

Much of the information given in these first chapters will serve as the basis for discussions to follow: the way the crews deal with the danger and the uncertainty, how the social structure aboard the seiners fits with the physical requirements of the process, the kind of self-image the fishermen derive from their circumstances, and other topics. These situations which the men encounter at sea are a major determinant in their understandings, perceptions, and behaviors.

These chapters, however, have described the process primarily as if each boat were involved in the search for the tuna alone. The next two chapters will deal with the additional behaviors and constraints on behavior which result from the fact that in reality each boat must operate within a system of cooperation and competition with the more than 150 other boats in the fleet, with the regulatory agencies which attempt to control the biology of the fishery, and with the governments of the foreign countries off whose coastline the tuna are found.

4 Information Management and the Communications Network

Communications

OF ALL THE factors which go into the fishermen's decisions about when and where to look for fish, the most important is radio communication between the boats themselves.

It is possible for a boat to search alone, using only experience and observation to find the fish. Some boats perform in this manner, or relatively so, and in fact their records are not significantly different from those of the rest of the fleet. There are certain fisheries where attempting to use information strategies to find the "best" areas does not seem to yield more than a random fishing pattern does (Dickie, 1969), and others where a reduction in the information potential among the fleet seems to affect the catch dramatically (Wadel, 1972). Because of the rapid expansion of the tuna fleet in recent years and the relative success of the individual boats, which has maintained a high rate of participation in the fishery, it is difficult to comment on the "real" efficacy of putting effort into information strategies. Most, however, do not fish alone but take part in a complicated network of affiliation, strategy, and competition through the exchange of fishing and other information.

Exactly why people bother with these networks at all, if it is empirically true that those who do not fully take part in them perform as well as those who do, is not certain. One possible explanation is that it *seems* as if a group who through effective communication systematically covered a large area of the ocean would stand a better chance of finding fish. This assumes that one is confident that his network partners will give him complete

104

and correct information, and that it will hold in the main that areas of fish discovered in this manner will be large and stable enough to warrant the rest of the network proceeding to that location. As we shall see, these are tenuous assumptions at best.

It could also be, as Barth has suggested, that skippers are naturally hesitant to ''take a flyer''—that even if one or two boats do well on their own, the skippers in the network have the satisfaction of knowing that they generally share the fate of a number of other boats, which is fine if it's good and understandable if it's bad. This is indeed a factor in the skippers' decisions, but in the tuna fleet it is only one of a more complex set.

Some, for example, have fixed ideas about their ''luck'' compared with others who operate largely without the benefit of the networks. They see the loners as ''lucky'' men who make up for the loss of information through special abilities, abilities that most others lack.

The skippers involve themselves in these communication networks largely, however, because the networks themselves are reflections of much of their personal and social lives and lifestyles. Much of the conversation within which the fish information is contained also serves as the vehicle for the communication of social ''messages.'' The skippers, like their crews, are at sea for long periods of time and for much of their lives. The skippers possess large amounts of status both aboard their own boats and in their communities ashore, but it is a demonstrative, conspicuous kind of status which relies on continuous presentation and assertion for its vitality. Participation in these information networks provides an opportunity for the skippers to maintain and manipulate their statuses within these various systems.

Whatever the reasons, the fact is that most of the skippers in the fleet involve themselves in this communications system. They have approximately five million square miles of ocean to cover in search of a highly mobile quarry, and as the fishermen say, ''Fish got tails''—you never know when they are going to leave and where they are going to turn up next. Most are of the opinion that the more information to which one has access, the better.

The Equipment

All of the boats in the fleet carry large, powerful single side-band radios capable under the right conditions of sending a signal from the West Coast of Africa to San Diego, California. Most carry more than one of these machines, using one as a primary set and the others as a backup. In addition to the single sidebands, which are now required by law through the licensing procedures of the FCC (Federal Communications Commission), many of the boats carry older double sideband radios equal in range to the singles but used only as backups because of their larger band width. The boats also carry a VHF radio transmitter, nicknamed the "yellow box." It operates off a different type of signal than the single sidebands do and generally carries only 25 to 50 miles.

Besides these principal pieces of equipment, all of the boats carry a "Mickey Mouse," a short-range transmitter with which the skipper talks to his speedboat drivers during the set (over which he can also monitor the maneuvers of other skippers in a set at very close range), and a variety of emergency signal devices. Some boats with a ham radio enthusiast aboard carry ham radio sets. These, however, are mostly used to call home to families and friends and not for the exchange of fish information.

Use of the Equipment

These are five general subjects of conversation over the radio: fish information, calls home, parts and repair calls, quota information, and "radio talk."

Fish information is the trading of information about fishing conditions. At night, after the fishing for the day is finished, crew members on many of the boats may call back to the U.S. to talk to family and friends. These are primarily personal calls, but they are also monitored by other boats and serve as a significant input into the ship-to-ship and ship-to-shore information process. All of the arrangements for repairs that necessitate the boats putting into port and all calls to order parts (which often must be flown to small South and Central American ports from the U.S.) are made over high-seas radio. During the first trip of the year, calls are made transmitting information concerning

106

the amounts of fish of the yellowfin species caught and the probable closing dates for clearing port "under the quota." Skippers in the same area of the ocean, often those in sight of each other, and friends and relatives among the skippers, often engage in a kind of rough banter which, while it is on the surface simply small talk and boasting, carries small bits and hints of information concerning the fishing process.

With the exception of the crew members who call home at night, the skipper is the only one who uses the radio. If the skipper is off the bridge when a call comes over the air, the crew will hustle to find him but will rarely even pick up the "mike" and ask the caller to hang on. On boats where there is both a Master and a "fish Captain" (skipper), the Master will sometimes answer for the skipper, but in general the Master in those situations has neither the knowledge of the social network of the fleet nor the status in it to communicate effectively with the caller. Each skipper knows most of the other skippers in the fleet by voice, and many keep written records of all the information they hear over the radio whether the call was directed to them or not. Aside from the exclusivity of their knowledge, many skippers guard their radio-operating function as a symbol of their control over the boat.

The style of the radio transmissions between the boats themselves and the boats and the shore varies with the person being called and the area of the ocean in which they are located. All calls to the U.S. are monitored by the FCC, and citations are given to the owners of the vessel if they do not follow fairly strict regulations regarding identification, breaking in on transmissions, and other matters. Most boats observe these rules when calling the U.S., but some figure that the dollars they pay in fines are worth the hour or so one often has to wait to avoid breaking in before another's transmission has been officially "signed off" and so they consistently ignore the regulations.

When calling the stations on the coasts of Central and South America, most of the etiquette regarding identification is used, mainly as a matter of expedition. Many of the shore-side operators don't speak the best of English, and radio etiquette is, after all, designed to promote efficient communication.

Between the boats themselves, however, radio "etiquette" is a different matter. It is very rare for any call sign to be used, and the whole conversation is handled as if it were being done over a multi-party conference telephone line. A typical conversation starts with a half-shouted, "Hey, Bud, ya on this side (frequency)?" The voice or some other sign, such as the particular nickname used, is recognized by the skipper being called and the conversation is on.

The tone and manner of speech during the conversations themselves is generally consistent. The speech is characterized by slow, measured phrases, oftentimes repeated several times: "I don't know, Bud . . . I don't know . . . I just don't know . . ." They are usually made to sound pessimistic, and the tone is one of a man who has his mind on other things. Direct questions about fish information are often made in a "by-the-way" manner, especially if the callers are not especially friendly with one another. Profanity is used liberally, and it is usually angry in tone but perfunctory in usage.[1]

Though the verbal "strategies" described below are intended to convey impressions of honesty, non-commitment, or whatever, the tone of a skipper's speech often transcends them. I would love to have a recording of a couple of comments made (over the radio) by skippers whose words were to the effect of "Oh, I don't know . . . I don't know . . . it's been all right over here, I guess" but whose underlying effervescence of tone said, "Man, did we get a lot of fish!" These nuances are picked up by other skippers and lead to second-guesses which, correct or not, often become significant in decision-making.

1. Researchers working in many other fishing communities around the world where radio communication between the boats is common (Löfgren 1972, Moustgaard, 1974) report many of these same conversational characteristics. The pessimistic tone is part of the strategizing as much as part of the actual substantive matter of the conversation, although many of the other characteristics of the speech are common to radio users in other contexts, such as "ham" operators and the military.

Many of the standard radio terms are used in ways different from their originator's intentions. The phrase "I'm out,"
for example, is usually equivalent to the caller saying that he is
finished talking and is going off the air. Many times, though,
especially in a heated conversation, this phrase will be used to
convey "and I really mean that!" or "what do you have to say
about that!" The person on the other end will respond to the im-
plied stimulus and often end his own speech with an inflection
characteristic of a question. The one who has just said, "I'm
out," will then come back on as if no indication of termination
had been given.

I mention these matters of tone and manner because a skipper's actions may in many cases be determined by what he *thinks*
the other fellow is doing regardless of what he is told over the
radio. Along with variables such as the previous history of the
relationship between two particular skippers and visual cues,
the information a skipper *thinks* he gets from tone, inflection,
and other auditory parameters is often a prime determinant of
his actions. The examples in the next chapter concerning resource
rights will bear this out.

Impressions of Resource Patterns and Competition

Before describing the communications networks themselves
I should expand upon the way in which the fishermen understand fish as a resource, and their impression of exactly how
much competition is involved in the search and set.

There is a division in the minds of fishermen between
"scratching"—finding isolated schools of fish—and fishing
in an "area"—a portion of the ocean where there is a congre-
gation of schools of fish. "Scratching" is generally seen as the
less desirable of the two for many reasons.

Isolated fish—both school fish and porpoise fish—are often
small catches. As mentioned earlier, it is almost exactly as hard
to set on five tons of fish as it is to set on 50 tons, and of course
the fishermen would always rather do the latter. Scratching involves a different kind of uncertainty from area fishing. There
is the problem of having to set many more times because of the

109

smaller individual catches. This involves concern over fatigue, equipment failure, and the existence of enough scratches to "make a trip"—that is, get a full load. Also, scratching is most often porpoise fishing, which involves more work on the part of the crew in terms of the use of the speedboats, backing-down, and other operations. Area fishing, while it may involve longer periods without fish at a stretch, involves a large payoff. Scratching, while reassuring the crew that at least they are putting some money in their pockets, puts it there in smaller amounts. Scratching also involves being away from the bulk of the fleet, which is usually if not already in an 'area' meandering in the same general direction in search of one. Scratching is often an indication that you have decided to go it alone, at least until someone within range does find an area.

In any case, the ideal is to find an "area" of fish. These areas are usually of one kind of fish or the other—either school or porpoise, generally the former—and are often homogeneous with regard to fish size, school size, and even behavior. Once again, behavior is important. If there is an area of porpoise fish, for example, but the porpoise that are carrying the fish are Costa Rican white-bellies, it may not be worth a skipper's time to go out of his way to get to that area. Likewise, if an area is composed of very small schools of very small fish, the skipper may decide to carry on his independent search until something better comes along. These kinds of factors are discussed in detail elsewhere. I bring them up here only to emphasize the following problem.

If a skipper is fishing independently or if he is scratching, he has only the resource itself to contend with. If, however, he is either fishing in an "area" or committed to searching for an "area," the problem becomes one of direct competitive and cooperative strategy with other skippers. The situation may be described by using a continuum of the zero-sum viewpoint (Anderson 1972, Stiles 1972).

Despite the growing quota restrictions and other limiting factors, the general opinion during the year I was at sea with the fleet seemed to be that there were plenty of fish to go around. This does *not* imply that the tuna fishermen see no need for resource conservation, but rather that *on the most abstract level* there is very little of the if-I-get-it-you-won't, zero-sum thinking. This belief on the part of the tuna fishermen reflects an attitude of optimism often found among fishermen, an attitude which has been noted by others including fisheries biologists who have experience with fisheries around the world (Gordon, 1954).

When a skipper is thinking of transmitting information of good fishing to another boat, on the other hand, many things start to pressure for the zero-sum mentality. A fellow with a slow boat, for example, knows that if he and a faster boat come on a school at the same time the faster boat will get there first and have rights over the school. He will think twice about transmitting information to a faster boat in his area, a form of zero-sum strategy. To take it one step farther, if a skipper comes on an area of fish that is dense and well integrated, which is often the case in log fishing, it is almost a truism that provided he has the storage capacity he can take all the fish in the area. To call another skipper over in a situation such as this is truly to involve a zero-sum decision, for any fish the newcomer takes is, so to speak, out of the other's pocket.

I should emphasize that all these are the fishermen's *impressions* of the occurrence of the resource. Any "factual" picture is hindered by the difficulty in collecting and the subsequent paucity of biological data on the tuna and porpoise populations. Most of the data is based on catch rates and examinations of the catches themselves. Data on highly migratory species such as tuna are expensive to obtain, and there are simply not enough research ships or facilities in the United States to give adequate attention to the problem. The fishermen have often provided space on their seiners for scientists who collected data as the fishing process was taking place. There are programs now in operation which offer rewards for information and cooperation to individuals for such things as the recovery and reporting of tagged fish used in migration studies. There is a program in the tuna fleet which provides for "charter trips," trips made with scientific personnel aboard which provide the boats involved with special rights with respect to quotas and other regulatory restrictions.

111

In spite of all of these efforts, however, the size of the task compared to the amount of resources brought to bear on the problem has resulted in less information than the scientists would like.[2] The fishermen's impressions I am setting forth here are informed by knowledge of the biological data, but are as much reflections of the social systems of the fleet as they are of the biological systems.

Under these conditions it might seem that it would never make sense to call out good fish information. This is perhaps true in the short-run economic sense. The reason it is not true in terms of the operation of the system as a whole, nor for the skippers as individuals, will become obvious as the following patterns of communications are laid out.

The Normative Communications Network

Of the things one ought to do by way of communicating fish information, two are paramount. First, a skipper ought to communicate exclusively and honestly with his "code group." Second, he must use information from and give adequate information to his shore-side managers or owners. (This second prescription, of course, is less applicable to those boats which are privately owned or under single-boat corporate ownership.)

Almost all of the boats in the fleet, even those which usually act as loners, belong to a code group. These are groups of anywhere from three or four to fourteen or fifteen boats who agree in principle to cooperate in the search for the tuna. In order to facilitate the transmission of information and to keep that information exclusive to the code group membership, elaborate "secret" codes are developed.

The accompanying example is a representative table of contents from one of these codes. The page numbers are included to give some idea of the relative amount of space provided for

2. There is, of course, a great amount of concern among fishermen, government and scientific agencies, and the general public over the conservation of animal populations of all kinds including fish. From the data we do have, the skipjack tuna seem to be abundant, in fact underutilized, and the yellowfin population seems to be responding to the regulatory efforts of the IATTC.

1. A Code's Table of Contents

each entry. The particular code which this table represents had approximately six thousand entries. Some sections were made up of self-contained messages, others of fragments with which a skipper could build a message. Each entry was coded with a four-digit number.

The weather section contained information on the sea surface, the tide-rips, currents, sky condition, wind condition, barometer readings, thermoclines, and comments about the general workability. Entries such as "It's nice weather for ducks" appear fairly frequently. Most followed continuums such as "Breezy . . . Breezy with whitecaps . . . Whitecaps but workable," and so on.

The relative number of Mexican coast locations gives some idea of the portions of the Eastern Tropical Pacific the fishermen in this particular code group used most frequently. The positions are listed by country or island group and are referenced by charted names of nearby coastal points, shoals, banks, and midwater locations that have acquired numbers or nicknames over the years.

The list of boat names is alphabetical, with spaces left at intervals for the addition of the names of new boats. With codes being revised every few trips, this is some indication of the rapid growth of the fleet which the fishermen expect.

The tonnage section is composed primarily of numerals. Exact position in latitude and longitude, courses both by magnetic heading and compass point, and exact tonnage figures are included here. There are also some phrases such as "this set," "today," "this position," "so far," "information for (time reference)," which are intended to fit with the numbers.

With the "fishing phrases" section, the codes start exhibiting the vocabulary of strategy and competition. Besides comments on what the boat is doing specifically ("in a set," "brailing," "putting out speedboats," and so on), there are instructions to go to a different radio (from high-seas to VHF, for example) or a different frequency, or to "come towards me." There are entries for "where did you get that dope?", admonishments about how confidential a piece of information is and the other people, if any, to whom it should be relayed, and unqualified remarks such as "What you heard is bullshit!" There are general observations on the number of boats in the area, news of any equipment that one boat or another may need, and assessments of the shark situations or other data which may determine the risk of setting in the area.

The porpoise entries describe the kind of porpoise sighted, their individual and school size, their behavior, and the number and species of birds traveling with them. There are in addition comments about what kind and size fish the porpoise are "carrying," how much of the porpoise school the boat was able to "wrap," and how many fish were trapped with the porpoise. The section is rounded out with a description of the "signs" in the area—birds, weather, flotsam, other marine life, and so on.

The school fishing section contains much of the same kind of information but with reference to the fish themselves: kind, size, numbers, behavior, the portion of the school wrapped. There are also several entries particularly critical for school fishing: water "condition"—its clarity, color, and the depth of the thermocline; the "workability" of the fish—their general response to the net, speedboats, noise, and dye; and the "friends" the fish have with them—"bullets," whales, junk fish, logs and other debris, crabs, squid, etc.

The "words" are just that—coded lists of words the skippers can use either to supplement the phrases contained elsewhere in the codes or to make sentences of their own.

Most of the entries in the codes are used fairly infrequently. The messages are almost never completely in code because it is just plain too much trouble. Original messages are generally of the form "I'm at 4378 . . . got 4568 on board . . . going 2343 . . . may stop at 0789 for awhile." When one boat is relaying the "dope" for several others in the code group, which they do frequently, the messages are simply number strings such as "Joe's is 4365 8970 5768 4368." Strings of this sort have an understood order among the code group members, which eliminates, for example, misunderstandings between the number 278 as a tonnage or as a course. Oftentimes, however, strings longer or shorter than normal get relayed and do cause misunderstandings or confusion. Also, since a relatively small number of the entries are used in general communication, the skippers have these memorized and do not always have to refer to the printed code sheets.

These codes are guarded jealously. There are several stories about people who offered crewmen large amounts of money to steal copies of their boat's code, but none of those of which I am aware are substantiated. It would not be a very intelligent action to take. With the web of friends and relatives on these boats, both the culprit and his patron would almost certainly be found out and neither would be able to get a job in the fleet again.

The bases of organization for these code groups vary. In instances where several boats are managed or owned by a single corporation, those boats will often share a code. With many of the skippers of the boats being close friends or relatives, a good portion of the code groups are organized around friendship or kinship. Some are composed of skippers who simply respect each other's fishing ability and have no other particular ties.

Like the crews themselves, the code groups are constantly changing. Skippers often either quit or are "kicked out" of code groups. Many times whole segments of different groups will break away to form a new one. There are several common reasons for this kind of rearrangement of code groups. A skipper, for example, may think that some of the members of his code group have been hiding information from him or distorting it in some fashion. Reversing the situation, a majority of code group members may feel that a particular member has been less than honest with them. Either of these situations may lead to the departure of a member.

On the other hand, a skipper may be offered a place in a more successful code group on the basis of his performance. He may become friends ashore with several members or perhaps one very prestigious member of a different group and be invited to join. He may go to work on a "company" boat and thus inherit the company's code group. There are also, of course, a variety of personal reasons for changing code groups. The kind of information exchange that goes on is certainly facilitated if the participants get along personally with one another, and personality conflict in the absence of any hint of a transgression of the rules of code-group behavior has caused many a move.

For whatever reason it occurs, switching code groups is looked upon as a chancy business for all concerned. The fear is that the "new" skipper will either take enough knowledge with him to share in the information in his old code group's messages, or more likely, pass information from his new code group to his friends in the old one. Both of these are in fact done, but it is usually much less insidious than it may sound.

In the normative framework of communication, messages from the boats to the companies ashore and back perform several functions aside from the routine maintenance arrangements for the boats in countries outside of the U.S. During the quota season the calls from the boats are the source of a good part of the information the NMFS (National Marine Fisheries Service) uses to compile its data on catch rates. They also, and this is especially important in the case of companies who own or manage a large number of boats, are the basis for the schedules of unloading, maintenance and repair, and provisioning which must be set up before a vessel reaches port.

The calls are also supposed to be an input into the skipper's information about the movements and whereabouts of the fish. This is potentially a good source of information. Besides information on their code group boats that a skipper may not have gotten for one reason or another, a shore-side manager can, or should be able to, provide information from scuttlebutt around the port—from unions, other companies, families, fishermen home early or in a different sector of the Pacific or even a different ocean, and many other sources. It is the job of the company to serve not only as a scheduler and recipient, but also as a transmitter of information.

The idea of these two communications networks, the inter-boat and the ship-to-shore, is normatively to provide the most efficient method possible of searching out, capturing, transporting, and processing the tuna. The actual networks through which the information is passed and the behaviors of the individuals in the system, however, present a somewhat different picture.

The Pragmatic Communications Network

While the system of code groups provides a seemingly orderly method of communication, the actual pattern of information sharing is much more complicated. The "actual" communications network is composed of a series of cross-cutting groups of which the official code groups are only one. These cross-cutting groups take a variety of forms.

In the code groups themselves there are cliques within which information is passed along the lines of what *should* be the norm for the entire code group, and others between whom there is less than perfect communication. These cliques are generally composed of friends or relatives who have "social stock" in both their own catch and the catch of the others in the clique. A good catch not only adds to the status of the skipper and crew making the catch, but also to the status of the other members of the code group by association. Even in the absence of good catches in any particular time period, status may be gained by the implicit knowledge that a particular skipper is a confidant of other high-

117

status skippers. In many cases, especially company code groups, this social stock is worth more to the skippers than is the "economic stock" whose value may tend to be increased through the more efficient search procedures which more complete cooperation might produce. The cliques tend not only to share more information with each other than with the rest of the code group, but they often stay in the same geographical area. In the terminology of the hunters and the chasers mentioned in an earlier chapter, most of these cliques are, as one might logically assume, composed of chasers.

It could be argued that this kind of partial information sharing occurs out of coincidence, that boats of the same code group who find themselves in an area together naturally concentrate on the search with their nearest partners. This is sometimes a valid argument; but it is valid just as often in the case of boats from different code groups. Independent of this consideration there are small groups within code groups who consciously and consistently work together.

Many of these same kinds of cliques also occur across code groups. Some of the same mechanisms that preserve the normative integrity of the code groups—fear of members taking information with them or continuing old alliances, various personality conflicts, and so on—at the same time produce these cross-cutting ties between code groups. If you cannot officially change code groups, you can unofficially alter your pattern of communications. Skippers are constantly coming into contact with one another either through chance on the fishing ground, or social contacts ashore, or some other means. While it is true that each skipper knows *of* most others, new friendships are forged or old ones recalled all the time. This happens at a faster rate than it is practically possible to change the code groups themselves, creating this "double standard."

Added to this is the fact that each skipper feels he is—and in many ways is in fact—independent from any controls, especially while he is at sea. The skippers value this independence, and part of being independent is being able to communicate with whomever you want. These two things together often lead to preferred communication with people outside your code group.

Blood relations also play a part in unofficial information exchanges. While it is mostly true that close relations—brothers, fathers, and sons—are in the same code groups, the industry is so filled with relatives that a skipper often has in-laws, cousins, uncles, nephews, and so on in different code groups. These people are often seen as ones to whom there is an obligation to supply information. These obligations and their transgressions lead to radio comments such as "He must have not told me. And he's *my own brother-in-law!*", the likes of which I heard fairly frequently over the air.

Just how much information a skipper can let out of his code group and not be chastised by the other members is determined largely by who he is, who he knows, and how he performs. One who is a "highliner" and the top catch man in the group, one who is a member of an important "owning family," or one who has strong social ties to other code group members can afford to give more information to boats outside the code group, although there is no one who has unlimited license in this respect.

Besides bonds of friendship and blood relations that cross-cut the code groups, there are various "local" agreements made when two or more boats are working in the same area. This usually occurs when the boats in question are relatively isolated from the rest of the fleet. Once, for example, we were off Columbia when the rest of the fleet was to the west and north of us quite a distance. We ran into two other boats who were not in our code group with whom our skippers had an acquaintance, and we agreed to cooperate in searching the area for school fish. The arrangement lasted only two days, but during that period we were essentially a small code group transmitting all the kinds of information that a normal code group would.

All of these groupings and the strategies that are employed within them are governed by two considerations: to whom you want to "give" fish, and what you think the other fellow is going to do with the information you give him. "Giving" fish to some-

119

one can mean actually calling someone over to let him braile fish that you don't need out of your net; or calling someone over to a log that is carrying lots of fish (an almost certain bet that the person called, if he comes quickly, will get some of the fish); or simply giving someone advice that the signs are good in your area. Each is an indication that you would like that person to get some of the fish which you yourself are getting, or plan to get. All are a form of sharing the resource.

Each time a skipper accepts information or fish from another he realizes that he has to some degree incurred an obligation to that other skipper. Much of the information which passes between the boats is calculated to have this effect, and many decisions are made with the matter of obligation in mind. I know of a case, for example—one of many—where a skipper was offered 25 tons of tuna (worth approximately $15,000) from a boat very close by. All he had to do was stream over and braile the fish out of the other fellow's net. The skipper to whom the offer was made refused it because the other skipper was known to be one who manipulated offers of this sort to gain large indebtedness from those who accepted them. He made an excuse, saying that he was onto another school and continued his search.

The other consideration, that of what you think the other fellow is going to do with the information, leads to what could at best be described as "partial honesty" in communication. It is said that an honest skipper will never be very successful in the fleet. Not that honesty affects the decisions of a skipper about where or when to fish; it does, however, affect the information other skippers give to *you,* the honest skipper.

The skippers are reticent about giving information to another skipper if they know he is going to pass it on to anyone who asks him about it. The tendency is to give information only to a skipper you know will keep it to himself or give it only to a limited circle of his confidants. You also hope that in turn for your doing him a favor in this manner, he will some time give you information that he would otherwise only give to his "circle." In this way a skipper's idea of where the information is liable to go when it leaves the fellow on the other end determines what the fellow gets told in the first place. And in general, "honest" men get slighted. The common problem is that because of the cross-cutting nature of the communications network, you can never be certain where the information you give out is going to end up.

This is more than slightly paradoxical, especially when viewed in light of the nature of the tuna resource and the economics of the industry. While complete information transfer would certainly change the distribution of the catch somewhat, it would almost certainly increase the efficiency of the industry as a whole. The main reason that the information is distributed in the manner described above is competition between the individual skippers—both for the resource itself *and* for the status gained relative to the other skippers and crews in the fleet.

The effects of this system are important for the owners of the boats and their shore-side managers. Especially in the cases of large company fleets, whose skippers are normatively sharing a code group, the system leads to considerable corporate inefficiency. Loyalty to the company is almost always overridden by status-seeking and other loyalties to friends, relatives, and the skipper's own crew.

Not—and this is a very important point in understanding the industry—that the system of communication as it is presented here is breaking anybody or causing crewmen's families to go hungry. Most men in the industry make a good living, and with proper investment can come out considerably better than men in many other occupations. But the system is, in my view, detrimental to the economic efficiency of the industry as a whole. In my view it is also, however, almost as integral a part of the smooth functioning of the *social* systems on the boats as are some of the mechanisms which will be brought out in a later chapter concerning the crewmen's interactions on board the boats themselves.

The Strategies

The actual strategies the fishermen use to direct the flow of information are as follows. First and foremost, of course, are the official codes. These are the primary and most prevalent means of selecting who receives your information. Their limitation is that they can only be used with the official code group, which is only one of the many networks within which each skipper may communicate on a trip.

If the person to whom you want to communicate the information is within approximately fifty miles and there is no one whom you specifically *don't* want to have the information within that radius, you can switch to your VHF or, at very close range, your Mickey Mouse. The instruction "go to 18 on the yellow box," besides being in most of the official codes, is often used over high-seas radio between any callers who want to effectively "seal" the information, at least on the first relay, within a fifty-mile radius. The problems with this method are that it is hard to know exactly who is within that radius, and that even if you know who is there you can never really be sure to whom they may relay the information. In VHF situations the callers are almost by definition not in the same code group, so the links between them are normatively, at least, more tenuous.

A strategy employed quite frequently is that of personal reference. Comments such as "You know that guy . . . that guy who was next to you at the Club the night before we left? He got 200 ton over this way the other day," or "You know the place I saw you last year . . . the second trip, it was . . . I hear there's good signs there" are heard often. Reference is often made to information already transmitted such as "You know what I told you yesterday? Well, I'm northwest of there . . . been running about as long as you have." This kind of tactic is used both with fish information and personal information such as scuttlebutt about who is getting what boat next trip or who is getting kicked out of a code group. This method is, of course, limited largely to personal acquaintances or relatives, and with the intimate nature of the fleet and the relatively closed nature of the social system ashore, it is never foolproof.

A fourth strategy is the use of other languages. A large portion of the fleet is Portuguese and a smaller portion Italian, and many of the skippers from these ethnic groups speak the native

122

tongues. While not everyone with the same ethnicity is someone to whom you might want to give information, it is true to a certain extent that code groups and other socially organized information groups tend to form along ethnic lines. Thus you often hear a skipper suddenly start talking, for example, in Portuguese. When he does, the person on the other end will generally respond in that language. The conversation will continue in Portuguese until one of the callers suddenly speaks in English again, automatically switching the conversation back to that language. This phenomenon also occurs in ship-to-shore calls. While this method is imperfect and may be employed for reasons other than privileged information (such as assertions of ethnic solidarity or personal ability of one sort or another), it is relatively effective in reducing significantly with very little trouble the number of boats privy to the conversation.

Some of the newer boats with more sophisticated radio systems have the ability to select their own frequencies rather than rely on the fixed channels which are determined by crystals installed in the radio itself. There are two types of radio systems of this sort of which I am aware. One uses a card pre-punched with "pirate" frequencies, and the other allows the user to select any frequency by simply pushing a series of buttons or turning a dial. Skippers who have these radio sets agree on certain frequencies before they begin their trips and use them as exclusive "meeting places." Anyone with a similar set, of course, would have the ability to find these frequencies by searching the various radio bands for conversations. For this reason these frequencies are changed frequently, as are the official codes.

Some of the skippers make a concerted effort to "break" the codes of other groups. I know of a skipper who broke two such codes on one trip the year I fished with the fleet. This requires a great deal of work besides skill and a certain knack, and not many skippers get information in this manner.

If the boats were entirely serious about information transfers they could buy scramblers, devices which convert radio signals into a form unreadable to anyone who doesn't have an "unscrambler." These devices are used on many smaller fishing boats of various types. To my knowledge, the year I fished with the fleet none of the boats in the high-seas tuna fleet used them.

This is not to say that the skippers are not competitive, or that they don't attempt to collect information on the activities of other boats besides that which is transmitted to them directly. The ways in which they compete and the channels through which they actively seek information, however, are organized around a set or rules different from those one would expect of an analytical, impersonal competitor. These rules of competition and information gathering are based on a complex set of social and personal variables which it is the purpose of this and other chapters to enumerate.

While the strategies I have mentioned up to now are all systems of information transfer, the ones which follow could better be characterized as actual evasive or deceptive techniques. The "information" they contain is built more out of the perceptions of the listener than it is out of the substance of the communication itself.

The first of these is the strategy of no response. The high-seas radios which the skippers use for most of their communication have a considerable range, thousands of miles under the right conditions. It is usual to direct a substantial amount of traffic to those in your own vicinity, they being more likely to provide assistance in your immediate endeavors. Given these circumstances it is rarely the case that no response stems from his inability to hear you; the exceptions would be when the boat being called is in a set, or otherwise unable to monitor the radio. Calls are generally sent out on several frequencies, and in any event callers usually agree on principal channels and times for their transmissions.

What is more likely, according to the fishermen, is that the person being called either is "on fish" or has information of excellent signs that he wants to check out before releasing the information. This realization is gained not only from deduction, but also from induction—from years of not being able to raise a boat for a few days only to hear in his first subsequent transmission, "Oh, we did pretty well here lately."

Another example of evasion is the noncommittal answer. This is extremely common, perhaps the most common tactic. Transmissions such as "I hear you're doing pretty well over by the tide rips," "Yeah, somewhere over there," or "Any signs around there?" "Well, yeah . . . we're doing all right" are heard all the time. Both the skipper's reputation as a fisherman and his reputation as a "truth-teller" enter into the interpretation of his remarks.

If, for example, a highliner says that he has been doing "OK" you'll usually find a general gravitation in his direction. Highliners don't have to broadcast their fortune to gain status in the fleets, and they tend to understate somewhat. In the event of a transmission of *any* good news at all from a habitual deceiver in an area which you have other reasons to suspect may have fish, it is usually taken to mean that he is getting fish.

It is extremely rare (and I have never heard an actual instance) for a skipper to broadcast better news than he in fact has. Besides drawing other boats into your area this constitutes something very different from the noncommittal answer. It might be argued that over-reporting on purpose is no different than under-reporting the same amount on purpose. But this is not true for the tunamen, for three reasons.

First, under-reporting can more easily be made noncommittal in form than over-reporting. While a toneless "Yeah, we got some fish" can be under-reporting, considerable purposeful use of tone and inflection is necessary to produce the impression that you in fact have *more* than the words themselves indicate. Second, over-reporting is likely to produce an expenditure of material and energy to no good avail. Those with no fish will spend valuable time steaming to a place with no more fish than the one they left. All of the skippers are in enough of the "same boat" not to be able to afford this kind of tactic, which would be likely to produce retaliatory action of the same kind. And third, this type of over-reporting would have the effect of falsely raising expectations. Uncertainty is one of the most troubling aspects of this occupation, and the stresses it produces would only be aggravated by the emotional and physical waste of

125

falsely elevated expectations. The skippers realize this and fairly studiously avoid over-reporting.

This brings up the last and most evasive communications strategy, actual lying and purposeful gross distortion of information. How much this happens, if at all, is hard to tell. At sea the boats are either within sight of each other, in which case there is no opportunity to lie (the case of third-party boats is subsumed here), or they are out of sight of one another, in which case anything is possible. Boats sometimes come upon one another shortly after a radio transmission, but because of the strength of the radio signal and general plotting of one another's positions, this is rarely a surprise happening. When a fisherman tells you of another's "lying" he generally means something on the order of a noncommittal response—technically a lie, but substantively different from purposeful overestimation or other more deliberate forms of distortion. I am sure, given that there is probably some kind of normal distribution of "dirty guys" in tuna fishing as in all else, that it happens. I would guess, from knowing the skippers themselves and the nature of the system, that it is fairly infrequent.

In some fishing fleets the amount of honest information passed between boats seems to be in inverse proportion to their proximity (Stiles, 1972). This is most often true in small, face-to-face fishing communities. Since most of the information passed among the tuna fleet is passed at a considerable distance, this may be less of a valid generality for the tuna fishermen. Although fear of discovery is certainly a factor, status levels and the strength of social ties are much more important factors in the determination of who gets which information. The amount of anonymity which the tunaboats' long non-concurrent trips and the multiplicity of the San Diego environment lend to the skippers also tend to lessen the impact of the discovery of "altered" information. Part of the reason I say this stems from reactions I observed when cases of distortion of some sort were discovered.

One morning, for example, we came upon a member of our code group who was in a set with what looked to be fifty tons of fish in the net. He had made a set on porpoise and yellowfin and was in the process of backing down, which means that he had been in the set for probably upwards of an hour and a half. He had told us earlier that morning that he hadn't seen anything for a couple of days, and at the same time had verified our position— at the time about thirty miles away from him. He could only have sighted the school he had set on *before* he talked to us on the radio.

A thorough explication of cases such as this will have to await the next chapter, which explains the nature of the resource rights between the boats at sea, but suffice it to say that the other fellow certainly could have given us more information than he had, either during the call that morning or in the period between the call and the time we came upon him. He was, in effect, caught red-handed. His reaction to this was typical of others I've heard in much the same situation. He made no effort to argue any case or apologize. He seemed slightly embarrassed, but only slightly. He made a few obvious jokes about such things as "people who don't believe anything you tell them" and "can't talk on the radio all the time," and the matter was more or less dropped.

This reaction, and our skipper's subsequent reluctance to pursue the matter with the other skipper (although he fumed a little about it in private, having personal stock in the communication), stem, I think, from the understanding among the skippers that it is their prerogative to take certain liberties with their information primarily for the purpose of insuring the success of their own boat first and foremost. It is also tolerated, though, in large measure because it is just a matter of non-commitment or radio silence. This puts the burden of deciding to alter any action or behavior on the listening skipper, whereas in cases of actual distortion or lying the burden is on the sending skipper. It is tolerated not only because everybody knows it happens and uses it themselves, but because it is a consistent behavior and does not lead to a malicious waste of resources. It does lead to inefficiency in the system as a whole, but the matter here is one of intent; is there an *intent* to waste, or simply an "error" of omission?

The System as Dissonance

These, then, are the strategies the skippers use to control the flow of information. A few additional remarks are necessary to understand, given the above normative and pragmatic guidelines, how the system of communications actually "works." The first concerns radio variability.

Besides the usual equipment failures, which is a relatively small factor given the back-up equipment the boats carry, there are many times external conditions—heavy traffic, "jamming" by foreign frequencies, atmospheric conditions—which cause gaps in the flow of information. One boat may be effectively cut off from another for varying periods of time by these conditions.

Second, there is human variability. Skippers often, because of the fishing process, simple forgetfulness, misunderstanding, and other circumstances, miss prearranged transmissions. This also creates gaps in communication.

Third, there are the gaps created by purposeful silence. This practice not only accomplishes its intended purpose of restricting others' knowledge of alternatives, but at the same time limits the silent skipper's knowledge of other alternatives open to *him*. He may listen in, but he cannot fully participate in the flow of information.

The combination of these factors could be described as "slop" in the system—gaps in information flow which, although few of them are purposive, have profound results on the character of the system itself in the following way.

The skippers themselves do not view most of the strategies mentioned above as things one ought not do. They in fact see them as their prerogative in accordance with the aim of doing the most good for themselves, either in terms of benefits for the crew, the company, or themselves personally. There is, however, a general tendency to attribute somewhat less desirable motives to others using the same strategy. Thus a skipper who decides to withhold information for a day or so until he checks it out more thoroughly does not see himself as doing anything wrong. When he discovers another boat has done the same thing, however—especially if the other fellow brought a lot of fish on board—there is always enough uncertainty about exactly *how much* liberty the other fellow took to evoke the comment, "That bastard must have lied to me."

Tie this in with the following situation. We were in a location off the coast of Central America and were on the way into port to take a sick man to a doctor. We saw some big schools of fish on the way in, but the weather was rough and we were in a hurry to get the man to the doctor. Another boat, one in our code group, picked up one of our transmissions which indicated that there were some fish in the area but that it was pretty rough.

We were in port about a day, and when we left we headed back to the same spot where we had seen the fish on the way in. The weather had calmed and we got lucky and had an excellent day on school fish. We had made some radio transmissions in the meantime, but the weather was rough and our signal was evidently weak. We reported our good fortune that night to the code group, and the same boat mentioned above picked up this transmission also. His reasoning then was as follows:

"The last transmission I got from these guys said they were at X position with no real good fishing. Now, almost three days later, they report at exactly the same position and say they have a lot of fish. And we didn't hear a thing from them in the meantime. Those bastards have been on fish in that same spot for three days and haven't told anybody!"

This reconstruction isn't mine—I got it from a crewman on the other boat after we got into San Diego some weeks later. The skipper of the other boat did not come over the air to chastise us, but this incident formed his attitude toward us, an attitude which precipitated a major confrontation which will be described in detail in the next chapter.

Thus the I-tell-the-truth-but-I'm-not-sure-if-he-does attitude—combined with, and to some degree caused by, various external factors—caused a transaction which not only would come to precipitate a confrontation, but which certainly affected the ability of boats of the same code group to work together in an organized search for the resource. This is a fair description of the way the system "works." It is a collection of individual units who for the most part see themselves as truth-tellers (and for the most part they are), but whose concept of the actions and motives of others become twisted into a picture which changes the nature of their competitive behavior and in turn the effectiveness of their resource exploitation system.

The Efficiency of the System

About a month out on the first trip of the year, a good many boats found themselves in a group off of the coast of one Central American country. The fishing had been slow for the fleet, and the presence of so many boats (ten or twelve in sight of each other) added to the tension.

One morning a certain code group was making their morning call when the discussion got a little heated. The problem was that one or more of their boats in our area had not come on the air for the code group communications for the last few days. One skipper was particularly irate. He said, "Now you guys have fucked everything up. We came over here, and those other guys think there are fish here and are coming full speed. They were going out there to look and now they're coming back again. Now we can't catch anything because there's too many boats here, and nobody's *looking* anyplace else either!"

The discussion continued on to other subjects, but three things were clear. First, the code group had interpreted silence to mean that the silent ones were on fish. Second, the fishermen think, and past a certain point it is true, that the more boats there are in an area the harder it is for any one of them to get fish. And third, strategic behaviors by the skippers can lead to inefficiencies in both the catch and the search. It was clear that this particular strategy had led, at least for that specific time period, to a diminishing of not only the fleet potential, but the potentials of the individual boats as well.[3]

Why, then, do the skippers use these strategies? Why do they, in the face of the potential benefits of full cooperation,

3. Anderson mentions the kind of inefficiencies which can result from this same kind of strategizing in boat-cannery communications (Anderson 1972).

choose strategies which essentially pit them against one another? Why, given that all these pragmatic strategies are used, does the fleet even have official code groups? Is there any light in which these strategies could be viewed as "necessary" to the fishing process?

Some of the answers to these questions were suggested at the beginning of this chapter: that being in communication with the fleet shifts the burden in some manner from the individual skipper to the fleet; that a skipper may not think he has the "stuff" to find fish alone; and that the communication performs social as well as economic functions.

Another answer is suggested in the chapter itself: that external circumstances, while they create misunderstandings between the skippers, do not override the basic belief that each skipper himself is (on the whole) telling the truth, and that others are doing, albeit to a lesser degree, the same.

Other reasons will be elaborated in subsequent chapters: that the resource itself is shrinking; that a basic motive in the skippers' behavior is their desire for status—a desire which cannot be fulfilled except with the cooperation of other boats in the search but at the same time cannot be fulfilled if that cooperation is too great; that various rights to the fish and the anxiety which accompanies fishing in close quarters overshadow the obligations of partners in the search.

Each of these is part of the "answer"; none is all, or even most of the answer. As with the rules for resource rights, the subject of the next chapter, the social and political systems are so entwined with the economic system that all are needed to explain the sometimes curious but *almost always consistent* behavior of the fleet.

5 Rights to
the Resource

THE LAST CHAPTER dealt primarily with the information networks which the skippers use in their search for the tuna. The present one concerns itself with the rules, both explicit and implicit, which govern various parties' rights over the fish should they be discovered in any given area and what happens when they are in fact found. It deals with legal strictures, less formal agreements between the boats themselves at sea, the varying degrees to which these sets of rules are observed, and the various sanctions used to deal with their transgression. The skippers' perceptions of these rules mold their attitudes toward their rights over the fish.

Legal Strictures

The most general and also the most problematic set of constraints on the fishermen involve the "legal" titles pertaining to the "ownership" and exploitation of the tuna resource.

The migratory nature of the tuna resource has been pointed out. Although it is theoretically possible to hunt the tuna in any portion of their migratory area, the major portion of the fishing is done in what is termed the Eastern Tropical Pacific, generally east of the 120 degree longitude line and between the 30 north and 30 south latitudes. The countries which border this area of the Pacific are, from north to south, Mexico, Guatemala, El Salvador, Nicaragua, Costa Rica, Panama, Colombia, Ecuador, Peru, and Chile. The favored fishing within this area is near the coast, within 300 miles, usually between the Galapagos Islands to the south and the tip of Baja California to the north. Here the fish are easiest to find, the weather best, and the facilities for parts, supplies, and repairs closest at hand.

The situations with respect to various national claims to the tuna resource, and the actions each nation has been willing to take to back those claims, are varied and continually subject to change. All the South and Central American countries, with the exception up to the present of Mexico, have for some years officially claimed a 200-mile "limit." Whether this is a territorial, a resource control, a fishery control, or some other limit is in many cases unclear. At the International Law of the Sea Conferences, which have been held in an attempt to develop a coherent plan of ocean resource ownership and exploitation, three definitions have emerged: that of a "territorial sea," a band of water bordering a coastal or island nation's shores within which that country has complete sovereignty; that of an "economic zone," a strip in addition to the territorial sea within which the nation has rights over fish, undersea minerals, and all other economic entities; and that of an "international seabed area," the portion of the seas not under any type of control by any nation. Many of the problems in the working out of these definitions and their applications arise from situations involving highly mobile or migratory fish stocks, of which the tuna are a prime example.

Peru and Ecuador, for their part, have made it very clear that they consider their 200-mile limit to be territorial. They have a history of confiscating U.S. fishing boats found within this limit with various resulting fines and admonitions. Chile, though it has in the past confiscated U.S. boats, has been quiet for the last few years and an official of their Fisheries and Food Technology Institute in Valparaiso, with whom I spoke in 1974, assured me that their government is more interested in cooperating in fisheries development than in policing "all that water." Chile has the longest coastline with the least occurrence of the tuna resource of all the west-coast South American countries. Colombia also claims the 200-mile limit, but it has relatively less stock in its marine as opposed to its land resources than Ecuador and Peru, and it does not engage in actively policing its waters.

The Central American countries also technically claim the 200-mile limit, but only Panama, and only in recent history in 1975, has confiscated or in any way molested U.S. fishing boats

133

for violating their waters. The Undersecretary for Foreign Affairs of El Salvador told me that his country, like Chile, has a greater interest in promoting fisheries development in cooperation with the United States than it does in policing its waters, which it doesn't have the means to do anyway. This attitude is typical of all the Central American countries except Panama, and Panama's actions may have had more to do with political differences over the Panama Canal than with interest in the tuna fishery.

Mexico, although it recently extended its limit to 200 miles, has for a number of years required a fishing license of foreign vessels fishing within fifty miles of its coast. Their program has been genuinely set up to help Mexican fishermen and to be cooperative with, if not in the best interests of, foreign fishermen. It required that at least 50 percent of the crew on foreign vessels fishing within that limit be Mexican, and that these Mexican crew members receive pay commensurate with their American counterparts. Mexico also, however, has a long coastline and a problem with policing.

Until recently the official U.S. Government policy has been to recognize only what they themselves officially recognize—a 12-mile territorial-resource limit. They have not told the fishermen *not* to respect the 200-mile limit, but they have tacitly advised them not to purchase the licenses which Ecuador and Peru offer for the right to trespass within that limit, which is an action tantamount to non-recognition. When U.S. tunaboats have been captured by these countries, the U.S. government has paid their fines and reimbursed the crews under the Fishermen's Protective Act of 1954. Sometimes the skipper or Master of the vessel has in turn been fined by our government—he being theoretically responsible for the "transgression"—and sometimes they have been given a hand-slapping admonition. It has been, to say the least, both in theory and in practice a grey area. In at least one instance of which I am aware, a tunaboat that had "escaped" during the night from a South American port was ordered by the U.S. State Department to turn around and go back to their captors until a diplomatic solution was worked out. They were also told that if anything happened to the two South American guards they had left tied up in a speedboat, their skipper would be held responsible.

These were the operative constraints as of 1974, the year I fished with the fleet and the time period for which my comments present a coherent system of belief and behavior. Since that time many other countries, the United States included, have passed laws claiming 200-mile limits of one kind or another. It is unclear what effect this will have on various international fisheries. Many conflicts will be resolved through bilateral or multilateral agreements, and others will be taken care of through licensing arrangements, but some, the tuna and other highly migratory species fisheries included, may be sources of difference for some time to come.

The Tuna Commission and the Regulatory Area

Overlaid onto this configuration of alternatives in space are the dictates of the Inter-American Tropical Tuna Commission (IATTC). The member nations of this Commission—the U.S., Canada, Mexico, Japan, Costa Rica, Nicaragua, and France— have formed the body as an attempt at conserving the yellowfin tuna resource in the Eastern Pacific. The Commission sets certain limits on the amount of yellowfin tuna which may be taken by each member nation within certain zones. Some countries, Mexico for example, have special exemptions allowing them to fish after the close of the ''season'' within the limits of the zone until the boats under their flag have reached their particular allocation. There is also a provision on a sliding scale according to boat size which allows for a percentage of each boat's catch to be yellowfin after the season has closed—on the theories that sometimes the schools are mixed and it is impossible to catch one without the other, and that smaller boats constitute less danger to the resource stocks.

The Commission acts by monitoring the catches of yellowfin among the member nations through a complex set of informa-

135

tion networks. They set a limit for the amount of fish to be taken each season based on what they deem reasonable to preserve the fish stocks, while at the same time serving the economic and political "necessities" of the fleets of the various nations. In the past these limits have been set with two discretionary increments to be added in the event that conditions warrant additional exploitation in that particular season.

Based on the *rate* of catches during the first "trip" of the year, the Commission projects a closing date for the season. The boats must clear into one of several inspection ports before midnight of that date in order to be eligible for a second trip "under the quota"—that is, for taking yellowfin within the regulatory area. After this second trip is completed the boats must fish entirely outside of the regulatory area unless they plan on taking solely skipjack, a bad proposition in both its mechanics and its economics. They must also depart on that second trip within thirty days of the season's closing date.

This adds a temporal aspect to the "rights" of the fishermen. Before the closing of the season U.S. fishermen have a "right" to fish more or less anywhere they want. After the season, which has been closing around the middle of March but will close earlier as the capacity of the fleet increases, they are effectively limited to trips "outside the line" with a certain leeway in the form of their "second trip."

How Constraining Are the
Official Constraints?

Each skipper works differently under this pattern of constraints. Each of course has his favorite fishing spots, or areas, and each is affected by his code group or other search alliances. Most of their attitudes toward the boundary claims of other nations can be summarized as follows.

Peru, Ecuador, and Panama have been the only real threats to mobility because of their territorial claims. Because the tuna migrate up the coast and come in from the west, it is often true that there is simply no need to travel as far as these countries' waters to make a catch. The 1974 season is an example. If, on the

136

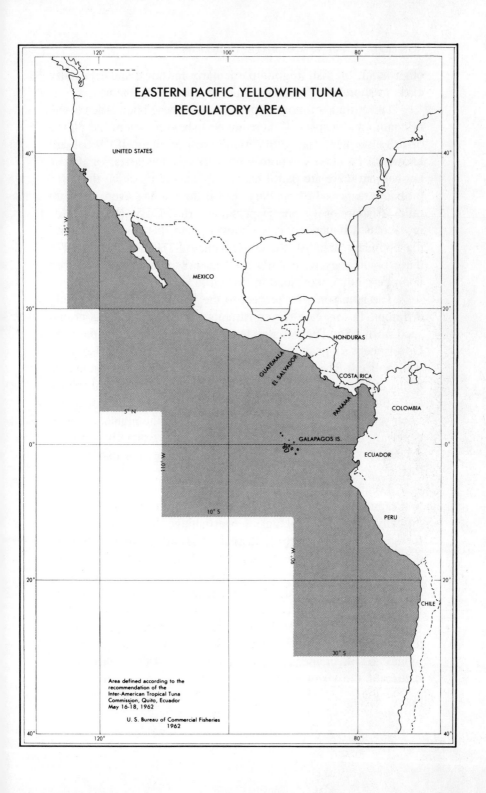

EASTERN PACIFIC YELLOWFIN TUNA
REGULATORY AREA

Area defined according to the
recommendation of the
Inter-American Tropical Tuna
Commission, Quito, Ecuador
May 16-18, 1962

U. S. Bureau of Commercial Fisheries
1962

other hand, the fish migrate particularly far north and especially close to shore, the Mexican limit may pose a problem.

The attitude of most skippers toward these boundaries is one of conditional respect. If there are no fish within them and plenty of fish elsewhere, they will certainly respect them. If the fish are known to be close to shore within these boundaries, or if it is known that there are patrol boats or planes in the area, they will probably respect the boundary. But if the fish are over, say, 100 miles offshore or if a boat is pursuing a run of fish which is leading across a boundary, it is almost certain that they will ignore the boundary and risk the consequences. The fact that in 1974 these boundaries were unilateral and not internationally agreed upon certainly contributed to this attitude.

The situation with respect to the regulatory area is slightly different. In this case the constraints placed on the boats are issued from a San Diego-based body with the authority of the U.S. Government's signature on an agreement behind it. It is also fairly well policed. The boats are less likely to violate the boundaries of the regulatory area than the claimed boundaries of other countries, but the same attitudes toward following a run of fish apply. Each year there are citations for violations of the regulatory area, generally occurring around the edges, and generally with the excuse that the boat was following a moving area of fish that was just too good to give up.

The fishermen's attitudes toward these resource conservation regulations are mixed. While most will agree, if asked specifically about the problem of overfishing, that there is a need for some form of control, there is a strong feeling of relative deprivation among the U.S. tunamen. Many times during the first part of the season they fish alongside other boats whose size or national registry will allow them to fish in the prime areas of the fishery for the entire year. The figures the fisheries scientists use to determine the tonnage limits for the quota are not as good as they could be, because of lack of equipment and money to collect adequate data and because of the highly mobile nature of the species. Added to this is the belief that certain countries could not possibly land the numbers of fish given to them in their "special allocations." These factors lead to a sort of sour grapes conformity with the regulations, which at the same time affects the attitude of fishermen toward competition with other boats.

I should point out that these constraints do not cover all the actual alternatives open to the fishermen. With more and more of the boats sailing under foreign flags, unloading in Puerto Rico, and being built with greater and greater ranges, it is becoming possible to travel to other areas of the world after the season has closed and even to depend completely on other fishing areas. Many of the boats, for example, are now going to the west coast of Africa after the quota is filled, and returning around Christmas for the season in the Eastern Pacific. The constraints listed above concern only those boats, still a majority, whose alternatives, at least in the minds of the skippers at sea, are limited to this latter area.

Resource Rights Among the Boats at Sea

The "rights" discussed in this section come into effect in three general situations: when two boats spot the fish at the same time; when several boats are in close proximity to one another in an area of fish; and when one boat is "on fish" and another approaches.

There do not seem to be any rules involving absolute distance from country of flag or home port. That is, a boat out of Panama off the coast of Costa Rica has no more rights to the fish there than does, for example, a Canadian boat. In the cases of the countries with extended territorial rights, of course, the situation is clear and binary: outside there are equal rights, inside there are no rights to foreigners. In the case of the countries with a claimed but not enforced boundary, the boats seem to be on the same footing, all other things being equal.

In fact, there is an ethic of fairness within inequality operating in the fleet. This particular sense of justice sometimes justifies a skipper's assertion of his rights to the fish in situations

139

where he might otherwise defer to another boat. It is my impression, for example, that boats from distant countries would probably respect some primacy of rights for local boats if it were not for the "relative deprivation" they feel with respect to many of the boats of the various Latin American coastal states, which have distinct quota advantages.

All other things are not, however, equal in either attitudinal or physical matters. Relevant to the *ability* of a boat to *assert* her rights over the fish are her capacity, speed, net size, machinery quality and consequent setting and retrieving speed, and her fish-finding equipment—all things which are far from evenly distributed throughout the fleet. A faster boat can reach a school first even though two or more boats may have spotted it at the same time. Capacity and net size give an automatic "right" to more fish simply because they can hold more, but they also give an advantage in using the argument that there is "just enough for me to make a trip," an argument that will be explained later. Setting and retrieving speed are important in the ability to "corner" the fish, and although fish-finding equipment, notably sonar, is not often used in the initial contact with the fish, it sometimes gives one boat the advantage over another at a critical time.

The U.S. boats are in general larger, faster, and have better machinery and electronics than boats from other countries. The U.S. fishermen are extremely proud of the size and efficiency of their fleet. Many of the innovations and most of the initiative for the fleet's development have come from within the ranks of the fishermen themselves. Subject to constraints that will be enumerated presently, they tend to hold the view that with respect to actual confrontation between two or more boats, their ability to catch more fish is a result of their own hard work and risk-taking and gives them the right to do so whenever and wherever they can.

All of these equipment differences, however, are only supplementary to the understandings discussed below. All are used as sources of power and legitimacy in transactions between boats vying for the same catch.

The General Rules

The first and most important of these rules is the "working first" rule. This is not simply a matter of getting to the school first, but rather of making a move intended to alter the movement of the fish or porpoise to get them into position to set the net.

In the case of porpoise fish, the deciding move is the launching of the speedboats. The first seiner with his speedboats into the water is assumed to have rights on the school. If, however, part of the porpoise school breaks away, another seiner may set its speedboats out after the runaway bunch. If the first boat sets and misses the fish, no matter how close the school remains to the first boat or the first boat's net, other boats have the right to set on the escapees.

These contingencies involve a considerable amount of judgment. If, for example, a skipper thinks that another boat has set its speedboats out much too early for the sole purpose of "claiming" the school, thereby diminishing their actual chances of capturing it, he will sometimes consider it his prerogative to set his speedboats out also. The schools are often spotted as far off as fifteen miles, and since the speedboats can travel up to four times as fast as the seiner, there is considerable leeway in a skipper's decision to put the speedboats out. If he puts them out too early he runs the risk of not being able to oversee their work and also of their running out of gas before they have finished working the school. If they do run out of gas too soon, or if the school moves toward the direction of the second seiner, the second skipper is generally considered within his rights to set on the school.

On the other hand, the skipper of the second boat may consider a renegade section of the porpoise school to have broken away, while the skipper of the first boat may consider the renegades part of the school, though harder to work. Some skippers are diligent about getting the whole school no matter how long it takes, while others are willing to let a few porpoise go in order to make a sure set on the remainder. There is the tendency in competition to assume that the other skipper is, or *should be,*

141

using the same decision parameters that you yourself are, the corollary being that if his are different they are wrong. In cases such as this, however, two skippers are often acting under very different decision parameters.

The exact moment at which a boat has "missed" a school is also questionable. Skippers have considerable leeway in the amount of towline they may let out in order to surround a school. The more towline they let out, the less likely it is that they will keep the fish in the net. Another boat may decide that the first boat has missed the school when the first boat's skipper has decided to risk letting out a lot of towline to try and get what he can of it.

The matter becomes more complicated in the case of school fish. School fish are found in "areas" more than are porpoise fish, and often the situation is one of up to ten or fifteen boats within a mile or so of each other in the midst of several separate schools of fish. The general rule in these cases is that the boat which makes the first turn onto a school, a turn that brings it immediately alongside the school or alters the school's direction, has the rights to the school. This also, however, is open to interpretation. One boat I was aboard was in this situation, and another boat made the first turn onto a school no more than 100 yards away from us. Our skipper started to turn away until several of our crewmen noticed that the crew of the other boat was still straightening out and running their cables, which meant that they wouldn't be ready to set for some time. The school was "spooky" and had been changing direction a lot, and our skipper decided that there was a good chance that the other boat would not be able to set on the school in time. We turned toward the school to make our own set. As it turned out, the school made several more maneuvers and ended up next to the other boat as he was finally ready to set, but the point is that our skipper considered the other boat's right to the school null on the basis of her unpreparedness to set. This is akin to the case where a skipper sets his speedboats out simply to "claim" the fish. Both illustrate the attitude that one only ought to have a right to the fish if he is prepared and able to exercise that right.

142

The ideal in school fish situations is to get what the fishermen call the "inside." Since the boats have to make the set circling to the left because of the configuration of the equipment onboard the seiner, being "inside" means being between the other boat and the school on the other boat's left or port side. It is often the case that two boats will spot a school at the same time and both turn toward it. If one or the other arrives at the school first, the "rights" are clear-cut. If they arrive at the same time, it is a showdown with two factors coming into play.

First, the boat on the left, or inside, will try to head slightly to the right of the school to put himself between the other boat and the school in a position to set. The boat on the right, however, has the legal right of way according to the International Rules of the Road for ships at sea. The boat on the left cannot force his hand because he is without legal rights, but the boat on the right cannot set unless the boat on the left moves out of his way.

The results of such a confrontation depend on each skipper's willingness to push his rights. It is a face-to-face showdown in every sense, an aquatic game of "chicken." And most often it is the more inexperienced skipper or the one with the least status in the fleet who backs down. To push a confrontation with a more experienced or high-status skipper may mean the loss of future search information for the new or low-status skipper, and few will risk that loss for a single school of fish.

Between skippers of equal ability and status, however, or between two skippers with a grudge of some sort, these situations can get tense. Among the smaller seiners from which some of the skippers have graduated into the high-seas fleet, it is not unheard of for a boat on the inside to refuse to turn away and observe the boat on the right's right of way, even after the boat on the right has dropped his skiff. There are stories of this kind of refusal resulting in the boat on the right setting his net in a straight line. The skippers in the tuna fleet, however, all realize that this kind of move would be both too costly and too dangerous to make on boats the size of the tuna seiners. They tend to be less aggressive because of the nature of their equipment.

The situation gets more complex in logfishing. There are areas off the coast of Central America where rivers flowing to the sea deposit large quantities of logs and other debris into the coastal waters, and these areas are prime for log fishing. So prevalent are log fish in these and other areas that a boat will often attach a buoy with a light or flag to a log or even to the carcass of a dead whale and simply drift alongside of it in the hopes it will pick up fish. If a boat comes upon a log that is "carrying" fish it will usually put out a marker immediately and then take its time preparing the equipment with extra care, having lunch, or whatever needs to be done in the belief that there is no hurry because the log will "keep" the fish for them.

These logs, the ones which are found with fish on them, are the ones most often tagged to drift with. The reasoning is that there are certain logs that are more likely to attract fish, and that often the fish will disappear only to reappear sometime later due to a sort of "ranging" behavior back and forth about the log. Because of this type of behavior log fish are considered very valuable. They are more to be "picked" than hunted. Even if you miss a school with a set you can be fairly sure that they will stay in the same area, around the log. This is in contrast to porpoise fish, which, if they are missed the first time, are usually off and running and impossible to catch again.

If a boat is alone and tags a log, the fish in the general area, within a couple of hundred yards, are considered its fish. A skipper with a log will usually, subject to satisfying his own needs, call another skipper to whom he is indebted or with whom he wishes to build up credit or do a favor to share in the find. It is considered proper that a boat be invited before setting on fish in close proximity to another boat's log. Again, this is a matter of judgment. If there are several boats in the area, or if the fish are scattered about considerably, anyone has a right to them. A single boat coming upon another with a log, though, is generally expected to wait for an invitation to set.

It is in the two-boat situation that the "enough for a trip" assertion is sometimes made. This is meant to indicate that there is enough fish on the log for the tagging boat to fill all his wells

144

but no more. Everyone involved realizes what this means: the end of a trip that may easily have been two and a half months; the chance to go home and see the family and get paid; the chance to get off of the boat. Balanced against this is the fact that a little in each boat's wells will allow each of them to get home a little sooner, but at the expense of one of them who could have gone right away. It is a strict zero-sum game. I have seen this request both honored and dishonored.

The one thing that one does not do, ever, is wrap another boat's tagged log. This is the greatest transgression, and the most clear-cut. There is no doubt or matter of judgment involved. The tagging boat will usually leave the set around the log itself until last, concentrating on fish near the log but not actually under it until the former are exhausted. The reasons for this are that skippers are of the opinion that it is possible to upset whatever it is about the log that is attracting the fish, and that there are often a large number of "junk fish" around the log itself which can make for considerable trouble when stacking net and brailing. If a skipper can make his trip without actually wrapping the log, he will. This means that the tagged log is usually more or less out in the open while the tagging boat is rounding up the neighboring fish. It is almost unheard of, however, for one boat to wrap another's tagged log.

Transgressions of the Rules

There are transgressions of these rules in varying degrees. Some arise out of differences of opinion while others are factually clear-cut, and in the more obvious cases sanctions can be substantial and swift.

There is a famous case, for example, that demonstrated the lengths to which a skipper will go to redress a wrong. It involved two boats, both out of San Diego, both of whom came onto the same school of fish at the same time off the coast of Mexico. One boat made the first turn onto the school but the other stayed right on his stern and as the school made a move away from the first boat the second cut "inside" and immediately dropped his skiff. The first boat, being physically cut off from

145

the school by the second boat's net, turned away to starboard and was forced to sit and watch the second boat surround the school. Needless to say the first boat's skipper was furious. His subsequent action, which is related with relish throughout the fleet, was as follows.

The second skipper had connected up both ends of his net and was starting to roll it back aboard. The nets being as large as they are, the half-net buoy was over a hundred yards away from the boat. The first skipper steamed slowly around to the second's half-net buoy, carefully nosed the bow of his boat over the corkline, and dropped both his anchors inside the second boat's net. He then put his seiner full astern and proceeded to rip the wrongdoer's $150,000 net into two pieces!

The case of course went to court, and the judgment went against the net-ripper on the grounds that the punishment far outweighed the crime. In fact, although the story is a delight to the fishermen, not many of them would be willing to say that the first skipper's action was a warranted or just one.

An instance which was considered an equitable though non-deliberate punishment for this kind of transgression is the following. The situation was much like the one described above. One boat had cut in on another and wrapped a school. The "losing boat" did nothing but learned a few days later that the other boat had lost its skiff in rough weather and was returning to port with less than a full load to acquire a new one, a process which would cut weeks out of their fishing time. This was generally considered "right," and a just punishment.

Any "punishment" of this sort is viewed ambiguously by the fishermen. An "act of God" punishment, like the loss of the skiff in rough weather, is generally preferred to a direct, aggressive, personal reprisal like the anchor incident. As will become clear in the discussions of competition, wage-bargaining, and recruitment in later chapters, much potential vindictiveness is curbed by the pervasive network of ties throughout the industry. Even though the crew on a wronged boat has perhaps been done out of both time and money by another, they generally view the other *skipper,* not the whole crew, as responsible for the ma-

146

neuvers of the boat—as in fact he is. By the nature of the social organization of the industry, the skipper is enough "outside" of the rest of the crew's social network to be open to criticism without the crew having to identify with his actions. The men also realize that to wish bad luck on or initiate action against another boat is to wish harm, at least financially, to a crew who are men exactly like themselves, more often than not friends and relatives.

On the other hand, it is generally true that the crew on any one boat are men who get along together and often share attitudes. Crewmen on a boat with a skipper who transgresses the rules were personally selected by him and are free to go if they don't find his actions to their liking. To this extent they are participants in his decisions. More than one fight ashore has involved a crewman "paying" for his boat's actions.

The punishments for transgressions of these inter-boat rules are of a different character from those found in transgressions of the more formal boundary and quota rules. While in the latter the punishment is either a fine or the loss of the catch in the holds at the time of detection, in the former it is both more subtle and more pervasive. A skipper who transgresses these understandings faces a loss of future search information from other skippers both in and out of his official code group, and a decrease in the number of other skippers who will be willing to defer to him by common understanding in cases of face-to-face confrontation. This type of punishment is much more costly, causing not only financial loss but also a diminishing of the skipper's "social capital" in the networks of the industry. This brings up perhaps the single most important set of variables in the applications of these rights, and that is the set of relationships btween the skippers and crews in the total economic and social network of the industry community.

The Social Network and Resource Rights

Any and all of these rules can be manipulated toward various ends. Sometimes one's rights over a school are deferred as a favor to a friend who has had a run of bad luck or who has done

147

one a similar favor in the past. Other times skippers will defer rights in the hopes of gaining another more powerful skipper's favor, which could mean a better berth or command of a newer, bigger boat in the future. These powerful skippers will themselves sometimes use their prestige to "bull" their way onto a school that normally would go to another boat in the same way that they use their prestige to transgress communications obligations. Some skippers will try to trade present rights for an access to information in the future from someone who normally might not feel obligated to give it to them. Others, strange as it seems, will actually pass up rights to fish simply to convey the impression that they are doing better than they really are.

I should emphasize again that any of these rights are subject to a skipper's or boat's ability to assert them. It is sometimes the case that a skipper, comparable to the skipper who follows a code group because he doubts his ability to find fish on his own, will defer rights to a boat he thinks is much more experienced or skillful than he. This is the exception, but it is often true that a new skipper will defer to one with a reputation although their actual setting abilities may be relatively equal.

Each skipper also has to take into account that he has three audiences to please. One is the group of skippers, from which he draws many of his friends and his code and his other search-group affiliations. Another is his shore-side employers or managers, who ultimately decide which boat he will run, or whether he will run a boat at all. The third is his own crew. For the first and last audiences he must practice a give-and-take in order to receive the necessary bits of information and favors he needs to make money for his own boat and in applicable cases, "the company." For the second, he must mix the proper amounts of aggressiveness on the one hand, to gain himself a reputation, and "group spirit" on the other to convince the company that he is their man.

From my observations most skippers sacrifice the latter to the former. That is, they are more concerned about their personal prestige, reputation, and the economic benefit to their own crew than they are about making money for the company, although the two of course go hand in hand.

Determining Resource Rights
Through the Social Network:
an Example

Some of these considerations will be brought out in the following example. The situation is one mentioned briefly in the last chapter and occurred between two boats in the same "official" code group and managed by the same company. They were fishing in the Gulf of Tehauntepec. First I will relate the details of the actual incident as I saw them from my vantage point as a crewman on one of the vessels. Then I will present additional information from the point of view of a man on the other boat to whom I talked some time later. Finally, I will add excerpts from the radio transmissions which took place between a number of the boats in the fleet and between our two boats and the parent company concerning the incident.

From Our Side. We were in the Gulf of Tehauntepec and had just come out from two days in a coastal port where we had dropped off an injured man. Three days before on the way into port, we had seen and reported some fish at a position considerably to the south, but the weather was rough and being in a hurry to get the man ashore we had not tried to set. We had communications in the interim, but nothing of import.

The weather was still choppy, but workable. We had 330 tons aboard, below what the crew considered the minimum acceptable break-even point, and we needed another 220 tons to fill up. It was late in the first trip of the year (we had been out 46 days) and the whole fleet, ourselves included, was trying to second-guess the season closing announcement, which could come any day and send us quickly on our way home to clear for a second trip. We were headed northwest when we got a call from a boat not in our code group but whose skipper was a good friend of our skipper. He was southeast of us about 20 miles and sent a "come towards us" message. We turned to comply.

Not half an hour later our skipper glanced out of the bridge window and saw a huge breezer of school fish on our port bow. As we looked closer we found that it was a large area of tuna

149

on a big tree trunk: log fish. We were, to say the least, ecstatic. We set on one school and got a clean 50 tons. We tagged the log with a lighted buoy and settled down to an apprehensive, expectant night drifting with the log. We had seen at least enough fish around the log to "make our trip." This being the case, we didn't call the information to any of the other boats we knew were in the area.

Just before sunup the next morning, as soon as we could see, we set on a big school of skipjack. We let out a lot of towline and had just started to winch it in when the steering broke on our skiff. The weather was still a little rough, and although we tried to aid the skiff with the speedboats (thereby allowing some of the fish to escape) we soon found the seiner swinging around upwing of the net, an extremely dangerous situation.

From the mast our skipper ordered the paper Master to get on the VHF radio and call one of our code group boats which we knew was in the area to come and help us out. This the Master did, but with one mistake; he didn't take the time to code the message in any way and sent our straight coordinates over the air. The message was received and the other boat replied that he was on his way. Shortly thereafter we got the skiff fixed and managed to get the seiner downwind again. The Master radioed our code group partner and gave him all clear and he said fine, that he was turning away to continue the search on his own.

Because of the skiff problems we only sacked up about 30 tons, but there were still fish all over the place around the log which was a hundred or so yards downwind of us. As we were brailing the fish aboard, another seiner appeared on the horizon. Since we didn't know who the boat was, our skipper took an ordinary precaution and ordered one of the speedboat drivers to go get the log and tow it right alongside the seiner, the theory being that the accompanying fish would then congregate around our boat and the newcomer wouldn't be tempted to set on them. This is a common log-fishing tactic.

Soon after this was done we recognized the approaching boat as a member of our company code group, one with whom we had not had a lot of contact that trip. Some crewmen on our

150

boat thought that he had "found" us using the coordinates that our Master had carelessly given out over the radio. The man on the other boat, whose comments I will present below, said they just happened to be passing our position. Our skipper got on the radio and told the other skipper the situation, saying that we had just enough to fill up on *our* log. The other skipper said fine, that he would keep on going.

I had gone down to help pack the wells when a big commotion broke out on deck. The other boat, after starting to turn away, had circled back and set on what seemed to be a major portion of the remaining fish about a hundred yards away from us. A green dye he was using to keep the fish in the net made it look like he had more than he really did (a very large, dense jag of fish will look like a light green spot), but that was neither here nor there; we had fourteen cases of apoplexy on board our boat!

Our skipper shot up to the bridge and was so hot and fast over the radio that it was hard to tell what he was saying, but one of the things was that he was never going to code with the other guy again, that being one of the less abusive comments. Our crew, while not as upset as the skipper, was pretty worked up. One of them mentioned to me that it really would have been hard for the other boat to pass up all that fish; another thought that although it wasn't exactly right he would have probably done the same thing. But in general the feeling was intense hatred. We were watching our "trip" being sacked up in the other boat's net.

We finished our set and started circling for the next one. Our skipper decided to wrap the log, partly because he was worried about losing some of the fish and partly to remove the fish from the other boat's grasp once and for all. This we did, and got about 100 tons! We also, however, got a lot of "bullets," a problem described in detail in an earlier chapter. This added once-and-a-half-again the amount of work and another two hours to our set. One of the other speedboat drivers and I pulled the log, still tagged, out of the net to get it out of the way. There were still a good number of fish in the vicinity. I learned later that during this set the two men in our skiff, who were within earshot of the other boat, had exchanged strong words with the other crew. The other boat finished their set and went on their way to the accompaniment of various comments from our crew, luckily out of range.

I was again below, packing the wells, when our skipper came over and said that he had just talked to the skipper of the other boat and had told him that we had enough to fill up in the set we had just made. He then laughed and said, "We *don't*, but . . ." and shrugged his shoulders and walked off. I thought that rather strange, but didn't think much of it until I heard another commotion on deck.

The other boat had returned and had done three very "bad" things. First, they had set extremely close to us, so close that their skiff didn't even have room to pull without running over our net. Second, they had set directly upwind and consequently were sure to drift down onto us. And third, they had wrapped our log, buoy and all! Our crew, even the oldtimers and the usually calm ones, were incensed. None of them knew about our skipper's call to the other boat, but even if they had, the combination of circumstances would have lit the fires.

The crowning blow came when the other skipper called ours on the radio and told *us* to move out of *his* way. News of this initiated several hostile suggestions among the crew concerning what we should do when he did drift within reach. Our skipper, not wanting to start real trouble and exhibiting an admirable amount of control and level-headedness, acquiesced and asked him to tell his skiff to come over and help ours pull us away. We still had a large amount of fish in the sack over the side, and this creates considerable drag in addition to danger to the net from the propeller. This the other skipper refused to do. We finally started our main engine and slowly moved away, our skipper saying that two wrongs don't make a right and that he'd settle with the other guy later.

That was the end of this part of the story. Both boats finished their sets and went on their separate ways.

From Their Side. This account of the same incident I got a month or so after we returned home, from a fellow who had been on the other boat. It provides substantial information for the analysis of the other boat's seemingly "deviant" behavior. It is, I should point out, the impressions their crew had of the motives behind their skipper's decisions, and therefore colored somewhat by the informant's perceptive constructs and hampered by whatever degree of lack of communication may have existed between that skipper and his crew.

When the other boat first saw us, they thought we were on school fish. It was only when they saw we had a log that they turned to set. This was all right, he said, because they felt as long as they didn't wrap the log they were entitled to go after fish in the vicinity, the corollary being that we had our "share" of the fish on the log itself. He did not know about the conversation between the skippers concerning our having only enough to make a trip and his skipper's agreement to turn away.

What he did know about was the conversation that had occurred after they had completed their first set and headed away. According to him, they returned because our skipper called and told them that we had enough fish *and that they could come back and finish the log if they wanted.* He said that was why they considered it all right to wrap the log, because we had called them back and "offered" it to them. He didn't remember that they had set upwind of us, but he did say that they couldn't release their skiff because they had their net in the water and couldn't take the risk of their seiner getting caught in their own net. Both of these comments are understandable, the first because the crew is often too busy to notice many of the factors and events in the set, and the second because it was a very real risk that their skipper had to balance against our request for the use of his skiff. All of these comments were justifications for his different interpretation of the "rules" of rights to the fish. What follows are more basic initiating factors in the disputed behavior.

He said, as I mentioned in the last chapter, that their skipper was angry at ours because of what he thought were lies about our situation five days earlier. Because of our reports of sightings before we went into port and our subsequent silence, he had made several comments to his crew to the effect that we had been on fish "like crazy" for those three days and hadn't told the code group. He also said that their skipper had been particularly incensed the night before the dispute because he had heard our transmissions with the boat that had given us the "come towards us" message. He had told his crew that there was another boat in the area whom he identified only as "one of (our skipper's) drinking buddies." He was under the impression that our skipper had called a friend into the area with good information before he had called our code group. This led the fellow to comment that their skipper did not smoke or drink and had never been very fond of our skipper, who indulged frequently in both. These comments, taken together with the other skipper's initial agreement to "keep going" (which I heard myself over the Mickey Mouse), lead me to believe that it was in essence these preconceptions concerning our skipper and his recent reactions which led to his setting next to us, not any real impression that he in fact had rights to the fish under the normal set of understandings operative within the fleet.

Later. Two questions stuck in my mind. Why had the other skipper changed his mind and decided to set the first time, after telling our skipper that he wouldn't? And why had our skipper called the other boat at all after their first set. The first of these questions is, I think, relatively easily answered.

The other skipper, through a combination of prior impressions of our skipper and misunderstandings about our information-sharing during that trip, came into the situation feeling that we had lost our right to claim the usual rights to the fish through what he perceived as our transgressions of the communications rules. He still needed a push in order to take the initiative and blatantly reverse his initial commitment to the rules, as evidenced by his promise to "turn away"; that push came in the form of his actual sighting of the fish and consequent rationalization that there was enough for both of us.

The second question, that of our skipper's call to the other boat after our second set, is more complicated. Its answer involves the three criteria by which he thought his actions would be judged: those of his own crew, those of the other skippers in the fleet, and those of the company. Judgment by any of these criteria involved the value of his own "social stock" as well as questions of economics.

News of the incident spread quickly, and all of the radio comments I heard were sympathetic to our skipper. Several skippers, most from outside our official code group who fished for different companies, called our skipper and in the course of conversation brought up the incident. Our skipper's tone during these conversations was one of mixed condescension and anger toward the disputed skipper—he had to express enough nonchalance to show that he really didn't need the fish and consequently wasn't all that disturbed and yet give the impression that the other fellow wasn't going to get away with what he had done. The reaction of the other skippers was generally one of "well, there are always guys like that around" mixed with condolences about having "lost" the fish.

The one heated conversation between the boats at sea concerning the incident was between the boat who had given us the "come towards us" call the day before the incident and the other skipper in the dispute. The former told the latter in no uncertain terms that he had been wrong in what he had done, and that "If you (the other skipper in the dispute) want to argue about it, you know where to find me (when we get in)." Interestingly, this defense of our skipper came after it had become entirely clear that we had been on a large body of fish very near our defender, fish which we had found because we turned to heed his call, and about which we had not told him.

With respect to our own crew, our skipper was on slightly shakier ground. He had always had, at least among the more pragmatic members of the crew, a reputation for being too loose with fish information. He was sometimes described as "radio-happy," as indeed he sometimes seemed to be. Part of this was due to his belief that everyone gets the most benefit out of a free flow of information, and part was due to his desire to increase his status within the fleet by giving out news of his fishing accomplishments. Even though the crew did not know the substance of the call to the other skipper, they did know that he had

155

spent time on the radio and there were a few comments to the effect that his radio-talk had lost us the fish. I don't think that this particular criticism bothered our skipper. He had defended his openness over the radio before, and sincerely believed that his policy was the best one. What did bother him was another aspect of his image before the crew.

This aspect surfaced directly only once, but with considerable vehemence. I was talking to him on my night watch several days after the incident and he said suddenly and very angrily that the other skipper "made a fool out of me in front of my own crew!" He was concerned that the crew would interpret his lack of aggressive action as not only having lost them money and time, but as an indication that he had backed down out of a lack of nerve. That is part of the reason that he did not tell the crew all about his call to the other skipper; that knowledge would only strengthen this impression on the part of the crew. The rest of the reason for that call lies in his relationship to the company, and through the company to the other skipper.

The night after the incident our skipper talked to the president of the company, himself an ex-skipper, on the high-seas radio. While our skipper got a lot off his chest he made no direct, specific complaint about the other skipper's actions that day. His conversation had the gaming aspect of many of the inter-boat transmissions. He brought up specifics only when they were needed to make his point or challenge the other's assertions. None of these specifics were in the form of explication of the incident, but were "examples" of the badness of the other skipper's behavior. He said that he wasn't going to code with the company group anymore, that they could "take the boat away" from him if they wanted but he wasn't going to do it. I think the president had already heard about the incident, so there was no need for him to refer to it directly either. Our skipper went on to say that he was tired of the sit-back-and-let-somebody-else-find-it attitude of most of the code group, especially when they did "things like that" to other guys in the group.

The president was very calm and almost supercilious about the whole situation. He pointed out that it was, after all, another company boat that had gotten the fish and that our skipper had money invested in the company. He was viewing the incident as a minor distributive matter within the total context of the company's operations. Our skipper, on the other hand, viewed the matter as one of principle. He emphasized this point to the crew after the call, stressing that he didn't care about "company money" but was out to see a fair distribution to each boat according to its skills in the process and cooperation with the other boats in doing what was "right." This was a good thing to say to the crew, of course, who were aware of the fact that the skipper had an interest in the company and stood to gain regardless of the outcome of the situation, while the crew had already lost. As one of the crewmen said to another fellow and myself the day after the incident, "It's not 'poor (our skipper),' it's 'poor (several crewmen's names)'."

The man from the other boat involved in the incident told me that their skipper also talked to the president a day or two later. The president had said "I heard you really scalped (our skipper) out there" in what was described as a chuckling tone of voice. The other skipper just grunted and changed the subject.

The president might not have treated the matter as lightly had the incident occurred with the roles reversed. The other skipper was an older man who had been with the company for quite some time *as a skipper*. Our skipper, on the other hand, had been running a boat for only a year or so. His brother was another skipper with the company, one with considerably more experience, including running our boat when our present skipper was only a deckhand. Also, our skipper's brother-in-law was the registered owner of our boat and an executive in the company. Thus, even though he was a very successful skipper, our skipper was susceptible to the "in-law syndrome"—the practice of granting an in-law a position and then failing to support him in adverse situations. This practice will be detailed in a later chapter.

Our skipper realized all of this and while he was on a par with the other skipper in actual ability (quite possibly better on school fish, with which he had an excellent reputation), he was a lower man on the totem pole at the company. At the same time

157

that the company values aggressiveness on the part of their skippers, they don't like to see dissension within their own skippers' ranks. Our skipper's second call to the other skipper may have been a form of reparation for his outbursts during the incident. It was also, of course, a reassertion of his own status and cavalierness. His actions during the incident, while they had been for the most part justified, were "uncool." His offer of the rest of the fish rekindled the impression that we were doing fine without them, and that he was the kind of skipper who found more fish than he could use and passed them on to others.

The Outcome. Both boats returned to San Diego under the quota and with respectable loads. What, then, were the "costs" of the incident, and to whom?

There was a direct cost to our boat in terms of the fish we "lost" to the other boat and the time we spent in the search after the incident. This amounted to possibly $45,000 (about $1,500 to each crewman on the average) and five or six days time.

Secondly, there was a certain loss of status for our skipper. He sincerely believed that "two wrongs don't make a right" and thus didn't take the most aggressive action which might have given him status in some people's minds.

Most important, however, was the "loss" in terms of future deferral of rights and the flow of search information within the fleet. Many skippers, those who didn't approve of the other skipper in the actions in the dispute, will be less likely to give him information in the future, thus decreasing his fish-finding power. Others who think that the incident was caused by our skipper's careless radio transmission will be hesitant to give *him* information in the future out of fear that he will be just as careless with *it*. Some skippers may defer rights to our skipper because they feel he got a bad deal on that trip, and some may be more aggressive with the other skipper because they either disagree with his actions in the incident or view him as one with whom they have to be more aggressive in order to be competitive.

Besides these various costs, the incident will serve to alter or strengthen each fisherman's impressions of how the rules of inter-boat rights to the fish ought to be applied. Many of the crewmen on our boat, for example, the skipper included, commented in a rationalizing sort of way that it wouldn't have been so bad if the other code group member who was on his way to help us originally would have gotten the fish, even if he had gotten them through the same means as the other skipper. His intentions and actions in trying to come to our aid would have given him a certain "right" to behave in that manner.

Some will undoubtedly interpret the incident as confirmation of the fact that being a nice guy and adhering to the rules doesn't pay. Others will see the incident as an example of what kind of costs could be avoided through proper adherence to the rules. The rules are, after all, not only a means to most equitably distribute the economic benefits of the resource, although they perform that function in a secondary manner, but also a means of regulating the interaction of the skippers and crews in the fleet—to express in the best way possible the perceptions of fairness and prescriptiveness of action held by the majority of the fishermen. Each man will judge the "correctness" of each party's behavior in the incident and adjust his own future behavior according to these perceptions.

Conclusion

There are several general points to be derived from these comments on resource rights. The first is that there are several senses of the word "right." One is the sense of ownership. This carries conditions, such as the obligation of the exploiter, if he is not the owner, to pay some form of remuneration for his exploitation and the right of the owner to determine who, if anyone, may exploit it.

A second sense of "right" is connected with the *ability* to catch the fish. This sense implies that you can reap the benefits of the resource more efficiently than anyone else, and in some cases that you are the only one who is able to gain any benefit from it at all. Closely allied with this sense is what might be termed the substantive economic sense—that through risk, hard work, and innovation one has "earned" the right to the resource.

159

A third sense of "right" is based on need, or in a loose sense, justice. Many of the underdeveloped countries, Peru and Ecuador included, assert that they have a "right" to the tuna resource because they need it more than the others who are vying for it and have fewer alternate ways to fill the particular need which the use of the resource fulfills. When one skipper defers to another because the latter has had a bad season, he is also using the concept of "right" in this sense.

Finally, there is a meta-sense of the word "right" that is used in such rules as the quota regulations. This sense assumes that no one has the "right" to outfish a resource, that fishermen only have any rights at all so long as they are not doing permanent damage to the rights of others or, in the end, to themselves.

It is important to enumerate all these various uses of this term, because the rules and their applications with which this chapter has been concerned are based on a particular view of the world, a view which holds various amounts of stock in one or more of these senses of "right." When two boats dispute each other's actions, when a boat is caught "inside the line," or when a boat is confiscated in "foreign" waters it is essentially a disagreement over which of these senses of "right" is the correct one with which to generate rules of interaction.

The second general point is that everyone tends to assume that others use the term "rights" and act under derivative rules of interaction in the same way that they themselves do—or at least that everyone else *ought* to. Thus a disputant tends to say the other fellow is "wrong" or "bad" rather than that he is acting under a different set of rules or assumptions. To do otherwise is very unsettling. It entails admitting that there is a different way to see the world, an admission which usually, though not necessarily, suggests a decision about whose principles are "correct." No one especially likes to make decisions such as this, or even admit that there are other possibilities.

What many times results from this, at least in disputes in the tuna fleet, is people arguing about or trying to ascertain facts when the problem is essentially that the parties are using different principles to interpret the facts. In the case of the incident

160

described above, the point actively argued was whether the other skipper had actually meant in the initial radio conversation that he wouldn't set, and whether our skipper actually meant that the other could wrap our log when he called him after his first set. What seemed to be implicitly at issue were the rules concerning entering another boat's area and wrapping another boat's log. What in fact was "causing" the conflict was the clash between our skipper's perception of the ownership principle and the other skipper's perception of the justice of our "paying" for our skipper's supposed transgressions of the communications rules with the loss of the fish he took from our log.

All of these rules and many of these principles are based on the fact that each man is interacting with others who possess certain attributes with respect to equipment, skill, charisma, connections, or obligations. While all of these considerations may not go into the initial actions in disputes, because of the heat of the moment and other factors, they certainly go into the eventual resolution of the dispute in terms of the rewards and punishments due each party, and also into the alteration of the perceptive constructs with which each party will view interaction in the future.

6 Recruitment and Alliance

THE BOOK UP to this point has been about tuna *fishing;* the lay-out of the boats and the organization of the trips, the seining process itself, the decision-making procedures in the search for the tuna, the communication network which facilitates that search, and the rules which distribute the tuna resource among the various participants in the hunt.

The following chapters are about the tuna *fishermen.* They trace the route of a fisherman through his employment on the seiners and his socialization into the crew as a social and occupational group. They describe how he is remunerated for what he does, and how he deals with the risk and uncertainty inherent in both that particular form of remuneration and the general nature of the fishing process itself. They set out the nature of the socio-political and psychological settings in which he finds himself while he is at sea, and the particular relationships with his environment ashore which are engendered by his participation in the tuna seining occupation.

Who Controls the Seiners?

There are three general categories of ownership and management in the tuna fleet: privately owned and managed, privately owned and company-managed, and company-owned and company-managed.

The ownership of a seiner may take several forms. Some are owned by individuals or in partnership. Others are owned by single-boat corporations whose principal investors may belong to the family of the skipper. Arrangements whereby several boats are owned by one corporation but with several outside investors as principals are becoming more and more prevalent. Some are owned outright by large corporations. In recent years

162

some of the large tuna canning corporations have become principal investors in some seiners. As of 1975, however, over half of the fleet was still owned by private individuals or single-boat corporations. Most owners and those representing owning interests, even in the larger corporations, are ex-fishermen or men from fishing families.

The management of the seiner is another question. Each seiner is an entity within itself whose needs must be forecast and met. The crew must be hired, the repairs and maintenance must be done, the provisions must be arranged, the unloading must be scheduled, and so on. Even for a small seiner, these matters consume a considerable amount of time and energy.

These arrangements have often been facilitated by "management agreements" whereby an entity in the form of a corporation or firm agrees to manage the affairs of a particular seiner or group of seiners for some form of consideration. This may lead to a situation where a seiner is owned by one individual or firm, managed by another, and skippered by yet a third.

With the privately owned and managed and the single-corporation boats, the owner—usually the skipper—is responsible for arranging financing, cannery contracts, berth space while the seiner is in port, repairs and maintenance, provisioning, and the performance of all the other tasks necessary to the operation of the boat. In the case of company-managed and company-owned boats all these arrangements are taken care of by the personnel at the company office, although the skipper of the boat is still responsible for making sure that their various charges are properly carried out.

In the minds of the fishermen there are only two categories of seiner, company boats and non-company boats, although the relationship between the managers and the owners is often unclear. The fishermen generally speak of the boats which are managed by a multi-boat-managing corporation as "company boats" even though they are not actually owned by the company. Often the fact that a company owns a small percentage of a boat which it manages leads to this kind of confusion.

Of the two categories, the non-company boats are consid-

163

ered the best ones to be aboard. It is said that their regulations concerning behavior aboard the boats (wearing shoes, no spitting on the deck, etc.) are less harsh and more subject to the preferences of the crew. The company boats have the reputation of being less willing to provide "extras" such as cash advances and are more impersonal in their dealings with the fishermen in general than the private boats.

A privately owned and managed boat, one which is known to belong to a private owner regardless of whether it is officially registered to a corporation, is never called a "company boat." Boats which are managed by a company which manages more than one or two boats, however, may or may not be referred to as company boats depending on the character of their management, which itself tends to change with turnovers in the company personnel and among the skippers of the boats. Boats which are owned outright or mortgaged to multi-boat corporations or canneries are always known as company boats—although they may not be referred to as such, the label being reserved for only those company boats which are run in an impersonal or strict fashion.

The year I fished with the fleet, the "company" boats tended to be the older, smaller, slower boats while the new boats with the latest equipment and the highliner skippers tended to be privately owned. I'm told that there have been times in the past when this situation was reversed, and with the increasing cost of the new tunaboats it may be reversed again in the future.

One of the major things that all of the seiners have in common, company-owned or not, is the role of the skipper. The skipper has the final say aboard the tunaboats. While they are in port, the skippers of the company-owned boats may have to defer to the owners or managers in small matters, and they are in fact subject to dismissal at any time. Once they have been hired aboard for a trip, however, they are given complete control of the vessel.

There seems to be no room in the make-up of a tuna skipper for taking orders, and most of them are capable of living up to this stance. Many of them are the perfect example of the aggressive high-roller fisherman although their personalities, of course, differ. One can go aboard many boats while they are at the dock and immediately pick the skipper out of the rest of the crew by his fancy, stylish clothes and the general deference which he gets from the rest of the crew. It is not uncommon for the skipper of a boat to have a partial interest in its ownership or in the company which owns or manages it.

The relationship between the owners or managers and the skippers, if the two are not synonymous, is generally one of mutual respect. Many of the managers and owners have been skippers themselves and in most cases share familial or ethnic ties with the present skippers. Each has a need for and at the same time is somewhat at the mercy of the other. The owner-managers, while they can order a boat in to unload and in some cases from one area to another while it is at sea, have little control over most of the actions of the boat once it leaves port often to be gone for upwards of two months. They are dependent on the skipper to run the boat well and bring back the fish which will enable them to meet their financial commitments. The skippers, while they enjoy almost complete control over their seiner, are subject to dismissal on a trip-to-trip basis and to the owner-managers' decisions on such matters as repair or reprovision expenditures. These interdependencies temper the nature of their relationship.

The Lure of Tuna Fishing

There are several characteristics of the tuna seining occupation which balance out some of the negative aspects described in previous chapters and serve as attractions for the industry's labor. First and foremost, the fishermen make a lot of money. It is common for a regular deck crewman to make between twenty and thirty thousand dollars a year, and for skippers to make between fifty and a hundred thousand. These are high annual wages relative to most other occupations, and especially high for an occupation which requires relatively little initial investment on the part of the fishermen.

That is the second attractive feature of the occupation. Provided, of course, that you are willing to spend eight to ten months of the year at sea and bear the risk and uncertainty involved in

165

the occupation (an important provision), there is a relatively small amount of initial investment in terms of skill or time involved in rising to a full-share position in which one makes that kind of money. The skills one must learn are difficult to learn anywhere else except at sea, but once one is out on the boats it is not difficult to rise to an acceptable level of proficiency in a year or so. Although to become very skillful takes years, the ratio of economic remuneration to experience in the regular crew positions rises very quickly and then diminishes slowly over the years.

A feature of the occupation especially appealing to younger men is its inherent adventure. Performing the various portions of the seining process and simply being at sea is very exciting, although like anything else the excitement tends to fade with the passage of time. Being at sea, however, is very pleasant most of the time, especially with the accommodations aboard the modern seiners. Visits to exotic foreign ports, encounters with different peoples and customs, the ability to bring home "sea stories" and imported gifts are aspects of the occupation which are very appealing to many men. I fished with 19-year-olds who had been up and down both coasts of the United States and Central America, all over the Caribbean, and to the West Coast of Africa. It is a nice feeling, even after the excitement fades, to be able to go into a restaurant in Panama or a hotel in Puerto Rico and be welcomed by familiar faces and old acquaintances.

One of the most important characteristics of the occupation is the sense of freedom it can give. This is especially true for the unmarried men, who can miss a trip or switch boats almost at will and not have to worry about where the next paycheck is coming from. The pay is sufficient and the labor pool small enough so that once you break into the occupation and work for a couple of years it is possible to amass enough resources in terms of money, possessions, and contacts to be able to live a very flexible lifestyle. The size of the labor pool and the difficulty of breaking into it, however, are also significant characteristics of the occupation.

166

Getting into the Occupation

The ethnic, familial, and social bases of the industry's networks cannot be emphasized too strongly. Virtually all of the skippers and key men on the boats are either Portuguese or Italian. Recent years have seen a rapid increase in the number of Mexicans and "down-south" men—from Central and South American countries—in the crews, but the industry as a whole, in the ranks of the owners, managers, skippers, and the general crewmen, is dominated by the Portuguese and the Italians. Besides controlling the boats themselves, men from these ethnic groups own the shipyards in San Diego where the seiners are built, the chandleries from whom their supplies are furnished, and many other infrastructural elements of the land-based portions of the industry.

This ethnic and familial commonality extends to the crews themselves. I was once aboard a boat on which ten of the fourteen crewmen were related within second cousin, and the method of hiring within the fleet tends to maintain the closed quality of the system. The normative structure of the hiring system is as follows.

The skipper is the final say on all hiring aboard his seiner. He has the power to hire and fire at any time. His word alone commits "the boat" to pay the crewman his share if the latter goes to sea, "the boat" being a term used to denote the economic unit which the seiner represents and which may also refer to the corporation which owns or manages it. When a fisherman says that the "boat" owes him money, he may actually be refering to the company. Even aboard the company-owned boats the skipper has the right to hire whichever crewmen he chooses, the company only recruiting men at the skipper's request or if he is indifferent in the matter—and even then the skipper has the last right of refusal on any crewmen the company finds.

In searching for crewmen to man their boats, the skippers tend to stay closely within their familial, ethnic, and social circles. One never advertises anonymously for crewmen. If a skipper needs, for example, a speedboat driver, he typically asks

167

around among his fellow skippers, his own key men, and his family and friends to find a likely candidate. At least up until this point in time, there has been close enough to a sufficient number of potential or experienced crewmen within these groups to enable the skippers to fill their crews from them.

The reason that the skippers choose their crews almost exclusively from their friends and relations is unclear. In San Diego, at least, it does not seem to be out of a lack of alternatives. There are plenty of men in San Diego searching for jobs aboard the boats, men from outside of the fleet's networks. One of the skippers suggested to me that selecting crewmen from the fishing community is the only way to ensure that the families of the crewmen will have someone to support them while the man of the house is absent. The pervasive nature of the ties in the community provides a security for the families which is lacking for the families of outsiders (Zolessi, 1974). Some researchers favor a more socio-psychological interpretation of the relative-friend hiring phenomenon. Anderson and Wadel state that "skippers and mates often mobilize their kinsmen . . . to fill shipboard positions . . . indeed, where crewmembers have no kinsmen in their crew, a substitute familial role identification appears to take place in stable crew settings. This seems to be a reasonable correlate of the tendency to view the ship as 'home.' The desire to conduct operations in a cooperative egalitarian atmosphere with minimal competitive clashes over decisions and authority, is also at work along the eastern Canadian coast. The inclination to recruit kinsmen may serve this aim" (Anderson and Wadel, 1972).

It seems to me, however, that the "homeness" of the boat and the feelings of solidarity it fosters are produced more by the condition of being at sea under dangerous conditions for long periods of time than they are by having one's kinsmen aboard. In the San Diego fleet there is in fact a noticeable "in-law syndrome" which occurs aboard the boats. There is a strong pressure on crewmen from their relatives and friends to help other relatives and friends get jobs aboard the boats. Relatives, however, especially in-laws, are people like anyone else and are just as likely to get along or not get along with each other than are other people, especially in the unusual conditions under which the men in the tuna industry have to work. What seems to happen is that very close relatives, such as brothers or fathers and sons, get along well aboard the boats. In the more distant relationships, however, there is a tendency for the man responsible for the hiring to treat the man whose hiring he facilitated in a manner different from the way in which he treats other men. They will often pile more work on the man or avoid giving him support or interacting with him as they do with other men. It is considered more desirable to get a relative a job on a boat other than one's own.

The fact that the fishing community in San Diego is composed largely of first- and second-generation residents, many of whom speak only their native languages, also has an effect on the hiring practices. Since the community must exist in a complex environment whose cultural values are in many cases very different from their own, it seems to be true that selecting a man who is culturally and especially linguistically like oneself may contribute to more comfortable surroundings, not in a nuclear family sense, but rather in a socio-cultural "family" sense.

As in all situations where potential employers are searching for employees and potential employees are searching for jobs, however, there are often gaps in the information system, so that the searching parties on either end do not find each other immediately. Because of this there are always men along the waterfront looking for jobs on the boats and skippers with a vacancy or two unfilled. In situations such as this, there is a specific pattern which one must use to board a boat and find the skipper, and most neophytes not connected to the industry in any way simply never get past the initial stages of the process.

In the first place, the skippers are not aboard the boats very much when they are in port. If they are aboard at all, it is from around nine in the morning until noon. Besides this the crew act as protectors for the skipper. If one doesn't ask the right questions immediately, the response from the crewman with whom he first comes into contact will usually be anything from a mumbled "I don't know" to, if there are more than one of the

169

crewmen present, an elaborate joking conversation with the job-hunter bearing the brunt of the remarks. The boats are tied up at various places throughout the harbor because there is simply no one place large enough to hold them, and many of the docks at which they berth are in the heart of the tourist area of San Diego. Work on the nets and light maintenance is done at dockside in these locations, and the net-mending especially is a great tourist attraction. At least a couple of the crewmen are aboard the boat for most of the day, and they enjoy the status which comes with their obvious connection with the big fancy seiners. They many times behave in the same in-group manner which may be seen in similarly visible groups in other occupations.

There is a good reason for them to "protect" the skipper by answering inquiries about jobs or the skipper's whereabouts with vague replies and jokes: there is almost always a steady stream of people coming by looking for jobs. In a way the crewmen are protecting themselves by diverting the competition, but the skippers do not like to be constantly bothered by job-seekers either, and they do nothing to discourage the crew's fun.

A certain amount of aggressiveness always helps, and if you go right aboard without hesitation when the skipper happens to be there and immediately ask "Is the skipper onboard?" you will usually be told where he is. Most first-time job hunters are too timid to go aboard the boats and they attempt a conversation with the crew from the dock. This rarely produces any information.

Once you make contact with the skippers, they are usually honest and straightforward about their situation. If they need a speedboat driver or an extra deckhand and no one has been sent to them from their regular network, they will listen to what you have to say. It helps to tell them that you will work "split-share" or at a tonnage figure below the regular rate, and it also helps if you have had some experience with the ocean. Many men during the course of my search for a job advised me to be honest about any lack of knowledge or experience I might have. They said that the skippers get a lot of people coming around who misrepresent their abilities, a situation which becomes very obvious as soon as the boat puts out to sea. Skippers regularly take on an

PLATE 10. *Tourists and Seinermen.* Much of the net-mending is done on the embarcadero in the heart of the tourist area of San Diego. Here two tourists step around the equipment on a stroll after lunch. The presence of tourists who often disturb the fishermen's labors makes it more difficult for the first-time job hunter to gather information.

inexperienced man or two as "split-share" men. Less is expected of these men, but the skippers definitely want to know what they are getting.

There are fishermen's unions in San Diego, but they have traditionally had little to do with hiring. Because the industry is so family- and ethnically oriented and because the skipper, who is most often in the same community systems as the crewmen, has by custom been the hiring agent, the concept of unionism has had a hard time getting a foothold in the industry. Although the occupation involves a considerable amount of danger, the crewmen are generally aware of the risks involved and take them voluntarily. They are also generally well paid, which makes the need for worker's organizations less pressing. The unions do perform important functions in the areas of fringe benefits and in the settlement of those disputes which do occur, but their role in recruitment is minimal.

The problem for the neophyte is coming across a skipper who is in need of a man. The boats move around the harbor quite a bit during their stay. They unload the fish, load provisions, take on fuel, and mend their nets all at different docks. There are anywhere from twenty to over a hundred boats in the harbor at a time in widely separated locations, and only a small percentage of them need men. No one but the skipper can even talk to you about a job, and catching him on the boat at the same time that he is in need of a split-share man is difficult.

It is especially hard for the new man because the fleet is small enough and the crews interrelated enough so that the news of a vacancy travels fast around the harbor, but only to those already connected with the fleet in some way. Often I have had people, gringos, tell me that they could not get a job in the fleet because their "hair was the wrong color," meaning that they weren't Portuguese or Italian. I think that this wrongly attributes a negative aspect to the skipper's hiring considerations. There are simply plenty of applicants for each job who get the news of vacancies through the "grapevine," a grapevine which goes mostly along the lines of ethnicity, kinship, and friendship. I myself was lucky enough to make friends with some of the men

172

in the fleet when I was looking for a boat, and they did not hesitate to direct me to open positions of which they were aware. After I had been to sea with the fleet, I also had Portuguese men and others come to me for information about positions.

Once you have made a trip aboard the seiners the entire situation changes. There is a large amount of boat-switching which goes on in the fleet, and people with whom one has sailed tend to spread out to many other boats in the space of a year or so, thus geometrically expanding one's network in the industry. Besides this, there is an incredible barrier-crossing which occurs once you have once worked in the fleet.

One of the first jobs I had in the fleet was unloading a seiner which had just come in from outside the line with a load of big yellowfin. I hired on as an unloader, one of the men who gets down in the holds and lifts the fish into the unloading buckets which are lowered through deck hatches with the brailing booms and into the wells. This is known as one of the worst jobs in the industry. You are in the approximately 30-degree wells standing on slippery fish trying to lift other slippery 100-pound fish chest high into the big unloading buckets for twelve hours a day.

We had to steam from San Diego about 100 miles up the coast to San Pedro where the cannery was located to unload, and we left late at night so as to arrive and begin unloading early the next morning. I noticed on that trip, and subsequently in many other instances where there was a new man aboard who had not been "in the fleet" before, that the crew paid almost no attention to me or whoever the neophyte was. The crews often do not communicate with each other very much in general at the beginning of a trip or at certain times when they are at sea, but their treatment of a new man goes beyond that particular phenomenon. Men on many boats will often not even bother to learn the name of a new younger man until he has shown himself "worthy" by performing some initiating work tasks.

On the way back to San Diego after we had unloaded, an old Portuguese fellow who had his bunk next to mine and had neither looked at, spoken to, nor in any other way acknowledged my presence for three days came up in the completely empty

173

fo'c'sle and sat down right next to me. As he began putting on his shoes he said, not looking at me but with a slight smile on his face, "Down in the wells, huh?" I said, not looking at him either, "Yeah." He gave a small chuckle, still not looking at me, and said, "Pretty nice work, huh?" I chuckled back and replied with a grunt. He then poked me in the ribs with his elbow, looked at me and smiled, and proceeded to talk about his fishing experiences for almost forty-five minutes.

I have seen this kind of behavior toward a new man many times. Fishermen will often ask a man about whose status they are not sure, "Are you in the fleet?" An answer in the affirmative and a mention of the last boat you were on and the skipper's name will usually be enough to start a conversation in the familiar "do you know?" style.

These behaviors, of course, are in no way unusual. We all talk most and more easily to those with whom we have common experience. The fishermen, however, have a smaller set of people with whom they share common experience than most of us. Rarely is this kind of commonality of experience and membership in a social network as institutionalized as a form of job-qualification as it is in the tuna fleet.

Getting a Share

A regular full-time fisherman in the tuna fleet is paid what is called a full share. Exactly how this amount is calculated is set out in a later chapter. Skippers get two to three shares, and the "key men" in the crew—the Mate, Chief Engineer, the Assistant Engineer, and certain others often get more than a full share— from a share and one-quarter to two shares.

Men who are connected to the system in some way—relatives or friends of fishermen, owners, or managers—usually start at a quarter share their first trip. If they work out satisfactorily they make the second trip at half share, then three-quarters of a share, and by the fourth or fifth trip they are finally full-share men.

Men not connected to the system in any way, however, often have to offer to go out for their first trip on the basis of what

174

is called "tonnage," usually agreeing to make the trip for one or two dollars per ton of fish caught. Certain considerations are made for men who go out under arrangements of this sort. They often are not asked to help unload the boat, and they do not have to pay a share of the trip expenses or their food, as the share men do. If the man stays in the industry or aboard the same boat, however, he is given a quarter share on his second trip and may even skip a step on his way to the full share.

Every man has to bargain with the skipper for his share. Some men in serious need of money will go out for less than a share even after they have worked in the fleet for years at a full share, although skippers who agree to this are generally thought of as taking unfair advantage of the man. A man who belongs to a union, which not all of the fishermen do, could take a situation of this sort to his union but the outcome would be doubtful. He most often would bring the case to the union after he had performed the work and had himself agreed to work for the lower figure. Certain skippers and companies have periodically been accused of taking unfair advantage of crewmen in this and other ways, and no one will dispute the fact that the skippers and owners hold a vise-grip on the fishermen's employment situation. Those who have in the past been disturbed by this situation have had a difficult time doing anything about it because of the multiplicity of relationships of different kinds which run through all levels of the industry, and the fact that even a three-quarter share is a pretty decent figure.

Raises in a man's share do not come automatically, even if he remains aboard the same boat. Many times it is understood that the skipper is happy with your work and is going to raise your share, but many skippers leave your share the same unless you ask to have it raised. The question of a man's share always arises when he switches boats. The new skipper will ask what the man got on his last boat, and if it was under a full share he will generally raise it a notch unless the man is in some way marginal as an extra hand or there is something undesirable about the man's past performance. Word of crew problems involving certain men circulate around the fleet constantly, and although a man who has performed badly in some respect is rarely black-balled entirely from the fleet, he may find it difficult to get a job at a larger or even at his former share.

In general, however, a man will rise to a full share in four or five trips—a little over year in the normal trip sequence—and remain there for the rest of his career unless he assumes a key man position.

Switching Boats

There is quite a high rate of crew movement among the sein-ers. This movement takes several forms.[1] There is individual movement. Crewmen will move off of a boat as individuals, either to hire on with another boat or to "take a trip off"—stay in port for a period of time. There is group movement. This occurs when two or more of the crew move off of a boat. In some cases, they will move as a group onto another boat. In other cases, once they are off the boat they will go their separate ways. Sometimes a skipper will go to another boat and the new skipper will ask some of the old crew to stay on with him. There is the movement of entire crews from one boat to another. This gener-ally occurs when the skipper is offered another boat to run, ac-cepts the offer, and takes his whole crew with him.

This crew movement creates some confusion for the unions. There are two principal unions in San Diego, and besides the men themselves every boat belongs to one of them. The unions re-ceive some percentage of the boat's gross receipts each year, typically one percent, making the boat's membership a valuable commodity. Theoretically, all the men on a boat belong to the union to which the boat belongs. The union to which the boat belongs is supposedly chosen by a crew vote, although even if a vote is held, which it many times is not, the result is usually in

1. This kind of movement occurs not only among the fishermen but also among the personnel of the companies which manage and own the boats, the canneries, the unions, and the various associations and organizations con-nected with the industry. Even the presidents and vice-presidents of companies often change firms or jump to another portion of the industry.

accord with the owner or skipper's wishes. The union officials themselves are ex-fishermen or from fishing families, and much of a boat's selection of a union is done on the same kinds of socio-political bases as the hiring of crews. In any case, whenever a man goes to a boat in a different union he is supposed to change unions himself. In fact he may or may not do so, and the result can be a tangle of affiliations and conflicting union-books.

There are several kinds of motives and circumstances behind these movements. Often these will occur in combination with one another to instigate a move on the part of one or more crewmen.

Personal conflict causes many men to search for a new boat. This can be conflict between a crewman and one of the key men under whom he must work, conflict between two crewmen on the same "level," or conflict between a skipper and the boat's owners or managers.

There are monetary and status incentives for switching boats. A man may be offered a post on a larger boat with the capability to bring home more fish each trip and thus make more money, or he may be offered a position on another boat at a higher share rate. A man may have a chance to assume a position as winch man, Assistant Engineer, or skiff driver and accept it because it gives him more status among the crew or a better work situation than his present position, even though it will not pay him more. It is common for men to move from larger to smaller or from newer to older boats for this latter reason. There is also a kind of impersonal status which one may get from being on a new, successful boat or one which is owned or run by a high-status member of the fishing community (Back 1951).

There are often pressures on the men from loyalties to families, friends, or a particular skipper to change boats. A relative who needs a position filled on his boat, or a friend who knows of a vacancy where the two could work together on the same boat, will often entice a man to switch boats. Crewmen will many times follow a skipper or Chief Engineer to another boat out of personal loyalty.

Different men also have different situational preferences. A man who moves off of a boat to take a trip off and spend some time at home, a man who moves from a boat which unloads in Puerto Rico to one that unloads in San Diego, or a man who moves to a smaller boat because they tend to be out for shorter periods of time are all exhibiting their personal preference for various situations within the fleet.

Finally, crewmen sometimes change boats simply because they are tired of the same old faces. I was told the story of one very successful boat many of whose crew had joined the boat when it was new and they were friends just out of high school. Even though the boat was consistently successful and the crew had no obvious problems, the friends eventually went separately to other boats saying that they had just been on the boat together too long, an expression, perhaps, of a fear that the continued close proximity would eventually spoil their friendships.[2]

Moving off of one boat and onto another is not generally viewed as unusual or undesirable by the crewmen or even by the skippers, who move fairly frequently themselves. It is viewed as detrimental by the more "systems-minded" managers and owners, who cite the intuitive justification that new crewmen must be trained into the crew which inevitably produces a reduced level of functioning compared with a boat whose crew has been together for some time. It is unclear how much truth there is in this. The nature of the seining process is such that it is primarily the skill and expertise of the key men which affects the success of the boat, and a new man in the ranks of the regular crew does not materially affect the workings of the process even in terms of the time it takes to "train" him, especially in light of the character of the "training" process, which will be examined in chapter 8.

2. Naomi Quinn (1971) suggests that crew movement is more often due to unsatisfactory experience with one's last crew than it is to expectations about one's new one. This implicitly assumes an adequate supply of positions into which to move while maintaining one's financial integrity. This condition is met by the tuna fleet in San Diego, and I agree with Quinn's suggestion.

In any case, the movement of crewmen between boats is considered normal, and even the "baiting" of crewmen from one boat to another is generally not looked down upon. Rather it is viewed as evidence of the competitive nature of the industry, which indeed it is. Successful skippers and men known for their abilities and skills often receive offers of jobs from other boats, and few are criticized for accepting them.

The relative frequency of movement is hard to estimate, but it is high. The 31 crewmen with whom I fished on my two boats are a fairly representative sample of the fleet, and the figures for them are as follows. Of the 31 men with whom I sailed, all but two are still fishing with the fleet. Of the other 29 only 5 ended the 1974 season on the same boat with which they began it. Only 4 ended the season with the same skipper with whom they began it, but these were not on the same boat on which they had begun the season. Of the 31 men, 9 made only single trips on the boats they were on during the year, 10 made only 2 consecutive trips aboard the same boat, and 12 made three consecutive trips. No one *made more* than three consecutive trips on the same boat, even though all but 7 fished every trip they could and many of the boats they were on made four or more trips.

It is interesting to note that after about a year and a half and after having been on two or three boats many of the men seem to end up back with the same skippers or on the same boats once again. This is reasonable given that the skippers do the hiring, that one learns of jobs through former shipmates at least some of whom may still be on the boat which one left some time ago, and that a man who is known to a skipper or recommended to him by one of his own crewmen will almost always be hired over a man about whom the skipper knows less.

The frequency of movement is less, as one might assume it would be, on the more successful seiners. Newer boats share this same low frequency of movement to a certain extent, but many men find that a boat's age does not correlate with its fishing success. Often the weight of economics, a dislike of the longer trips which the bigger, newer boats tend to make, or a desire to join a crew around whom one feels more comfortable will outweigh the status and physical comforts of a newer boat.

Conclusion

The recruiting and hiring practices of the tuna industry, then, are characterized by an emphasis on personal contact and alliances between friends, relatives, and acquaintances within the fishermen's ethnic community. Given a certain level of skill, the determining factors in employment often seem to be other than those which maximize economic variables or benefits to the fishing process itself. The usual question is, ''Who do I *know* who could do this job?'' There is some doubt, expressed by many gringos, that skippers get the best men for their crews by hiring only within their ''system.''

This system is possible partly because the success of the seining process varies greatly with the skill of the key men but less with the skill of the rest of the crew. The skippers can afford to hire less experienced or skillful men as general crew. It is also possible partly because the nature of the occupation requires men with qualities different from most other occupations. A man who is not quite as quick or as strong as another but who is persistent, patient, and able to endure the long months at sea and take pride in performing well as a fisherman may very well be a better crewman than a college-educated ex-football player. Men with the former attributes seem in fact to be better fishermen than men with attributes which characterize successful and admired men in the community ashore, although the two are certainly not mutually exclusive. It seems to be true that the success of the fleet in the past has depended at least as much on the men who have had the ability to go to sea and catch fish as it has on the men who have stayed ashore and integrated the fishery into the business and financial community.

It is also hard to ignore the fact that the fleet has, at least in the last ten years, been very successful. The recruiting and hiring methods have in fact produced a system of ''production'' which is both economically and socially successful. It is hard to knock success.

180

Finally, the fishing life requires much more than the qualities of the fisherman himself. It requires that his wife and family also be able to adjust to the fishing lifestyle. The close familial and ethnic ties within the fishermen's communities ashore enhance the ability of wives and families to adjust much more readily to these requirements than those into which most of us are socialized.

7 Economics, Risk, Uncertainty, and Suerte

OF THE IMPRESSIONS that the non-fishing public in San Diego have of the tuna seinermen, two are prominent. The first is that they sail on big, expensive boats and make a lot of money. The second is that the way they make a living involves risk, uncertainty, and luck ("suerte"). It may seem strange that matters of economics are together in this chapter with descriptions of rituals and religious beliefs. But arranging them otherwise would have misrepresented the way the fishermen perceive the monetary value of their efforts, and also the way the peculiar nature of their occupational lifestyle affects their economic behavior.

The Distribution of Benefits

The seinermen are what is sometimes termed "co-adventurers."[1] They are workers whose livelihood depends directly and with a very low level of predictable elasticity on the fruits of some common endeavor.[2]

There are two remuneration principles which exist side-by-side in the fleet. Most of the boats which work out of San Diego operate on what is called the share system. The principle of

1. This term and its application to fishermen come from the United Kingdom. Fishermen in sections of the various fishing industries there were classified as "co-adventurers" rather than laborers and thus were exempt from many of that country's labor laws.

2. By "low level of predictable elasticity" I mean that the men's pay is connected to their success rather than to the effort they expend. The crew may spend two months at sea and make fifty sets yet not come back with enough fish to make expenses. It is impossible to predict except on the basis of past experiences, which are difficult to tie to future events, whether or not the boat will catch fish. In this sense there is no production function for this and many other fisheries except that of the stochastic type (See Lewis 1975).

182

this system is that the excess of receipts after each trip's expenses are met goes to those with an investment in the catch according to some predetermined distribution. This investment may be in the form of labor, capital, or expertise of one kind or another. Monetary reward systems of this type are common in most traditional and many modern fisheries (Tunstall 1962; Firth 1966; Quinn 1971).

Who pays what part of which expenses, to whom the residual is given, and the exact proportions of its distribution differ from boat to boat. Generally the rule is that all expenses incurred during or as a result of a particular trip are collected under the category of "trip expense" and subtracted from the gross receipts for that trip. The remainder is termed Net Divisible Income. The NDI is then split between the "boat's" share, which goes to the owners, and the crew's share. The crew's share is divided by the total number of man-shares yielding the value of One Gross (crewman's) Share. The total galley bill is then divided equally among the crewmen and subtracted from the gross share figure, leaving each man's gross earnings.

There are various subtleties in the distribution of the crew share. Crewmen who go out "split-share" receive one-quarter or one-half of One Gross Share. Because of this, the divisor used to obtain the value of One Gross Share is often different from the one used to divide the Total Galley into each man's share of the food, liquor, and so on. If, for example, there were fifteen men on the boat but that number included two half-share men and one quarter-share man, the divisor used to determine the value of One Gross Share would be thirteen and one-quarter, while the divisor for the Total Galley would be fifteen. Thus the presence of split-share men is to the full-share men's monetary benefit. The split-share men are paying a full share of the food while not reaping a full share of the profits.

While the owners or managers of the seiners are the only ones with direct access to the figures necessary to calculate these amounts, the latter are supplied to the unions which in turn make up wage and cost breakdown sheets for each of their members (see accompanying example). The "boat" produces

Model Share Breakdown*

Receipts	Yellowfin	Skipjack	Trip Expenses	
Gross Weight				
(lbs.)	1,000,000	1,000,000	Fuel and Oil	$60,000
Rejects	16,000	24,000		
Net Weight	984,000	976,000	Clearance and Entry	
Price per Ton	$575	$545	Salt	
Total Receipts	$282,900	$265,960	Welfare Fund	
			Pension Fund	
			Fish Inspection	
Net Divisible Income		$458,860	Association Fund	
			Cargo Insurance	
Crew Share (40%)		$183,544	P+I Insurance	
Less: Alien Shares		$2,940	Unloading	
Gross Share		$180,604	Foreign Port,	
			Canal Charges	
Number of Shares (15)			Messages	
Value of One Gross Share		$12,040	Hull and Outboards	
			Medical Supplies	
Total Galley		$10,500	Radar Repairs	
Galley Share		$700	Powerblock Repairs	
			(Combined)	$30,000
Net Share		$11,340	*Total Trip*	
			Expenses	$90,000

*For a typical 1,000 ton net capacity seiner, with a crew of 16 including one "down-south" crewman, and a 60 day trip.

these sheets for non-union members. The largest single entry under Trip Expense is Fuel and Oil, usually accounting for over half of the total for that category. Various insurances and association fees are prorated based on a yearly figure. There are no "heavy" repair or purchase charges, and no place for mortgages or major refittings under "trip expense." All of these items are taken care of by the owner out of the "boat's" share of the NDI.

Certain of the crew, usually the key men—the skipper, Master, Chief, deckboss, and sometimes the Assistant or mast man—receive more than one share. Skippers commonly get two to three shares. Chiefs get one and one-half and sometimes two. Paper Masters, Mates, deckbosses, and Assistants get a share and one-quarter to a share and one-half. Any excess over a full share is usually paid to these men by the owners out of the boat's share. The shares are figured ''as-if'' each man were receiving only one share, and the figure is then multiplied by the number of shares for which a man signed onboard and the excess is paid by the ''boat.''

Most of these figures vary over time and from boat to boat and are the subject of continual bargaining. The unions are generally responsible for pursuing and contractually cementing any changes in remunerative arrangements. The percentage used to calculate the boat's share from the NDI, for example, may vary with changes in the boat's age or mortgage situation. The owners and the unions argue constantly over exactly which expenses should be included under Trip Expense. There was a recent dispute resulting from the desire of the owners to include one complete speedboat per seiner per year under Trip Expense. The unions were against this, contending that it is not always the case that depreciation of the speedboats occurs at that great a rate, and that replacement as opposed to maintenance of the speedboats was not a proper item for Trip Expense.

Other figures, like the number of shares a crewman received, are dependent on bargaining between the man himself and the skipper. The unions would like to be able to determine or at least control bargaining procedure, as they would like to have a hand in the hiring process. The customary control and independence of the skippers and owners, and the tradition if not the practice of *compadrazgo* among the crews, however, mitigate against any ''interference'' in the relationship between a skipper and his crewmen. When a man asks for a job he is usually asked how much the last skipper he worked for gave him. If the man is young and learning or especially skilled he may ask for an increase in his share. If, on the other hand, a man is hired as an extra or has some sort of blemish on his record, he may be offered less than he received with former employers.

Many of the disputes which the union is called in to settle

involve a boat which a man claims promised to pay him a larger share than was in fact paid him at the end of the trip, or a boat which claims that a man misrepresented his abilities or lied about his share on his last boat and thus is not entitled to his originally agreed-upon share.

Bargaining also occurs between skippers and boat owners. If an owner would like to lure another boat's skipper away they may offer him two and one-quarter or two and one-half instead of the two shares he is getting from his present company. He may in some cases be offered some portion of the ownership of the boat itself or stock in the company which owns or manages the boat. What is important to note is that unless a man rises to a key-man position, he will receive no more than one full share no matter how long he has been in the fleet, on a particular boat, or how skillful he is; and that he may expect to rise to full share status within two years of his initial employment in the fleet. Most of the San Diego crewmen are in this full-share category.

With the growth of the number of crewmen from Mexico and other Central and South American countries aboard the boats, and the movement of many of the vessels to foreign flags, an alternate method of payment known as the tonnage system has increased in usage. Under this system the crewmen are paid a prearranged number of dollars for each ton of fish brought aboard while they are signed on the boat. No deductions are made for the "trip expense" or for food, although charges for liquor, payments made to hired watchmen in foreign ports, wages for galley boys, and other 'luxury' expenses are divided evenly among the crew, as food costs are under the share system.

Most key men and most San Diego crewmen on boats operating under this system receive a tonnage rate roughly equivalent to what they would make under a share system. These rates range from $10 to $15 per ton for a full-share man, depending on the particular company or boat. The tonnage rates for skippers and other full-share-plus men run proportionately higher.

The tonnage rates for non-San Diego crewmen, on the other hand, run much lower. Top money for these "alien shares" (see share breakdown) is $6, and in rare instances $8 or $9 per ton. It is relatively rare for non-San Diego crewmen to be paid on the share system. The skippers and owners who determine these rates rationalize these differences in several ways.

First, they maintain that non-San Diego crewmen are not as skilled, knowledgeable, or experienced as San Diego men. In many cases this is true. Second, they say that even this smaller wage is more than the men could hope to make in their countries of origin. They also point out that living and other costs are frequently much lower in these crewmen's home countries. These things are also generally true. Third, it is a fact that these men are in most cases willing, if not content, to work for these smaller wages. Whereas the men from San Diego have union organizations available to back them up, the down-south crewmen are completely on their own. During the year I fished with the fleet, some attempts were being made to organize crewmen in Panama and Puerto Rico. These efforts may eventually meet with even more success than the San Diego unions have, because of the relative economic and status deprivation of the down-south crewmen, but at present these men realize that there are a good number of equally skilled men from their own countries waiting on the dock every time a seiner puts into port and that they are at the complete mercy of the skipper for their employ-ment. Finally, there is pressure put on each skipper from other skippers to maintain these wage levels. Skippers have told me that often they have wanted to pay an exceptionally good man more but have been kept from doing so by other skippers, who argue that it would set a bad precedent and hurt them in their efforts to keep operating costs down.

There are advantages and disadvantages for both the owner-managers and the fishermen in each of these payment systems. Under the share system, both the ''cost'' of labor and the boat's share of revenues for any given amount of catch goes down as trip expenses increase. On a boat whose net divisible income is split 60 percent for the boat and 40 percent for the crew, the boat's share of the revenue decreases 60 cents for each additional dollar of trip expense while the labor cost decreases 40 cents on each dollar. Under the tonnage system, for any given catch figure labor cost remains constant while the boat's share decreases one dollar for each dollar of additional expense.

Under neither system is productivity tied directly to any cost except labor. A 100-ton set does not "cost" the owners any more than a 25-ton set except for labor, and that cost is exactly proportional to the difference in productivity between the sets.

The tonnage system is usually more economical for the owners, although for reasons other than the internal workings of the system of payment itself. Boats using the tonnage system are generally boats working out of southern ports with down-south crewmen who are hired for less than the tonnage equivalent of a full share. It is in fact true that a boat with all full-share men on tonnage which made an unusually long trip could leave the owners considerably less well-off than the same boat on a share system. Since the men fishing under a tonnage system are not sharing as much of the financial risk of a long trip as they do under the share system, that burden is more upon the owners. The only "cost" of a long trip to the fishermen under the tonnage system is the opportunity cost of his time at sea—which is at least financially negligible.

The fishermen themselves view these systems in different ways. Some say the share system is good because it gives them the chance to share in the extra benefits of a short trip, although most concede that it also means they share the burdens of a long one. Some like the tonnage system because it relieves this latter risk, and also because "a man always knows where he stands" with tonnage. With the share system one has only an approximate idea of how much money he will make until some time after he returns to port, often not finding out for certain until after he has left on his next trip. The expenses must be calculated, the cannery reports received, and all the operations needed to calculate the share amounts completed before the fisherman finds out exactly how much his share on his last trip was worth.

The Relative Values of
Position and Proficiency

There are four general principles under which a man can either hold a full share or advance from one share to another.

The first is the possession or acquisition of a scarce skill or attribute, either within the fleet as a whole or onboard a particular boat. The paper Masters and Mates are paid more than a full share, for example, by virtue of the Coast Guard requirement that there be certified personnel onboard and the fact that there is a scarcity of certified crewmen within the ranks of the fishing community. They receive a share and one-quarter simply because they hold papers. Being certificated is a scarce attribute, although a certificate does not necessarily indicate skill at sea.

The second source of "value" to the boat is proficiency. A man will be paid accordingly if he is recognized as being good at some skill necessary to the efficient functioning of the boat. Chief Engineers, for example, while not exactly in overabundance, are paid in excess of a full share primarily because theirs is a very necessary, difficult, and responsible position. Likewise, a deckboss earning a share and one-half or an Assistant earning a share and one-quarter, these being the upper limits of a negotiable pay interval, are men being paid for their exceptional skill.

A third principle is that of social connection. This is exemplified by the owner-skipper who called his crew together one morning to announce that he thought his teenage son, who had made only one trip, was now worth a full share and would henceforth be paid accordingly.

The fourth source of value is longevity, or seniority. Many crewmen are paid a full share or more primarily because they have been in the system a long time. Most often in this category are older men who are past their physical prime and are not in key-man positions. Their skills are not scarce, their jobs are those for which there exists a considerable pool of proficient substitutes, and they may or may not be in the sub-circles of the community which would allow them to take advantage of

189

social connections. They are employed at a full share because they are the old men, the fathers and uncles of the other crewmen, and are men who even though they may be past their prime ought not be passed over.

These are the categories of "value" given by the fishermen for advancement to or presence in a particular pay category. Once again, however, it must be noted that all full-time fishermen generally rise to a full-share position relatively quickly and remain at that level for the rest of their careers.

Within the ranks of the full-share men there is continual banter over the value and obligations attached to each person's duties, and sometimes-playful sometimes-serious arguments over who is and who is not "earning" his share. An argument broke out on one boat I was aboard between a first-generation Portuguese speedboat driver and a gringo skiff driver. Many of the first-generation Portuguese, Italians, and down-south crewmen, especially those who do not speak English, are adept at the actual fishing process but lack understanding of the mechanical devices used in it. Besides being less concerned over the state of the machinery than are many locally trained crewmen, they are hesitant to put themselves in what they see as a subservient position in order to learn more about it. In the cases of language differences, they are often simply unable to pick up more than a minimal amount of knowledge.

The skiff driver, a gringo, who in the case cited here was also one of the two men on the boat who knew the most about outboard engines and thus served as the onboard mechanic, was irate at what he saw as the lack of concern on the part of a particular speedboat driver for his equipment. Something had broken on the fellow's speedboat and the skiff driver had been called to fix it. The latter claimed that if the speedboat driver had done what he was supposed to do in the way of routine maintenance the breakage never would have occurred. He went on to say that if the speedboat driver wanted to earn a full share (which he did), he should learn to take care of his own speedboat, including fixing it if it broke down.

The speedboat driver retorted that he wasn't hired as a mechanic, and that he earned his share out in the water and not onboard messing with the equipment. He said that the skiff driver had been hired because he knew about outboards and could fix them and should earn his share by doing so. The skiff man retorted back that he earned his share driving the skiff, and that his mechanical skills were dispensed as "extra" effort to keep the equipment in shape.

This argument occurred at a time when the whole crew was tired and upset from a long day with no fish. The skiff driver was in fact known for his handiness around the boat with all types of equipment and his readiness to perform whatever job was necessary. It was also generally recognized that the speedboat driver in question did more than any of the others to maintain his speedboat. Both men were signed aboard for full shares. While this argument was precipitated by particular circumstances, it was an example of two crewmen presenting their perceptions of the value of their respective attributes, abilities, and responsibilities so that they fit into a consistent pattern which preserved their own integrity and self-image while at the same time fitting into the shared understandings about the distribution of necessary tasks on the boat and their value. This is an on-going process which may be observed in almost any occupational group.

Another example of perceptions of value and obligation is that of the cooks. Among the San Diego-based crews it is traditional for the cook to play a part in the set, as well as having a duty to prepare food. His usual job is stacking the rings along the port side of the net deck to insure that they run off smoothly in the next set. He is usually expected to help with sorting during the brailing, but in many cases is excused by the skipper to go and prepare the food.

As is the case with most positions, it is possible for the cook to do more or less work in the set just as it is possible for him to be more or less competent or efficient—or spectacular—in the preparation of the food. His duties on deck are always referred to as what the cook does "besides" his "regular" duties, even though they are uniformly expected of him. For their efforts most cooks, even those just starting out, receive a full share. Everyone realizes how important the cook's job is, but at the same time the position suffers from the stigma of not being one of the "active" jobs. The cook's job lacks the vigorous action of many of the other positions and he is paid a full share by virtue of a set of abilities different from most of the crew.

A cook on one of my boats once refused to go on deck and help clean the net in a particularly troublesome "bullet set." He was angry about a collection of things that are not relevant here. The deckboss came down to the galley and told him to go on deck and help. He refused, saying that he was the cook, not a deckhand. The deckboss replied that the cook earns his share by doing more than just cooking. The cook still refused, and the deckboss left.

In fact, this cook had helped in situations such as the one described in many other sets on the same trip. The deckboss knew, however, that the sort of help the cook had given in the past was "above and beyond" what it is commonly understood that a cook should do for his share. The cook in this case was using the common understanding about a cook's duties as a source of privilege, while still preserving the impression that he was "earning" his share even though he was refusing to work on a particular project.

These arrangements and expectations concerning duties and privileges differ from boat to boat and vary with particular mixes of crewmen and their attendant skills, seniority, attributes, and social connections. Cooks on down-south boats, for example, are rarely expected to do any but very minor deck work. They are not expected to get on the netpile or handle the fish.

Besides varying the amount of effort put into a particular position, there are other ways a man may adjust his perceived effort to his perceived reward. Some down-south crewmen can in a sense "make up" for their lower pay by attempting to take advantage of their status or skill to assert rights of privilege, authority, or personal influence. The number-one speedboat driver on my second boat, a strong and competent young Costa Rican, obviously enjoyed the status his position and competence gave him in such endeavors as maintenance on the speedboats and a preferred position on the netpile relative to the San Diego crewmen, who were making up to twice his tonnage rate. Even though they can sometimes assert their power, however, most still feel a sense of relative economic deprivation, although it rarely surfaces. Many comments were made to me by down-south'ers about so-and-so from San Diego's lack of skill in various portions of the process or lack of perseverence or strength, followed by "and *he* gets $13 a ton!" The fact that they can exert claims of influence, authority, or privilege in some instances does not often make up completely for the fact that they are paid and to some extent treated differently from the San Diego crewmen.

Value with Respect to the Rest of the World

Aside from the intra-boat division of remunerations, the fleet as a whole is generally well-paid. Below are the average income figures for men in the fleet from 1966 to 1971.

Year	Average Total Wages
1966	$12,991
1967	12,977
1968	15,545
1969	18,941
1970	26,445
1971	26,124

Being averages, the figures are affected by the high earnings of the skippers. Roughly adjusted, however, the figures for 1971 would yield about $60,000 per year for skippers and $18,000 per year for the average full-share crewman, still relatively high. These latter men, those outside of key man positions, are generally men who could not earn anywhere near these amounts in an occupation on shore. They are very aware

193

of this fact and have evolved a fairly clear concept of why they are paid as they are.

They will, of course, point out that there are many skills involved in being a good crewman. General seamanship, wire and rope splicing, net making, fiberglass repair, general painting and carpentry, the ability to "see" fish and distinguish between varieties, numbers, and sizes—all these are skills involved in the fishing process. They are, however, with few exceptions things that almost anyone could learn to a fair level of proficiency in the space of a year or two and which ashore would be worth considerably less than they are at sea in terms of remuneration for their performance.

Secondly, they will tell you that they are highly paid because theirs is a physically dangerous occupation. This is certainly correct. Various notions of "risk," physical and otherwise, enter into the considerations of all those who are involved in the industry, from the owners to the speedboat drivers. I will say more about this presently.

By far the most prevalent justification given by the crewmen for their high pay is this: they are paid to be at sea for a long time. They say they are well paid because they are away from their families for frequent, prolonged periods of time. They say they are paid for "missing" life ashore. Some compare it to being in jail, and others say the money is compensation for being "forced" to be alone at sea, away from family, friends, and the alternatives of life ashore.

A significant factor in this seafaring situation is boredom. As several crewmen said to me after a two-week period without so much as a good sighting: "We're paid to be bored!" On my first trip we fished 27 of the 57 days we were out. On many of those days we would set once for three hours and search for the other ten. One deckboss recently told me that his boat had only 6 days of fishing out of 50 on their last trip. To combat this boredom on their off-hours the crewmen read books, play cards, fish or shoot at sharks while drifting at night, carve, clean and polish turtle shells or swordfish bills, and anything else they can find to do. The movies and video tape systems help somewhat, but

even these are limited and are reserved for after-dinner entertainment. There is no way to combat the tedium of long days
spent searching for signs of tuna. The fishermen see their isolation and boredom as a part of their job for which they receive
"rewards" in the form of high pay.

Finally, the fishermen will tell you they are paid to make
investments, bear risks, and deal with uncertainty. Most fishermen readily tell you about the year they only made $5,000, or
the trip for which they received no compensation and had to
pay expenses out of their own pockets. They leave the benefits
of the good trips and good years to be communicated implicitly
through their actions and by their possessions. They tell you
about the unforeseen equipment failures, the sudden accidents
and injuries, and the weeks of frustration without fish. Of much
deeper personal concern to them than the monotone of boredom
is the myriad of unexpected and uncontrollable situations, situations whose occurrence must somehow be dealt with by their
own beliefs and behaviors.

Risk and Uncertainty

Exactly how risky, how uncertain is tuna fishing? The
answer lies in defining the difference between these two concepts
and indicating what *kinds* of risk and uncertainty are involved,
and to whom they are most salient.

Risk is inductive—a matter of probabilities. To calculate
risk is to use past experience and knowledge of present conditions to predict future outcomes. Risk may involve physical
danger, a financial gamble, or even the hunch that if you leave
your wife for too many more fishing trips she may not wait home
for you anymore. Risk is salient for both the owners and managers
ashore and the fishermen at sea, but it is conceptualized differently by each.

Uncertainty, on the other hand, is a measure of "surety."
It is a matter of faith, of confidence. It stems from a lack of
knowledge, or control. While there are indices which try to
quantify uncertainty (for example, stress, fit, degrees of freedom, confidence levels), most of us don't calculate uncertainty;

195

we *feel* it. While risk is a phenomenon conceptualized over time, uncertainty tends to be one which is temporally-bounded. The risk involved in an action or venture remains relatively constant over time and is assignable from known variables; one's confidence in his own abilities or the outcome or consequences of a particular event often depends on temporally-limited psychological variables and may be changed radically in a short time-space by seemingly unrelated inputs. Uncertainty is the effect of wondering if the cable will break and take *your* arm off in the next set, even though you know that things like that happen relatively infrequently. Uncertainty is the effect of wondering if *your* boat won't find fish, even though you know that most boats seem to manage. Uncertainty is the effect of wondering if *your* wife will be home when you return when you have friends whose wives weren't. Calls from home, news of mishaps from other boats at sea, conversations with other crewmen, incidents which refresh memories of past situations; all these kinds of inputs affect both the psychological state and the physical functioning of the fishermen.

Because of the differing natures of these concepts, risk is generally more salient to the managerial personnel ashore while uncertainty is the nemesis of the fisherman at sea.

Whose Point of View?

The managers and owners of the tuna industry tend to view the fishing process within a time frame of years. Within the "seasonal" frame, a sub-frame which corresponds to a calendar year because of the Christmas holidays and the IATTC regulatory period, they have maintenance and cannery schedules, accounting obligations, and personnel decisions. In the longer time frame they have mortgage obligations, growth or expansion decisions, and the various infrastructural concerns inherent in the political and economic needs of the fishery.

Because they have these long-term obligations they are forced to assign probabilities, anticipate earnings, and project cash flows. The companies tend to figure mortgage-carrying abilities and other obligations on the basis of a conservative

196

estimate of their boat's fishing success. They will, for example, expect their boat to bring in 2000 tons in a season while assuming only that amount of obligations which could be covered by 1500 tons. The excess (if one appears) which one might consider "profit," they consider their compensation for having "risked" their capital. It is important to note that these owners do not "plan" on receiving this excess. It is an avoidance-of-loss rather than a profit-making strategy. When asked why they should have gotten X amount of profit in one season, however, the payment-for-risk answer is the one they give. Fishermen are traditionally known for plowing this kind of "profit" back into equipment and machinery, and the men in the tuna fleet are no exception. Organizers of research and lobbying groups which work in the fishermen's interest have commented to me that it is hard to get the fishermen to support them financially because they spend all their spare money on their boats.

Some of the time, of course, the boat fails to reach the tonnage needed to meet even the conservatively estimated obligations. But because they have accurate records of past years' catches and fairly accurate means for gauging present conditions, the managing personnel are generally able to subsume these failures under their calculations of risk. Financial uncertainty to them is a matter of timing more than of end result, and its effects can be distributed over time.

The Fishermen's Point of View

The fishermen's time frames are more complex than those of the owner-managers. In terms of the fishing process itself, their time frame is trip-oriented. Their concern is going out, obtaining a certain amount of fish in a reasonable amount of time, and returning to port.

At the beginning of a trip everyone is hopeful for a full load and a 21-day trip. As the trip wears on, however, various "target" figures tend to emerge. The first such target to appear is that of expenses. The crews on the share boats have a fair notion of how much fish they need to cover their trip expenses. They mumble and grumble until they have that amount. If the

197

fish are coming aboard slowly and the trip is dragging out, the next figure which tends to emerge is the tonnage with which most of the crew would be satisfied in lieu of a full load. These are very specific figures and are verbalized among the crew, especially as the trip wears on toward 40 days. As this last figure is approached or met, concern once again turns to the trip length. While the 21-day trip was a common hope at the outset, as the trip goes on that figure increases. Wishful thinking seems in most cases to settle on about a 60-day trip.

During the trip there is very little mapping of effort-to-catch or even of time-to-catch. If a boat makes a few good sets early in the trip, there are comments of "X tons isn't bad for Y weeks." Some crewmen, when the fishing is bad, will assert that "you've got to catch X amount of fish each Y amount of time to make it in the long run." Both of these comments, however, tend to be reactions to discrete situational pressures which give rise to either temporary hopes or temporary fears. The more general attitude toward effort and reward balances income and time at sea in terms of good or bad days or trips. Sixty days seems to be the temporal break-even point. An acceptable amount of fish in that time is seen as a satisfactory trip.

These attitudes are all affected by the nature of the work. The work day is in a sense "regular" aboard the boats. You get up with the sun, perform whatever routine maintenance is necessary, look for fish, and make a set if you are "lucky" enough to find any. At sunset, unless you are in a set, you quit. The sequence goes on much the same day-after-day.

The crew realizes that there is really very little they can do to control either the state of their environment or the timing of the fishing process itself. They usually have the skills to deal with situations which arise in either, but they have no control over their occurrence. If the glasses aren't left unattended, if the holes in the net are sown after each set, if new splices are made and cables replaced periodically, there is little else the crew can do but run through each day in the normal manner and hope to spot fish.

The distinct mode of work which has developed aboard the

198

seiners works well within these circumstances. Nothing outside the set itself is hurried. The work is spaced out a little each day, mostly in the morning, and generally adheres to the random-work order which will be described in a later chapter. No one really wants to "scratch" for fish. All want to find an "area" and load up, but all realize that finding an area involves a large amount of luck. The entire process of running the search and getting through the day is gauged to the very real possibility of the trip lasting 60 days. One of the risks the crew takes is that at the end of this time they will have their target figure of fish aboard, and from past experience they know reasonably well what this risk is. The uncertainty with which they have to deal, however, is the almost complete lack of knowledge or control over when, where, or under what conditions and with what consequences the fish will come onboard.

On one of my trips, for example, in twelve instances there were intervals of from two days to a week between sets. Twelve times—one third of all our sets—we either "skunked" or didn't get enough fish to brail. Once we went fifteen days without bringing any fish aboard at all. After fifteen days, skippers tend to get "hungry," and their acceptable setting standards in terms of weather, school size, and other variables tend to diminish considerably. This affects the conditions under which the crew must work. After two months, however, we returned to San Diego with almost a full load. That was generally considered to be a "good trip."

Aside from their behaviors and attitudes on the trips themselves, the fishermen view longer-term financial matters in different ways. Some are "locked into" making as many trips as possible in a season by obligations at home such as a big home mortgage, large family, or free-spending wife. Many of the first-generation Portuguese and Italians work as much as they can and save every penny in order to return to the old country and live in style (with, say many of them, a small fishing boat of their own to keep them busy and make a few escudos or lire). Still others are bitten by the bitch of capitalism and just can't seem to stay off of the boats—they get itchy at home thinking of all the money they could be making at sea. All, however, seem to view their financial success in terms of yearly averages. They are concerned about the dollar amount per trip, and the total of those amounts at the end of each season. They do not say, "I spent X amount of hours at work, or time at sea, for Y amount of dollars." They instead say, "I made X dollars fishing last year" or "I shared out at X dollars last trip."

Many of the fishermen, especially the older ones with no children at home and their homes and other financial obligations discharged, have target figures for each season. They will work the "quota" at the beginning of the year and make their target of a couple of thousand dollars and then take a trip off. If they get tired of staying at home they can try to get a boat for the last trip of the season from about August or September to November and be home again for the Christmas holidays. A skilled crewman, especially one with mechanical ability, can get a job fairly easily. Some skippers will even hold a job for a man, hiring another in his place for a single trip. Even an average crewman, however, with a little hustling can get a "trip out."

Although their average incomes are usually adequate, the men do not know exactly how much they will make, how their income payments will be spaced throughout the year, the lengths of their trips to sea, the amount of work they will have to put in to reap their wages, or the timing of their activities at sea. They deal with the financial effects of this uncertainty partially by concerning themselves only with end products, in per-trip or per-year figures. Their incomes have up until this time been sufficient to enable them to do this.

An exception to certain of these attitudes is the skipper. Although he is subject to the same "fisherman's luck" as the rest of the crew, he has a much greater pool of information with which to deal with the uncertainty and calculate the risk. He has total control over the vessel and her crew, if not over the environment directly. If despite all the crew's efforts the boat makes a bad trip, the skipper is likely to feel it most. He bears the ultimate responsibility for the safety of the boat and its fishing success, and a bad trip may very well cost him and his crew their jobs. To be essentially solely responsible for a multi-million dollar craft and a half-million dollar catch three or four times a year is a considerable burden, especially when "fish got tails"— you never know where you will find the tuna, when they will disappear, or where they will turn up thereafter.

Although the skippers have access to a large pool of information, they share very little of it with the rest of the crew. The opinion of most skippers is that it is better for the crew to have to deal with the uncertainty of a lack of information than with the feelings of relative deprivation which might stem from the knowledge that others are catching fish when they themselves aren't, or that others are on their way home while their own boat is still just half full. Most skippers will, however, selectively distribute some information about the successes or failures of other boats to bolster or in other ways effect the morale or interaction of the crew.

The skippers also tend to have a different attitude toward the matching of efforts to rewards. Having access to more information and a greater personal control over the process, they are of the opinion that the more effort they personally put out the more fish they will find. While most crewmen can only spend the requisite amount of time on the glasses with a sharp eye to gather "information" for fish-finding, the skipper has the radios, code groups, weather machines, sonars, written records of past sets and successes, and many other sources of information at his disposal. He could, if he utilized them all to their maximum, work twenty-four hours a day. No skipper can do this, but they have exponentially more opportunity to contribute to the search than does the rest of the crew. An unsuccessful trip is much more likely to weigh heavily on the skipper than on the crew, even though the skipper may have done everything humanly possible to collect information annd have made all the "right" decisions from it. Uncertainty thus bears somewhat differently on the skippers; though they seem to have much more control over the fishing process, they often end up in the same boat as their crew, cast there by chance, the companion of uncertainty.

Physical Risk

While the skippers are perhaps more subject to the emotional stresses of financial risk and uncertainty, they are for the most part removed from concerns of physical risk. They are, like the Chiefs, Masters, and sometimes the Mates and Assistants, in positions which keep them out of physical proximity of the most potentially harmful equipment and processes. The people who "risk" the most in this sense are the speedboat drivers, the deckboss, the brailers, and secondarily anyone on the fish deck or netpile from the time the neg begins to roll through the block to the time the skiff is hauled aboard.

The speedboat drivers are launched into an often rough sea from a seiner traveling at fifteen knots. They have to drive their boats at full speed through waves, swells, and winds up to twenty-five or thirty knots. They often have to jump a wake and grab and fasten a dangling line while the seiner is going full speed in order to come back aboard. Back and kidney injuries are a significant risk for speedboat drivers, and broken lifting slings, freak waves, and heavily rolling seiners are an uncertain feature of their job. For the brailers, standing on a pitching skiff and trying to fill a two-ton brailer with a heavy 30-foot handle and to maneuver it on board the seiner is both risky and uncertain. The deckboss is by definition the person who handles the most dangerous jobs on the boat. He puts on the cable clamps, which involves climbing over the side of the boat and standing on tons and tons of rings held by a single cable; he is the first one in the water to clear roll-ups or a net caught in the rings; and he is expected to be the man in the forefront of any dangerous or emergency situation.

The people in these positions, and to a lesser extent the entire crew, are constantly subjected to situations which, though obviously dangerous, have a quality of "fate" in their events. The cable that breaks and shears off a metal stand six inches from your head; the ammonia condenser that explodes ten minutes after the crew ceased work right next to it to go to lunch; the 200-pound shark that falls, unseen, from the powerblock sixty feet above and lands right next to you instead of right *on* you—

events like these, combined with the awareness of accidents involving other crewmen on other boats who weren't so lucky, tend to put an edge on even the most skillful and confident fisherman. That edge is anxiety caused by uncertainty.

Risk and Uncertainty Again

For workers in the tuna fleet, then, there are several types of risk. In addition to financial risk and physical risk, there is social risk—the personal risk that each man who has close family or personal connections takes by participating in an occupation that requires as much time away from home port as distant-water fishing does. Each sector of the industry is subjected differentially to each of these types of risk, and each has different resources with which to assign weights and probabilities in order to try and determine the future flow of events.

Combined with each of these kinds of risk is uncertainty—the effects of a perceived lack of control or knowledge of the timing, sequence, and effects of future circumstances. Uncertainty is also felt and dealt with differently by each sector of the industry.

The personnel ashore bear a much greater financial burden than those at sea. Their names are on the papers promising payment for the huge capital outlays which the industry requires. On the whole, however, they are able to calculate, budget, and control cash flows well enough to circumvent the problems in timing that uncertainty contributes to the process. The men and women in this portion of the industry do not in general have to deal with the physical and social aspects of risk and uncertainty. Their risks are confined to the financial realm.

For the fishermen, on the other hand, the physical and social aspects of risk and uncertainty have effects at least as great if not greater for them than those arising from the financial aspects of their occupation. These men have far less actual control over the factors which go into the processes involving physical and social risk and uncertainty. Their means of dealing with these risks and uncertainties are, rather than accounting procedures, matters of belief systems—understandings about how one goes about controlling the uncontrollable.

Suerte

There are two general belief systems which the seinermen use to attempt to control these uncontrollable factors, to deal with their "suerte"—their luck, chance, or fate. The first system if that of conventional religion.

The seinermen—whether they may be Portuguese, Italian, Mexican or "down-south'ers"—are mostly Catholic. This is the dominant religion in their countries of origin and the one that they and their families practice in San Diego. For the Portuguese and Italian communities, the formal religious practices strongly reflect the communities' involvement in the tuna fleet. I will draw my examples from the Portuguese community, because it is the one in which I lived during the period of my research and the one whose involvement in the church I could observe most closely.

There is a Catholic church located in "tunaville," the area on Point Loma where many of the Portuguese fishermen live. Sermons are given in Portuguese, a fairly recent development made possible by the arrival a few years ago of a Portuguese-speaking priest. The church is within easy walking distance of the entire community, and those attending are almost exclusively Portuguese. The activities at the church are geared to the fact that the majority occupation in the community is tuna fishing. Invocations and prayers for the safety of the men and a good catch are given each Christmas before the fleet sails on the first trip of the season, and prayers and offerings are made throughout the year while the men are at sea.

The church also caters to the Portuguese and to tuna fishing in other institutionalized activities. The biggest socio-religious event of the year in the community, for example, is the Festivo Espirito Santo, the Festival of the Holy Ghost—or in "standard" Catholic terminology, Pentecost. The Festival culminates in a parade which runs through the community from S.E.S. (Sociedade Espirito Santo) Hall (commonly called "Portuguese Hall") to the church, and after a service, back again. After the parade there is a feast of sopas, a traditional Portuguese dish honoring Saint Isabel, the patron saint of the parade. In a large

PLATE 11. *The Festivo Espirito Santo parade.*
This festival and parade are one of the major socio-religious events of the year in the Portuguese community. The local police halt traffic for the paraders.

PLATE 12. *The festival queen and her retinue.*
The queen's "guards" are members of one of several fraternal organizations in the community. The patch on their shoulders reads "Past Faithful Navigator." The party immediately behind the queen is the festival president, traditionally a tunaboat skipper.

PLATES 13 *and* 14. *The fishermen's children.* Children of all ages from fishing families participate in the parade, some with a little help from their mothers.

PLATE 15. *Community and Occupation*.

This model seiner is a symbol of the importance of the tuna fleet in the life of the community. The church in the background is St. Agnes', the Roman Catholic Church in "tunaville," where the festival procession attends a rosary before returning to Portuguese Hall for more festivities and the traditional meal of *sopas*.

yard adjoining the Hall there is dancing to music played on ethnic-Portuguese instruments, and there are booths selling beer, homemade pastries, and food of various kinds and offering games of skill and chance.

Although the festival is primarily a religious event, the tuna fleet is inextricably involved in the entire proceeding. There are several festival queens chosen for the parade, all traditionally fishermen's daughters. Most of the small children who also have a large part in the parade are fishermen's children. The Grand Marshal of the parade is traditionally a tuna skipper, as are several of the other dignitaries in the parade. Much of this mixture of religious and occupational qualities may be due to the fact that ethnicity and occupation are simply coincidental in the community, but major portions of the event are institutionalized to represent the interdependency of fishing and religion in the lives of community members.

This interdependency, that of religion and occupation, is much more salient to fishermen—and also to farmers—than it is to people in most other occupations. Since fishermen are forced to deal with natural forces in a much more direct way than men in most other occupations, and since there seems to be such a large component of luck or chance in the search for fish, fishermen's belief systems tend to be much more directly connected to matters of income than those of workers in other occupations. The place where these belief systems and their connection to the fishing process present themselves most clearly is aboard the boats at sea.

Belief Systems at Sea

Many things from Catholicism—the "official" belief system—are evident aboard the boats themselves. All of the boats have a chapel on board. Until recently these chapels were separate cabins which housed an altar, carved statues representing various saints and religious figures, silver chalices for Holy Water, candles, and various containers for offerings. In the early years of the fleet, when the boats were still constructed of wood and were less luxuriously appointed than the boats today are, the chapels reflected this greater simplicity. As the accommodations and interiors of the boats got fancier, however, so did the chapels; they acquired lush carpeting, expensive paneling, studied lighting, expensive ornaments. Most of the boats built in the last two years have reduced the chapel from a separate cabin to a large alcove in the main passageway through the crew's cabins, but the general character of the objects and appointments remains.

Every seiner also has two other reminders of "official" religion. One is a relief wall representation of the Last Supper which hangs in the galley. The other is a picture of a young man at the helm of a ship in a storm-tossed sea. Behind him is a ghostly figure of Christ with his hand on the young man's shoulder pointing "the way." This picture always hangs in the pilothouse or chartroom. While it varies in size from boat to boat, both it and the Last Supper relief, which varies in color and texture, are regular fixtures aboard the seiners. Many of the men wear crucifixes, and others keep small pictures or statues of religious figures in their bunks or cabins. Some carry Bibles and other religious reading material aboard, although these seem to be in a small minority.

The use which these chapels and other objects get is another question. I never—and I watched for it—saw anyone in the chapel on my first boat, which was a separate cabin, or in front of the alcove which served as a chapel on my second boat. The one exception was the Mexican cook on the second boat. He tried to keep a candle on the altar burning throughout the trip; it went out quite frequently, and because he was the only one who relighted it, it remained extinguished a fair amount of the time.[3]

3. Most of these men are not regular churchgoers when they are at home. As in the case among families in many religious groups, the women and children make up the bulk of the attendance at services throughout the week. On special occasions and in particular circumstances such as weddings, confirmations, and funerals, most of the men attend, but even the men who wear crucifixes and have religious figures in their bunks when they are at sea often do not attend church regularly when they are at home.

The use of these objects seems to be governed loosely by need. Although I never saw it happen, I have heard several accounts of crewmen lighting candles—sometimes on the bridge— in particularly bad storms or heavy weather. The men talk often of saying more "hail Mary's" in times of slow fishing, equipment failures, or bad weather. One man's wife had given him a small cross with the instructions to wear it inside his hatband for good luck. It remained on the desk in his cabin for most of the trip, but it appeared in his hatband near the end of the trip when the fishing was slow. The concept of invoking some form of external power or control when specific situations warrant it becomes more subtle and complicated when other beliefs and behaviors are brought to light.

Superstition

There are generally three categories of belief and behavior which deal with the circumstances of the boat itself or of the fishing process. The first is that of preventive measures. Many of the "official" religious customs—the blessings in the church before the boats leave port, the objects brought aboard the boats, the usual prayers said every night, the special ones said on Sunday—have this preventive character.

The second category of belief and behavior concerns itself with explaining undesirable events or situations. In this category there are several beliefs to which the term "superstitution" seems particularly applicable.

Some think, for example, that beards mean long trips. I know of boats where no one was allowed to have or grow a beard for this reason, and others where crewmen shaved off beards in the latter portion of long trips because of this belief. On a boat I was aboard the belief was brought up one evening at dinner and everyone laughed and joked about it. The next morning three of the crew were clean-shaven. Hatch covers from the wells which have fallen upside down have been blamed for bad luck in filling the particular well which they cover, or for bad luck in general. I was told that in the old days if a hatch cover fell upside down, the crew would simply batten it down and not even attempt to fill the well it covered. Whistling on the bridge is believed to bring the wind according to some, and bad weather in general according to others. I found this out the hard way. I couldn't understand the looks I was getting on my first boat when I would walk up and down the bridge on my watch, whistling merrily. I finally asked one of the crewmen to whom I was fairly close why I was getting the evil eye, and he told me about this belief.

One interesting belief, usually expressed in a joking manner—as are many of these superstitions—is that bad luck, and particularly equipment failure, occurs when one of the crewmen has not paid a prostitute, or has in some other way been unfair to her. Crewmen have a good deal of fun debating who the offender might have been.

There are many other beliefs like this—for example, that the color black on a boat (in the way of clothing or some other object) forbodes death or injury, or that crossed utensils in the galley will bring bad luck—but all have the same character: they are brought up after the fact as explanations for undesirable situations or events. Whereas one could say, "If I go to Mass ashore and say prayers and my Hail Mary's, I will be safe and have a good catch," one would generally not start that sentence with, "If I don't grow a beard or drop any hatches upside-down, and am nice to prostitutes." While the first type of statement tends to be preventive, the beliefs in the second type are used to explain events or situations which have already occurred.

The third category of beliefs concerns actions which one can take to actively change or affect a particular situation or problem. Some of the superstitions discussed above have elements of this attribute—it is believed by some, for example, that certain fishermen are good luck for particular wells on a boat, and that man will be allowed to place the first fish in that well. One of the clearest and most interesting examples of this kind of belief was demonstrated to me one night off the coast of South America.

The Ritual

On one of my trips there was a point where the fishing was intolerably bad. We were off the coast of Colombia, the weather was hot, and we hadn't brought any fish aboard for almost two weeks. We didn't have what anyone considered an acceptable load on board at the time, and we had been at sea for a little over a month. People were getting edgy and a little testy, especially amid radio reports that other boats were catching fish.

Most of the crew was on the bridge one day looking for fish when one of the young first-generation Portuguese crewmen came on the bridge with two eggs in each hand. He said nothing but went quickly across the bridge touching the eggs to each crewman's back as he went. Then he disappeared below. There were a few glances exchanged, but no one said anything.

Later that night I was reading in my bunk, waiting to go on watch. Most of the rest of the crew was asleep. I smelled something burning, but it could have been a cigarette so I ignored it and went on reading. The fo'c'sle where my bunk was located ran athwartships, from one side of the boat to the other. There was a passageway to the crew's lounge leading forward, and a passageway to the rest of the cabins leading aft, both in the middle of the fo'c'sle. There were doors on either end of the fo'c'sle which were open because of the heat.

Soon after I smelled the burning, the cook, a young Costa Rican, stepped into the fo'c'sle from the door on the port side where my bunk was located. He was carrying a two-pound coffee can from a string and there was smoke coming from the top of the can. (I later learned that the burning material was rosemary). He was followed by the young Portuguese carrying the same eggs he had on the bridge earlier that day, and a gringo crewman of about the same age who was carrying the silver chalice from the chapel filled with water. All three passed by my bunk, which was about at their eye level, without a glance, their faces blank. Behind them at the door was an old Portuguese fellow, the father of another one of the crew, who smiled at me and then disappeared.

212

The three men went through the fo'c'sle methodically putting first the smoke, then the eggs, then a sprinkle of the water in every space they could find; bunks, closets, drawers, lockers, everywhere. When they had made their way to the other side of the boat they disappeared forward into the crew's lounge. A few minutes later they emerged and went straight into the passageway which led aft. They had neither spoken nor been spoken to, although I saw at least one other crewman whom they had awakened with the smoke stick his head out from behind the drawn curtain on his bunk.

After a minute or so I got up and walked down the passageway where they had gone and down to the galley. The three men were nowhere to be seen. I went up onto the working deck and met another young first-generation Portuguese, the son of the man who had smiled in through the door just after the three had entered the fo'c'sle. He smiled nervously and we exchanged a few remarks, and then he asked me a little sheepishly if I'd seen "What those guys are doing," and nodded down below. I said I'd seen them go through the fo'c'sle, but that I didn't know where they were at the moment. He said they'd gone down to the well deck, engine room, and shaft alley. After a short silence, he asked me if I believed in "that stuff." I shrugged and he said (with some bravado) that *he* didn't but that the young Portuguese who was one of the three did. He said that the other fellow and the Costa Rican both believed in it.

As he said this, the three emerged from the stairwell and proceeded across the working deck in the same manner I had seen them go through the fo'c'sle, putting first the smoke, then the eggs, then the water everywhere. Once again they passed close by us but said nothing. After finishing with the working deck they climbed up on the netpile and repeated the procedure. They ended up on the port side of the net by the chains, and after climbing into the skiff for a short period they disappeared behind the netpile at the very stern of the boat. By this time they had gone over the entire boat, from crow's nest to bilge and from the bow to the stern.

213

After a few minutes the three appeared from behind the netpile. The Portuguese was carrying the chalice, and the others were empty-handed. They seemed relaxed, and the Portuguese member of the trio went forward to the chapel with the other young Portuguese to whom I'd been talking while the other two stopped where I was standing. The gringo looked at the cook, made a fist, and said "fish tomorrow." The other nodded, and said to me half-apologetically, "Some people believe in this." The gringo said he believed it, that he hadn't until he'd seen it work on another boat he'd been on. The cook said he'd seen the eggs "work" before in Costa Rica. His grandmother, he said, "practices things like that." He said she makes you clean by passing the eggs over your body and then breaking them. He mentioned that he'd seen a vision of a dead relative once when he'd been watching his grandmother doing that.

He started to say, "Just like now . . ." but the gringo put his hand up as if to stop him, then lowered it again and walked away toward the chapel. The cook continued, saying that just then when they had thrown the rosemary and the eggs off the stern they had seen a flash of light. After a moment's silence, he said, "You have to have faith in these things." He excused himself and went around the port side of the deckhouse to his cabin.

The gringo came back a minute later and sat down beside me. We looked at the sky and the ocean for a minute, and then he said, "Hmmm, I'm still sort of in a trance." We sat there for a minute more and then I got up, he followed, and we both went forward to our bunks.

When I got back to my bunk I recalled that the day before I had heard the gringo who had been involved in the ritual saying something about "getting rid of the bruxos," which means witch, or spirit. He and I and the young Portuguese who had watched the portion of the ritual with me on the working deck had been talking, and the Portuguese had then said that somebody in San Diego had told him about something being wrong aboard our boat, and he mentioned the word "praga." I knew that "praga" meant curse, and had heard the term used several times when someone was complaining about something not going right, in phrases such as "Praga on this thing." Once, when I had been on the netpile stacking net with several of the first-generation Portuguese, a portion of the net still in the water had tangled around one of the cables and we had a small roll-up. The skipper had gotten pretty mad about the whole thing, but it wasn't anybody's fault. In frustration he had yelled, "Praga on this boat," a comment which made a few of the men around me visibly uneasy. I didn't think much of it at the time, attributing their uneasiness to the skipper's general anger.

I said nothing about the rosemary ritual at the time, nor did I do any questioning. We saw no fish the next day, nor the next. It was five days before we made a set. During that time the tenseness aboard the boat was still there, and I didn't want to "rock the boat." Neither, apparently, did anyone else. There was almost no reference to the ritual among the crew. On the fifth day after the ritual we made a good set, 40 tons, and thereafter did very well and were on our way home less than 20 days later.

About the time we started home I was talking to the cook on my watch and asked him about the ritual. He explained to me that the burning rosemary (the traditional material used in Portugal for this purpose) had been to "smoke out" the bruxos, or evil spirits. The eggs were a symbol of goodness and cleanliness, and cleansed the boat. The water, which came last, was a blessing, a sort of "preservative." Up until a very few years ago, the crewmen would follow these actions by greasing or oiling the rails of the boat so that the bruxos could not climb back aboard. He said that he knew of these things partially from his grandmother, a curer in Costa Rica, and partially from things he'd heard and seen on other boats in the fleet. He said that the young Portuguese who had carried the eggs knew about the process from his experiences in Portugal, and that the ritual itself was a mixture of what the three men involved thought should be done. The mixing of belief systems inherent in the

215

use of these particular objects and procedures is an example of those systems adapting to particular needs and circumstances: the chalice, a tool of the Catholic faith; the smoke and the material used to create it, a traditional Portuguese ritual practice; the eggs, a symbol from both Portuguese and Central American spiritualism.

I asked him what "brought" bruxos aboard, and he said that it varied. Sometimes someone "wishes" a praga on the boat, and that brings the bruxos. Sometimes they come with an object placed aboard the boat. (A variation of the ritual, according to other men in the fleet, is to ritually "find" some object in which the praga is assumed to reside and cast it over the side. The boat is then "purified" in the manner of the ritual described above.) And sometimes, he said, the bruxos just appear.

This ritual never seems to contain any suggestion that the boat or its crew had done anything to bring on the praga. There is a very vague notion that some personal affront, or competitive behavior between boats (as described in previous chapters) can lead people with some kind of power to place a praga on a boat. Never, however, is the person or situation named or any reference made to an offending act or person. While many of the superstitions (such as the growing of beards or the upside-down hatch covers) whose purpose is to explain a particular situation refer to a particular offender, the praga and its accompanying bruxos and cleansing rituals are directed at a completely impersonal object the purpose of whose "visit" is unclear—except, perhaps, in the minds of individual crewmen.

The cook then asked me if I remembered on which day of the week they had performed the ritual. I said I thought it had been a Sunday. He smiled and asked if I knew that every big catch we had made since then had been on a Sunday. Before I could answer we were interrupted by several other crewmen coming up the stairwell.

That night I looked at a record I'd been keeping of the catch distributions for each day of the week. The results were as follows:

Day	Total catch (tons)	Increments per individual day
Sundays	290	105, 85, 100
Mondays	20	15, 5
Tuesdays	5	5
Wednesdays	12	11, 1
Thursdays	0	0
Fridays	25	20, 5
Saturdays	80	40, 40

Belief Systems and Uncertainty

It was obvious at the time the ritual was performed that the men involved were hoping to catch fish immediately thereafter. Not only did they express this in those words the night of the ritual, but they were obviously disconcerted the few times small references to the ritual were made by other crewmen in the days following its performance.

In the absence of the desired result, the cook did what people often do, not only on fishing boats or in matters of rituals such as the one described here, but in any situation of dissonance between belief and circumstances: he looked for some evidence which confirmed the desired consequences of his actions. In this case he certainly found what one might consider strong confirming evidence.

In this sense, rituals like this one and many others "work." One can always find some evidence or sign which indicates that the desired result in fact was brought forth. It is also true that the so-called "laws" of probability are on the side of the believer. Few boats come in with empty holds. Few go for more than a couple of weeks without catching any fish. In most cases by the time the beliefs and rituals are invoked it is probable that at least some of their desired effects would have occurred soon anyway. To look at these beliefs and actions only in terms of their achieving their stated goals, however, would be to miss a large component of their value to the people who are involved with them.

217

As the cook said the night of the ritual, "You have to have faith in these things." He meant, I think, not only that if you don't have faith the rituals won't work, but also that one needs these things to believe *in*. The extremely small amount of overt attention paid to the ritual by the crew, especially in light of the fact that it didn't seem to "work" immediately, was due to two things. First, there was a desire to avoid confrontation with the performers of the ritual, part of a general avoidance pattern which will be discussed in a later chapter. Second, and more important, *everyone* on the boat *wanted* the ritual to work.

When you are out in 100-mile per hour winds and 30-foot seas, you want those candles you light to "work." When you are in a position of responsibility at the end of a long, long trip and still don't have a full load, a situation which could cost you your position, you want that cross you put in your hat to "work"; when you hear the small strands of a cable pinging next to your head on the same day that you hear over the radio that a cable broke on a boat near yours, dropping the main boom on four men, breaking one's back, one's leg, and injuring two others; in all of these and many other situations, you want your belief systems, or anybody else's for that matter, to "work."

It is a matter of money, certainly; you want to make a good catch in a short time because that means a good share and more money in a year. They are in a sense situational matters; many of the rituals and beliefs are invoked only in times of need. These belief systems are also, however, a means of convincing oneself that, in the midst of a great deal of risk, and more particularly, uncertainty, that there is someone or something in control of both your life and your livelihood.

8   Learning, Sanctioning and Confrontation

ONCE A MAN is hired aboard a seiner he must fit the requirements of the fishing process, his social circumstances, and his
personal needs into a workable cognitive and operational orientation. This chapter is about the styles of socialization within
which most crewmen accomplish this task.

Areas of Knowledge

There are three general areas of "knowledge" in which
each crew member must attain a certain level of proficiency.
The particular mix of competence and style in each of these areas
varies from man to man and from position to position.

The first area is knowledge of physical processes. The
skipper must know how to direct the skiff to keep the big boat
off the net. The navigator must know how to take a sight and convert it into a position. The engineer must know how to make the
mechanical repairs necessary to fix the machinery. Everything in
this area is material which can be "taught" in the sense of reading it in a book or having it explained by another man.

The second area is that of cognitive orientation. This is
knowledge in the sense of a mode of incorporating information
about problems, situations, and processes and acting on that
information. Each of us employs different degrees, for example,
of rote and analytical reasoning in determining our behavior
(Cole, 1971). While all decision-making is in a sense analytical,
some of us enumerate alternatives, attach weights, find causes,
and explore alternatives differently from others. Some act on a
stock response based on a recall of previous like situations,
and if the task cannot be categorized with some previous situation, they do nothing. There are, of course, many modes of

information-perception and decision-making strategy, but the point here is that like facts themselves, these modes of incorporating information and acting upon it are learned. The product of this learning process is one's cognitive orientation. It is unclear the extent to which "knowledge" in this sense can be "taught."

The third area is that of experiential knowledge, that portion which is gained from having performed some process in the past. This area is different from mechanical knowledge in that each of us brings a different background into any given situation which makes us perceive it differently from others. Each man can say, "My experience with that is . . ." and complete the sentence differently from many others. He does not mean he was taught differently, but that the performance of some activity has given him a particular insight and has shaped his thoughts. He may not understand or be aware of the mechanics of a process, but he knows the framework within which the process seems to work most smoothly. It is separate from one's cognitive orientation in that no matter how many ways we imagine things could happen, there is always a way we don't envision. This experiential component is salient for both the rote and the analytical decision-maker, and by definition it cannot be "taught."

These three areas are components of the learning process. Their importance varies with the specific subject area (experiences may be very important, for example, in "learning" social behaviors) and with the operation aboard the boat to which the learning is applied (learning of physical processes is very important for the Chief Engineer).

The relative "value" of each of these areas for the fishing process is difficult to judge. The physical one is essential. Without it the system will not work. The experiential one is important in correcting mistakes and solving problems, but it is not always necessary for the system to function. A cognitive orientation is always present in one form or another, and although its many possible configurations may vary widely in their effects (such as promoting or hindering innovation), any one of a number of modes will provide adequate means for the system to continue.

I make this division because these three kinds of skill, or knowledge, exist in different degrees and are of different importance in the operation of the physical and social processes aboard the tunaboats. The degree to which each is present and in what form is crucial to the system of resource exploitation and the system of social interaction in the fleet. This will become clear with a knowledge of the patterns of learning, sanctioning, and confrontation aboard the seiners.

Methods of Teaching and Learning

By far the most prevalent attribute of the learning process aboard these boats is that it is markedly nonverbal. Very few things are explained to a new crew member in their entirety. A minimum amount of instruction for a certain aspect of a process is usually given, and from then on the man is more or less on his own.

While the *instruction* prior to the action is negligible, however, the *direction* given during the performance of the process itself is extremely loud, impatient, and often abusive. The skipper and the deckboss are the prime sources of this sort of angry-toned, sometimes personally degrading direction. While others in the crew depending on their particular combination of skills and attributes may exhibit this verbal assertiveness, it is generally only the skipper and the deckboss who are able to use it to actually modify behavior.

Even though this verbal assertiveness may not command compliance, a new man soon "learns" that to communicate during the set one should do it at high volume. At the same time he learns that the volume and abusive character of the exchange does not necessarily imply real scorn, and often not even real chastisement for him personally or for his actions. This realization is necessary in order to eliminate the inevitable anxiety a new crew member feels about both his performance of his assigned tasks and his "social standing" among the crew. Some men grasp this situation more quickly than others. I know of more than one situation where a man has left a boat or even the industry altogether because he failed to come to an understanding of this "system."

Note that there is a difference between what happens during the set and what happens at other times; that is, what is permissible in terms of direction and instruction. The loud and abusive quality of the exchanges during the set disappears completely as soon as the fish are aboard. That the distinction between these two periods is so complete and marked is the reason I call the process during the set "direction," and the process at other times "instruction." They are both attempts to modify behavior in some way, but their characters are completely different. There is very little verbal *instruction* outside the set.

A corollary to the nonverbal nature of the instruction is its watch-and-see character. If, for example, you ask how to perform some setting activity at any time other than when the activity is actually being performed you are almost always given a few short remarks followed by, "Wait and watch. Then you'll see how it's done." Even if you are being "taught" to make net, operate the autopilot, or help around the galley you are not *told how* to do it, you are *shown how*.

A third phenomenon is what I call the random-work process. The random-work process is characterized by a general lack of systematization in most of the work that takes place aboard the boats aside from that performed during the sets themselves. This is evident in work done both at sea and in port.

I first noticed this phenomenon when I was working as an unloader aboard one of the seiners in San Pedro. Not only was there no instruction prior to the activity for the newcomer, me, but there was very little preparation in the form of assignments for any of the regular crew or the other unloaders. Some people seemed to know exactly what was going on and started right in. But others—a majority of the crew—just seemed to gravitate in the general directions of activity performing little duties here and there. When the fish buckets finally started coming aboard everyone settled down into a job, partially with the help of the skipper who made a last-minute round of the below-decks.

Later, when I hired out on my first fishing trip, the boat was in port for about three weeks before the season opened. During that time the crew would show up, most of them, to work in the mornings or however long that day's job required. In working with the crew—the boat was not the same one I had unloaded— I noticed the same behavior. The crew would gather in the galley to drink coffee while one or two of them rounded up paint brushes or puttered with fittings. After awhile the work would begin in various places around the boat. Throughout the day people would wander from job to job, dropping in occasionally to have a cup of coffee in the galley. If I didn't go up and ask what I could do, even if I was standing right next to work being done, I found I could stand there for an hour without anyone saying anything to me. I usually asked what I could do so I didn't spend much time standing around, but even after three months with the boat I noticed that one could, if he didn't ask or start in, stand and watch work without anyone *telling* him to help.

The general feeling aboard the boats, one which serves as a source of pride for the fishermen, is that every man knows his job and can do it without being told. In this vein it could be that I simply didn't know the jobs, and I would bow to this reasoning were it not for the fact that I observed many other crewmen, both novices and fishermen of many years experience, doing the very same thing with no one overtly attempting to modify their behavior either.

There are three things to point out concerning both the random-work phenomenon and the character of the "teaching" aboard the boats. First, it is not clear that the fishermen have the command of the situation which the lack of instruction might indicate. Second, there is a distinct tendency to avoid telling another crew member what to do. Outside the context of the set this tendency is even evident on the part of recognized authority figures such as the skipper and the deckboss. And third, there is no set system of teacher-student relationships.

The Reasons for the System

There are several reasons for these attributes of the learning process: the nonverbalness, the watch-and-see attitude, the

223

emphasis on everyone knowing his job, and the aversion to telling other men what to do. One of the most important reasons is related to the general level of education in the fleet.

Probably the most pervasive thing years of experience in an educational institution does is to teach one that actions and processes ought to be thought out, that analysis of causes and effects can and ought to be done before an action is performed, and that the results of this thought process can be transmitted effectively through verbal and written communication. Most of the men in the fleet have simply not had prolonged exposure to this kind of cognitive orientation. The median level of education on the first boat on which I was a crew member, which I would estimate is close to the median for the fleet, was somewhere around ninth grade. I use the median calculation because the paper masters and navigators often have significantly greater amounts of education than the rest of the crew. The facts that these men must many times work as equals with the rest of the crew, and that most of the activities and communications within the system revolve around interactions of the crew as a whole, make it necessary to avoid bias because of a few individuals.

Because of this relatively low level of formal education (in many cases coupled with a language barrier which makes it not at all surprising that any communication is nonverbal) the men are not comfortable in situations where one is required to absorb a large number of concepts without immediate reference to an actual situation. That kind of abstract learning process would be characteristic of school-type instruction. They are used to more action-oriented socialization and learning situations.

There is also simply no provision for formal instruction apart from the actual work situation. The only school available is the learn-by-doing one. The men are at sea so much of the year that when they are at home they tend to stay away from the boats as much as possible. When they do have to be at the boat they generally talk about their exploits rather than the virtues and failings of their fishing methods, so that their conversations have a low instructional value. Listening to them may teach you to *act* like a fisherman and is therefore important in

224

the learning of interactional norms, but it does not teach you to *be* a fisherman.

Once the boat is at sea, one is almost immediately into the fishing process. Four days after we left on my first trip, most of which time was spent readying the boat, I was in a speedboat chasing tuna. In my case there was little time for preparatory instruction but plenty of opportunity to learn by doing. In the most important operations, however, watch-and-see and learn-by-doing can be far from perfect methods of instruction. There is a necessity for speed in most of the processes and the extra dangers of having to set in rough weather or cope with equipment malfunctions, and these circumstances further weaken the ability of the neophyte to absorb the actions going on around him and consequently to learn from them.

This lack of instruction is sometimes due to a certain amount of job-holder's jealousy. Positions on the boat are held by virtue of a complex set of combinations of ability, attributes and "connections," but no position is permanent or inviolable, not even the skipper's. If either the owner, the skipper, or the crew in general wants you replaced by another man there are many, many ways to accomplish that goal. This jealousy is understandable in light of the fact that if many of the crewmen had to find employment ashore they could not earn more than a third of what they earn on the tunaboats. Many are unsure of their ability to get a "ride" on another boat despite the large amount of movement between boats in the fleet, and this uncertainty and knowledge of their lack of alternatives combine to make them less eager to impart information to a man they see as a potential competitor.

Another factor in the lack of communication between the experienced and the inexperienced is often the attempt on the part of the more experienced man to conceal his lack of knowledge. In many jobs the levels of expertise necessary for efficient operation of the system is far below that of a complete understanding of all the processes involved. I noticed crewmen taking refuge in the watch-and-see response when I would ask them (before I comprehended the effects of my inquiries) questions

225

about portions of the process about which it later became obvious they knew nothing. When I noticed that I was getting this sort of response I started looking for it in others' conversations and found it frequently, even from some skippers whose job, it is normally assumed, is to know everything. The common understanding that one ought to know what to do without being told, and the fishermen's pride in this rule, serve to provide a shield for those with incomplete knowledge.

Finally, much of the lack of communication that goes with the lack of instruction stems from the feeling that one man ought not tell another what to do. This even applies to the correction of mistakes made during the set if the opportunity for communication does not arise until after the set is completed. Part of this feeling is due (that is, it has been put to me in these words) to the notion that a man at sea for two or three months with all the deprivations and all the pressures does not need someone correcting his work on top of everything else. More comprehensive reasons for this will be discussed in Chapter Ten. What is important for the learning process is that the break in communications does occur.

I do not want to convey the impression that these fishermen are uneducated, insecure, jealous, evasive men, with all the connotations which would normally accompany those kinds of adjectives. Certainly they display these characteristics from time to time, but so do many other people. Nevertheless, each of these attributes does contribute to the general pattern of learning and socialization.

Despite the seeming lack of instruction in the learning process, the system of resource exploitation works quite well. It makes the companies and individual crewmen relatively handsome livings and it copes admirably wth the external limitations imposed by governmental bodies and provides an adequate supply of tuna to the public at a reasonable cost. There is a relatively high injury rate at sea, but it would be hard to show that a significant portion of the injuries occurred as a result of the poor training of crewmen.

There are, to be sure, various problems inherent in the

processes employed aboard the boats. There is a tendency in the fleet (as there is in other fleets and occupations) to innovate just far enough to solve these problems, putting off until "next time" unsolicited improvement. While there are certainly innovators in the fleet who are constantly trying to come up with better ways to do things, their efforts often fall prey to the fact that improvements, as opposed to solutions, come more slowly and are accepted more slowly in the midst of an aura of success and well-being. Innovation in the instructional process may be a victim of this sense of security.

All of these characteristics of the learning process have consequences for the acquisition of knowledge by the new crew member in the three areas mentioned at the beginning of the chapter. They tend to make the learning of mechanical components a slower process. They tend to produce a cognitive orientation which stresses rote rather than analytical components. Finally, they tend to force the newcomer to rely on experience as the only complete set of data from which to learn.

Sanctioning

There is little explicit *positive* sanctioning in the form of rewards aboard the tunaboats. There are the rewards that result from outstanding performance over the long term, in the form of a higher position on the boat, a larger share, and respect from one's fellows. There are always the standard "good job" comments given after a good set, but these are rarely given individually. Everyone is happy and satisfied when a good set is made, and non-directed "rewarding" comments are common. The times are rare, however, when one man is singled out for commendation. Part of the reason for this is that the teamwork necessary to the process is so pervasive and the forces on the equipment so great that not only does everyone have to do his job well for a good set to be made, but if anything goes wrong— or even in the course of a normal set—it is hard for the actions of any one man to make a significant difference.

Most of the sanctions discussed below are negative sanctions related to transgressions of some procedure or norm. These

227

transgressions fall into several categories. Transgressions in each category are differentially subject to various sanctions.

The first of these categories is mistakes in procedure occurring during the set. They are in the form of a speedboat driver not paying attention or not listening to the skipper's directions, crewmen losing lines or cables overboard, the skiff driver running over the corkline, or the skipper letting the skiff go too early or too late. Everyone on board runs the risk of making some mistake of this kind. Even the cook, who besides his galley chores is on many boats an integral part of the net-stacking process, is subject to these mistakes and thus to the sanctions invoked to correct them.

The second category is mistakes in general work procedures. These are things such as the misuse of tools, incorrect keeping of engine room records, improper lashing or stowage of equipment, and other routine but nonetheless important matters.

The third is transgressions of the collective preference. The cook on one boat, for example, insisted on cooking all of the meat well-done when the crew liked rare meat. With the important role food plays in the daily routine, this was a serious problem. Also falling into this category are those actions taken by key men which are not to the liking of the majority of the crew. Although there is an underlying and well-understood hierarchy of authority aboard the boats, there are also group pressures from an egalitarian ethic which can be brought to bear against the key men. These will be set out elsewhere.

The last category is that of social mistakes. This is the most elusive category because it contains things which often have more 'oughtness'' than tangible necessity for the operation of the boat in any of its aspects. These are things such as excessive belligerence, lack of consideration for other crewmen, excessive drinking on board, avoidance of certain work tasks, improper joking or friendliness with certain crewmen, or ignorance of such things as ''proper'' seating arrangements at dinner or the movies, which reflect status positions within the crew.

Most of the sanctioning done during the set itself is verbal.

It is roughly the same as the "direction" described earlier, and is rarely useful in any instructional sense. Most of the verbalization performed during the set, sanctioning or otherwise, is loud, sometimes abusive, and rich in profanity. The bulk of the talking is done by those with official position, but anyone who can "afford" it in terms of his particular status relationships may make himself heard.

Profanities which refer to one's family are considered more offensive than others. On one boat the phrase "son of a bitch" was used once by the skipper to a first-generation Portuguese speedboat driver. The man, who had in the same set been called much worse things in terms of *personal* reference, took this as an insult and said to me later, "You don't call a man a son of a bitch. You can call him other things, but not that." This was not an isolated incident. I had other conversations with crewmen who indicated there was a hierarchy of profanity, each word differing in its permissibility depending on the situation. Family reference, and usually even direct personal reference, are avoided.

Those who cannot afford to speak their displeasure loudly express sanction in an under-the-breath manner to crewmen close by. It is common for the crew on the netpile, for example, who are generally those with the lowest status, to comment in tones just as abusive and angry but lower in volume about crewmen in other areas of the deck. Their companions to whom the comments are made are most often members of one of a man's cliques within the crew, although this is not always the case. This verbal expression, while having little effect on the performance of the tasks themselves, makes the victims anxious. It also tends in its under-the-breath form to promote inter-clique stratification.

One of the first things the crew will tell you upon coming aboard is not to take the yelling seriously or personally. They say that people tend to get excited during the set and yell a lot, but that they rarely mean what their tone and volume implies. It is one thing, however, to be told this and quite another to practice it. Even the most experienced crewmen exhibit annoyance at the skipper's loud and abusive verbal direction as well as insecurity over conversations between crewmen in a small group when they think they themselves are the subject of discussion.

One of the most interesting forms of sanction was a mystery to me for a long time. Periodically, at the beginning of a meal when a particular person sat down at the table the entire crew would start tapping either a plate or a glass with their utensils. Their facial expressions would not change, nor would they look at the person. After a short time it would stop, and the meal would continue. No one person seemed to start it, and not a word was spoken.

After a considerable period of trying to correlate this behavior with *anything,* to no avail, I asked one of the men what it was about. He laughed and said that it varied. If someone had done something especially well it could be a form of commendation. If someone had broken a rule of some sort, for instance having been discovered sleeping on the netpile, it was a chastisement. In the case of the skipper, especially if he was late to a meal because he had been getting fish information on the bridge, it could be a form of general appreciation for his efforts.

I think it is true that not all of the crewmen know of the particular incident which prompts this action in every case, but it is institutionalized to the degree that when anyone starts tapping everyone else follows suit. The qualities of this sanction, which appear in many of the other interactions aboard the boats, are that it is a case of the entire crew acting as a body, and that it has no *direct,* overt reference to the crewmen being sanctioned.

A third form of sanction is censure. This most often takes the form of the isolation of an individual either verbally or behaviorally. For example, the crew will not initiate conversation with a certain crewman who is behaving in a way that transgresses a rule or norm. They will generally speak to him if *he* initiates a conversation, because it would constitute a personal affront not to do so; but the general patter of conversation which reinforces the crew solidarity and is so much in evidence during periods of normal operation makes it obvious when one man is being left out.

Public disclosure is a fourth and one of the most blatant and effective means of sanctioning, and it has more effect as a corrective mechanism than any of the other sanctions. It always occurs at a meal or some other gathering when all of the crew is present. The disclosure is always made in a third-party frame of reference, and it is never addressed directly to the offending man.

For example, on one of my boats there was a problem concerning the watch schedules. The Master on that boat made up these schedules. The problem had existed for some time, and the Master had been rather slow about correcting it. The crew was in general agreement that something ought to be done. The Master in this case was a "paper Master," one who is only on board to meet Coast Guard requirements and does not actually control the fishing process. As in the case of verbal sanctions in the set, the initiator of the sanction was the deckboss, a man with some status who could afford to take the lead. At a noon meal he said, loudly but to no one in particular, "I don't know what the problem is with the watch schedule. It doesn't seem like it would be hard to fix." There followed general muttering in agreement, but no comment from the Master. The deckboss continued, "It just means switching a couple of guys. I thought it was supposed to be fixed already."

The Master said nothing and kept eating. Immediately after the meal, when half the crew had gone on deck, he spoke up as if the subject hadn't been mentioned and said that he hadn't quite decided how to do the schedules yet. He made a few joking comments with the remaining members of the crew, which included the deckboss, and went back to the bridge. The new watch schedule was out that night.

In another case we had taken our skiff driver to port with an infected hand. The new driver, who had been the skiff assistant previously, took over and proceeded to make several mistakes, ones which he continued to make over a period of several sets. They were of a nature that could be corrected simply if he had asked someone else who knew about the skiff—there were

231

several such people aboard—to help him, but he didn't. Finally, again at the noon meal, the Assistant Engineer, himself a former skiff driver said, "You know, they used to have that same problem with the skiff on the (boat name), and the driver finally learned (brief explanation) and the whole problem was solved." He said this to a man in the opposite direction at the table from the new skiff driver, but in a voice designed to let the whole table hear. Later that afternoon I saw the driver talking to the Assistant and the mistake was not made again.

The same two elements are present in this method of sanction that were present in the plate-tapping. The whole group was present, and the remarks were not directed to the offending individual.

The last method of sanction is that of private advice or admonishment. This is hardly ever used. While it sometimes occurs between close friends and occasionally (often through one himself not "in" with the crew) with a newcomer, it rarely occurs between positions of higher authority such as the skipper or the deckboss and the offending crew member. An incident is recounted in another chapter where a deckboss steadfastly refused to order the cook to perform a task, even though the cook was being extremely defiant, the deckboss was within his rights, and the deckboss was a man of considerably higher status with the crew in many respects. The reason why this direct confrontation is the least used of the sanctions, and the reasons for the common characteristics found in other sanctioning procedures, are the subject of the next section.

Learning and Sanctioning as Confrontation

Throughout the learning and the sanctioning processes there are two common threads: one of assertiveness, skill, and individuality, and the other of avoidance of individual confrontation and an accompanying emphasis on group action. There are two circumstances that contribute to both of these aspects.

The first of these is the cultural characteristic called *macho,* or *machismo*. Macho is usually connected with maleness; in

232

behavior it is exhibited through a strong assertion of individual prowess, pride, and infallibility. Macho is generally identified with Latin people or Mediterranean countries, but its characteristics are recognizable in many cultures.

While much of the learning of the macho style comes through childhood processes of socialization, a strong reinforcing factor can be found in environments where the individual feels a lack of control, inferiority, or a loss of prestige. The behavior of the tunamen, for both ethnic and occupational reasons, is influenced by all of these factors. The crewmen on these boats are either Italian, Mexican, or Portuguese, thus comprising cultures which "teach" the macho ethic through early socialization. Long periods at sea leave the fishermen weak in the understanding of many of the norms and values they need for efficient functioning in the complex community in which they live ashore. These two circumstances combine to produce an aversion to personal criticism together with, and perhaps the product of, a sense of insecurity.

The same attitudes also help explain the elaborate sanctioning procedures which attempt to avoid any personal criticism or submission which may lead to confrontation. A role as student to a more knowledgeable teacher, for example, is a subservient one no matter how insignificant the subject matter. Because of this there is little demand for instruction aboard the boats. In this way personal attitudes shape the learning process.

Another circumstance which contributes to the particular character of the sanctioning and learning process, one which has no connection to early socialization or conditions ashore, is the dangerous and depriving nature of the occupation itself. A skipper once said to me, "I yell a lot during the set if things don't go right, but after the set is done I don't think it's right to keep on a man. They have it hard enough and do a good job without that." In a general way this ties in with the slow, half-day work style and the random work nature of most of the non-setting activities: the fisherman endures enough and works well enough to earn his pride, a pride and resulting confidence that ought not be dented by another man.

The fishermen are involved, however, in an occupation with a violent life-style that necessitates quick, vigorous, decisive action. When fifteen men live and work within fifty feet of one another in the absence of external diversion or alternatives for two to three months, there are always situations which create problems necessitating action. And there is, finally, a job to be done. The systems of learning and sanctioning outlined above have evolved to accommodate to these circumstances.

Socialization as a System

The degree to which it is "realized" that these mechanisms are connected to these circumstances, and the degree to which they are "necessary" to the workings of the physical and social pressures aboard the boats, is open to speculation. In certain areas the intent is obvious. Some skippers have told me that they don't allow liquor aboard because it can cause problems. On some boats the crew agrees not to play poker until the trip home, and to play other games for very small stakes which are agreed upon before the game even starts. In cases such as this the fishermen will tell you directly that they are trying to avoid conflict-producing activity. There are many boats, however, on which the liquor is unlimited and the crew gambles the entire trip, mostly without significant incident.

With the mechanisms of learning and sanctioning the question of awareness gets more difficult. The crewmen do not sit down and say, "OK, let's talk about this situation so Joe will straighten out." No one will admit, "I won't tell this guy anymore because I don't know that much myself." They "realize" to the extent that they will, as the one skipper did, tell you that "you can't keep on a man after the set," but whether they "realize" the extent and regularity of the system is not clear. On the other hand, the question of the "necessity" of the mechanisms gets easier. These mechanisms, unlike those of liquor and gambling regulations, seem to be the same on all boats.

It is not, of course, necessary for the crew to be aware of the system, and certainly not necessary for them to be able to verbalize it, for it to be working. Each of us has principles of

234

behavior but few except the social scientist ever pause to place our own and those of others into a system. Within the limits of the participant-observation method, that is what I have attempted to do here.

A larger question is the influence of these systems on the effectiveness of the tuna fleet, both as a socializing agent and as a resource exploitation method. They have profound effects on the new recruit to the industry, the technical development of fishing as a process, and on what could be described as the inertia inherent in the industry. The three components of the learning process mentioned at the beginning of the chapter are helpful in looking at some of these effects.

The new recruit to the industry learns primarily by experience. He is socialized to the fact that he must learn by doing and at the same time is chastized for his efforts during the set and ignored afterwards. His experience is his primary base, but the "lessons" of that experience are not consistent with one another.

The consequences of these systems for the technical development of the industry lie in the learning of the physical processes of the seining method. While they eventually socialize individuals into the use of the equipment, they do not promote innovation in either the design or the use of that equipment except in the solutions to persistent problems.

Finally, these systems affect the cognitive orientation of those within the industry. They tend to impart the idea that one ought to do as others do. They teach that the way to learn is to watch others rather than to reason out the best way with the experience of others as an input. The systems of sanctions, as they are "designed" to do, promote conformity in behavior. This way of "thinking"—using rote rather than analytical approaches to problems and situations—makes for inertia rather than innovation.

Once again, I want to caution against interpreting these statements as condemnations of the industry. The U.S. tuna fleet is the most technologically advanced and one of the most efficient fishing fleets in the United States. This is due, however, to a complex combination of factors, such as the complexity and industrial base of the area in which it grew up, the requirements of harvesting the resource which acted to promote further development, the particular storage and marketing characteristics of the tuna itself, and of course the vision and hard work of many men in the industry.

These are the modes of socialization through which most of the men in the tuna fleet "learn" about their occupation, with all of its attendant work-oriented and social norms of behavior. Some learn the "system" quickly and fit well within it while others do not. Mavericks with respect to both the procedural and the social rules aboard the seiners exist, but they are far outnumbered by those who learn the system and abide by its rules.

Although the tunamen learn to fit themselves into a community lifestyle which may seem harsh in many ways, it is in fact one which allows each individual to see himself as a full participant in a common endeavor. The non-directedness and group emphasis of the sanctioning procedures, the avoidance of confrontation on the part of all including the key men and the skippers, the tradition of each man being self-sufficient and knowledgeable in his job—all of these factors lend themselves to an egalitarianism that the crewmen will point out as a significant feature of their occupation. The preference for private over company boats, the remuneration breakdown which was detailed in the last chapter, the lack of contractual obligation—all of these things and others besides are manifestations of the desire for and prevalence of an egalitarian ethic.

All men, however, fishermen included, are not equal. They are not equal in personal attributes or ability, they are not equal in their positions in the larger community ashore, and they are not equal in their knowledge of or facility with the systems of behavior which they encounter aboard the boats themselves. The next two chapters are about the distributions of power, deference, and individual satisfaction with the seining lifestyle created by these inequalities.

9 Social Structures at Sea

THE TRADITION of a strict shipboard hierarchy prevails among most seafaring groups. To carry out the mission of the vessel; to provide for the safety of the ship and its crew; to deal with those whose behavior threatens the accomplishment of either of these goals; because the sea is a dangerous and unpredictable environment which necessitates the greatest skill and split-second decisions and reactions; and because the ship's environment is isolated from all other authority structures, a community in itself—these are the reasons usually given for the maintenance of a strict hierarchy of status and authority at sea.

These kinds of traditions and understandings evolved primarily through the history of merchant and naval seafaring. Seamen in these situations were often less-than-willing recruits. Shanghaiing, impressment, and conscripted service were not conducive to a spirit of comradeship or cooperation. The pay was low, the work dangerous, and the hours—and often months—long and tedious. The accommodations were worse than poor, and the men in the positions of rank often saw themselves as something more than mere mortals, dispensing a probably doubtful benevolence and taking a less than charitable view of the worth of the common seaman.

What happens to these traditional attitudes of hierarchy and authority when we have a situation where men are at sea for long periods of time, in perhaps more dangerous and trying physical circumstances than most seamen either now or in the past, but whose backgrounds, relationships with one another, control over their entry and exit from the situation, the remuneration are very different from those of the traditional seafarer? How does tuna fishing differ from the traditional "myth" of seafaring, and where is it similar?

This chapter and the next are about the power distributions, social structures, deference patterns, segments, cliques, and conflicts on board the tuna seiners, about behavior patterns which have evolved out of their own particular history and circumstances.

The Need for Direction and Authority

Unlike merchant seamen whose job it is to transport cargo across the ocean, the tuna fishermen must expend considerable energy and expose themselves to the dangers of an additional process which adds another dimension to their occupation: they must catch the fish. This extra dimension places several constraints on the interaction which occurs both within and outside of the work procedures themselves.

There are radically different requirements in terms of skills and attributes for the various tasks aboard each seiner. The skipper must be a strategist who has the ability to remember hundreds of names, locations, and relationships and synthesize them into a coherent plan to locate the fish. The brailers and speedboat drivers must be agile men with quick reactions and the manual dexterity to handle their equipment and boats at high speeds and in rough weather. The navigator must have a command of mathematics and be able to work with sophisticated electronic equipment. The deck crew must be skilled in working with netting and cable, fiberglass, wood, metal, and various synthetic materials. The Chief Engineer, and to some extent the entire engine room watch, must be able to operate and repair sophisticated diesel and gasoline engines, several-hundred-kilowatt generators, complex refrigeration systems, and various other hydraulic, electronic, and mechanical equipment. All must have the physical stamina to withstand the rigors of the fishing process. The range of skills and attributes these fourteen or fifteen men must possess—and many of them can switch easily between jobs—is very wide. Because the requirements of the fishing and navigation processes are so diverse, however, a good deal of planning and coordination is needed to make them into a workable system, coordination which the men themselves must implement.

238

Added to this is the fact that many parts of the various processes occur in spatially distinct and often widely separated areas. In the chase after the porpoise, the speedboats are often several miles from the seiner itself. The skiff is several hundred yards from the seiner throughout most of the set. The men on the netpile, the men on the bow, and often even the skipper on the mast and the men at the hydraulic console are hidden from each other's view and out of verbal contact. These conditions make it particularly important that there be a system of common understandings among the crewmen regarding the various portions of the process: who performs them, in what order, on whose direction or cueing, and with what contingencies.

Finally, it must be remembered that the voyages of the seiners are characterized by risk, uncertainty, and often adverse physical and socio-psychological conditions. In circumstances such as these men often exhibit a need for a "higher" authority in which to place their trust and confidence. Certain of these "higher" authorities, in the form of belief systems, were discussed in Chapter Seven. It is often the case, however, that men will place their trust and confidence in other men, men who because of some behavior, skill, or attribute make themselves worthy of this trust in the eyes of the crew.

All of these factors—the diverse requirements of the fishing process, the particular situations of spatial arrangement and communication possibilities, and the desire of the crew for stability and direction—press for a system in which certain of the crew acquire "power" of various kinds over the fishing process and in the interactions between the crewmen themselves. Added to these factors, which are internal to the system of tuna fishing itself, are the requirements of the larger governmental system under which the boats in the fleet operate. These sets of constraints lead to the patterns of hierarchy and power distribution which are found aboard the tunaboats.

The Status Structure

As pointed out earlier, the seiners are required by the Coast Guard to have a licensed Master, Mate, and Chief Engineer

239

aboard. Some are also required to have a licensed Assistant Engineer. These men, by virtue of their licenses, are the "officers" aboard the boats.

Some of the men in these positions are officers in name only, the "paper" officers discussed in Chapter One. Paper Masters and Mates are still common today. If the skipper does have Master's papers, the Mate usually does the navigating, runs the console during the sets, steers the boat, and generally takes care of the bridge. When there is in addition a paper Master aboard, the Master takes over these functions and it is not unusual to find the Mate on the netpile or on engine room watch.

The Chief Engineer's position, on the other hand, has always required a considerable body of knowledge which is still very necessary to the process but which the fishermen themselves have not had, and for the most part have had no desire to attain. The skippers, the real directors of the enterprise, were and still are almost entirely Portuguese or Italian, and even paper Master and Mate positions are often filled by older fishermen of these ethnicities who have either tired of the manual work or have simply wanted to increase their own status. The Chief's position was and still is, however, occupied in most cases by men from outside the controlling ethnic groups in the industry.

There is a particularly large amount of technical expertise and mechanical ability required of the Chiefs. While it is not difficult to learn the material necessary to pass for a Master's or Mate's license in a relatively short amount of time if you already have the experience of several years at sea, it is extremely difficult to do the same with the material for the Chief's license. Besides this, the Chief (and sometimes the Assistant) is in a direct supervisorial capacity as head of the engine room watch. Paper Mates and Masters rarely act as supervisors, even for the deck watch. That job generally goes to the deckboss. This makes it important that the Chief be able to deal with other crewmen as well as with the fishing process itself, abilities not so necessary for the "paper positions." There are no paper Chiefs so far as I know.

With respect to licenses in general, the Coast Guard recognizes that the situation aboard the seiners is different from that aboard a merchant ship. There are normally two parts to the examination for a license; an oral interview and a written test. For fishing vessels only—and this fact is clearly marked on the man's license—one is allowed to take the entire examination orally. This provision was lobbied for and obtained by the American Tunaboat Association and the various labor unions. Their successful argument to the Coast Guard was that while many of the fishermen, particularly those of different ethnic backgrounds, had all the necessary skills for the license they lacked the reading and writing ability to negotiate the test.

Besides the provision for different examination procedures the vessels themselves are officially classified as "uninspected vessels" by virtue of their fishing status. This also makes the requirements for all licenses a bit softer. Most of the certificates hanging on the bulkheads of the tunaboats also carry the limitation "For Uninspected Vessels Only."

These are the men who are officially in charge of running the ship. The Master is the titular head of the enterprise; the Mate theoretically does the navigating; the skipper is in charge of the day-to-day decisions and the fishing process; the Chief and his Assistant are in charge of all things mechanical, electrical, hydraulic, and chemical aboard the boats. In a court of law, Master-Mate-Chief-Assistant would be the chain of command. The "paper officer" situation and the different character of the licensing procedures compared to those for most vessels of comparable size, however, contribute to the egalitarian atmosphere aboard the seiners.

There is one other position which should be included in this group even though he is not licensed, and that is the deckboss. He is normally parallel to and between the Chief and the Assistant in institutionalized status. While the Chief in is charge of all the machinery and the engine room watch, the deckboss is in charge of all work on the rigging, net, deck, and the deck watch and directs the operations in the retrieval of the net. Because his function is solely in the fishing operation and does not have to do directly with the running of the boat, he is not required to be licensed.

In terms of the processes aboard the seiners, however, his job is an important one and his position and subsequent status is as a director, or supervisor. Besides the licensed personnel and the skipper, the deckboss is the only one on board with institutionalized supervisorial powers, and the only one besides the Chief who exercises those powers on a regular basis. If a skipper changes boats, his Chief and his deckboss usually go with him even if the rest of the crew does not. Since the primary requirements for the job are that the deckboss be skillful and work well with the skipper, the bond between the skipper and the deckboss is often stronger than most other interpersonal bonds on the boats.

Besides these formal, institutionalized positions which are the same on all the seiners, there are several semi-institutionalized positions which vary from boat to boat. These have to do with particular skills necessary to the process, and their form and substance varies with the particular personality in the position.

The foremost of these is the cook. His job requires a set of skills different from any other position on the boat and necessitates his working a different set of hours and in a different location from most of the crew. He gets up earlier, remains in the galley all day, does not take watches, helps only minimally in the fishing operation, and is not licensed in any way. His performance in his job is, however, crucial to the well-being and attitude of the whole crew and thus to the fishing operation itself. The cooks have tremendous potential power stemming from this fact, as we have seen in examples in earlier chapters.

The mast man, skiff driver, and on some boats the number one speedboat driver are also semi-institutionalized positions. The mast man is the leader in the visual search for signs of tuna, theoretically the best man on the boat for that job. Comments like, "He has eyes like a hawk," and "He's up there (on the mast) all day—never lets up" are common in reference to mast men. The skiff driver not only drives the skiff in the setting

242

operation but is in charge of the brailing and responsible for all the maintenance and operation of the skiff in whatever job it is doing. The number one speedboat driver is the leader in the chase after the porpoise and the man who is sent over the side if a speedboat is needed for any other purpose. Although he is usually closely directed by the skipper, his skill, knowledge, anticipation, and ability to work with both the skipper and the deckboss are valuable assets to the process.

These semi-institutionalized positions are usually determined by abilities rather than by attributes as some of the more formal positions are. The power connected with them varies with the particular person holding the position.

A paper Master, for example, either holds papers or he doesn't. The power he gets from this attribute is a discrete amount. A mast man, on the other hand, will get much more or less status or power out of his position depending on whether or not he finds any fish. The same thing applies to the cook and the skiff and lead speedboat drivers—their ability and performance in their positions determines the power they derive from the positions themselves.

The other five or six members of the crew—those who do not hold any of these institutionalized or semi-institutionalized status positions—are the men who drive the other four or five speedboats and the one or two who work as general hands on deck. The speedboat drivers usually constitute the remainder of the deck crew and the general hands fill the engine room watch list, although many times these men are interchangeable. Everyone except the cook and the skipper takes a watch at night or whenever watches are necessary, with approximately half of the crew going to the engine room and half to the bridge.

This last set of men—the "regular" crew—has a pecking order of its own. There is often one man who is understood to be the assistant to the Assistant Engineer. He takes control of minor portions of the operation and maintenance of the machinery. There is likewise an "understood" assistant to the deckboss, and he directs small portions of the deck work. There is not only a number one speedboat driver, but a number two,

243

three and so on. These numbers not only reflect the order in which the boats line up in the chase after the porpoise, but also roughly correspond to the duties of each driver. The number one speedboat driver, for example, will do little or no maintenance on the speedboats while the number three and four drivers will do all the refueling, tying down, and other minor duties associated with their operation.

It is very important to remember, however, that in addition to matters of status, structure, and hierarchy—which are all very real phenomena—most of the interaction aboard the boats is governed by a strong egalitarian ethic. The conflict between these two things—the "need" for and the existence of hierarchy and authority on one hand, and the egalitarian ethic on the other—results in a system of behaviors which reflects interactional powers and their distributions among the crew.

Types of Power

There are three types of power that play major parts in the interaction aboard the tunaboats. Some may only be exercised through institutionalized positions, while others may be exercised by anyone with the proper resources. The first type of power is *authority:* the right to control the behavior of others by virtue of an institutionalized position such as Master or Chief, a position which theoretically carries the power of an external sanctioning agent. Any challenge to a lawful command of the Master, for example, even if he is a paper Master with no real function in the processes of the boat, could be prosecuted in a court of law. The Master, Mate, Chief, and sometimes the Assistant formally possess this power in a strict legal sense, and the skipper and deckboss possess it by common understanding.

The second sense of power is that of *privilege:* the ability to perform or not perform some duty or activity normally associated with a particular crew position or work task. The number one speedboat driver is using this kind of power when he leaves the maintenance of his speedboat to others. The older crewmen who stack the corks or work the bow winch (considered preferred jobs), even though they are not especially skillful at

244

these jobs, are exhibiting this power. The crewman who sits in the skipper's seat at meals or at the movies when the skipper is absent is using this power, as is the man who stays home with his family or flies home from Panama while the rest of the crew helps to repair or unload the boat or make the crossing from Panama to Puerto Rico.

The third sense of power is that of *personal influence*. This is the ability to influence face-to-face interaction or the behavior of others from outside a position of institutionalized or formal authority. The man who takes charge of any work situation even though a man of more "formal" authority may be present; a man for whom people make way in the galley and the passageways; a man whose opinions gain adherence from the other crewmen; these men are using their personal power of influence.

There are several things to note about these various kinds of power. There is a distinction between actively asserting power of one sort or another and being the object of others' understandings about the possession of power. A skipper, for example, often need not ever visibly assert his power of status-position because it is commonly understood that he possesses that power. Some, on the other hand, may attempt to assert power over others only to fail because those others do not share the same understandings about the formers' possession of that power. One Master with whom I sailed continually voiced his opinion in the presence of multiple offenders that a Master (he himself was a paper Master) ought to keep people out of his chart room. The men sitting in the chart room would smile, grunt or say nothing, but nobody ever moved.

Each of these kinds of power occurs in increments and in combination with others and is differentially effective in different situations. The paper Master mentioned above, while he had some degree of authority as Master, could not use it to alter certain behaviors. Had he also enough power of influence, however, he might have been able to keep people out of his chart room. One Mate with whom I sailed had this power of influence and set crewmen to squirming with nothing more than a glance. People possess power of these three kinds in various amounts and combinations, and their positions in the boat's hierarchies depend on the mix each man possesses and the particular situation involved.

The three kinds of power are also transitive in varying degrees. A Master who gives an order to a crewman is effectively transferring some of his formal power and vesting it is his appointed agent. Authority is relatively transitive in this sense. The power of privilege is less transitive. A man who claims a privilege because, say, of his close relationship with the skipper can sometimes be the source of a claim of privilege by one of *his* friends on the same basis. The understandings about the transference of this kind of power, however, are much less clear and less binding. The power of personal influence is almost completely intransitive. Because it does not rely on any sanctioning agent outside of the person himself, it is very hard to extend to another man. Men who themselves possess the power of personal influence may sometimes grant power to others, but more often than not their ability to do so is derived from their possession of either authority or the power of privilege.

Attributes of the Powerful

The possession of these various kinds of power results from combinations of abilities and attributes particular to each crew member in much the same way as does one's remunerative status. One attribute which contributes to one's power, of course, is the possession of a formal status. The paper Master I mentioned earlier, although he could not command direct compliance with his orders in cases such as the clearing of his chart room, did receive "making-way" deference from most of the crew. He could go to the front of the chow line, and people stepped aside for him in the passageways. His abilities were not special, but he had an attribute: Master's papers.

A second source of power is ability or skill in some necessary process on the boat. I knew a Chief on one boat who commanded no physical deference from anyone in the way the Master mentioned above did, but who commanded instant compliance to any request for work on the engines by virtue of his reputation for knowledge and expertise as Chief Engineer.

A third source of power is age or seniority. Some crewmen possess powers of privilege simply because they have been around the longest. Even though they may lack the strength or agility for certain jobs (realizing of course that what they lack in these areas they may make up for in knowledge or experience, they often command privilege and deference simply because of their age or seniority on the boat.

A fourth source of power is friendship or kinship ties. This is a very important source of power, given the structure of the industry. A friend or a relative can get you a job on a boat, a better position on a particular boat, grant you privileges, and in other ways materially affect your status and certain of your powers.

A fifth source of power is simple physical stature. Power derived from physical stature can exhibit itself in many ways. The deckboss on one boat on which I worked never had to worry about people making way for him; he was 6'4", weighed 200 lbs. (most of which was in his shoulders), had bushy jet-black hair, a long turned-down moustache, and a slanted scar over one eye. He was in fact a friendly and good-humored fellow, but always looked as if he would rather tear you in half than look at you. That appearance got him a lot of places without any trouble, a fact he realized and of which he took good advantage.

Physical stature also gets one power in more subtle ways. In an environment which is harsh, with a strenuous job to be done, and among men who naturally envy power and strength, it makes employment easier to find and position easier to acquire. This is true not only for fear of a man's size or strength, but because the components of trustworthiness and capability which people like to attribute to their leaders are more easily fulfilled by men with physical stature.

Manifestations of Power

There are several specific ways in which crewmen's power stemming from the various attributes or abilities may manifest itself. These are forms of deference; that is, power creates the ability to have or make people defer to you or your judgments in various ways. Assertions of power without any resulting deference is bluster, and is most often obvious as such.

The most common kind of deference is that granted upon a specific request or command. Crewmen who launch their speedboats on the skipper's command, pull a certain section of the net on the deckboss's command, or go forward to fetch a line at the request of another crewman are exhibiting this kind of deference. This is deference in the sense of obedience.

Another kind of deference is that of physically making way for another man. When certain men pass through a hallway, walk up to the coffee pot, or go to climb a ladder, others get out of their way. This kind of deference is very prevalent, very obvious, and the people between whom it will occur very predictable.

A third kind of deference is verbal acquiescence. There are certain men who may interrupt a conversation when they wish, talk when and to whom they wish, and most importantly always gain agreement, at least verbally, to whatever argument they might be presenting. Forms of address such as "sir," "captain," or "mister" are also in this category.

Finally, there is deference in physical status-location or position. Leaving the skipper's place open at the table, not going onto the bridge or into the chart room, taking a lower bunk, or commanding a berth in a two-man room are examples of this kind of deference.

The last three types of deference I mention here may seem trivial or unimportant to the reader. We, most of us, perform these deference behaviors every day in elevators, with clerks in stores, and in front of "no parking" and "employees only" signs. When these same actions take place regularly, in a closed space, and with the same individuals as objects for months at a time, however, their performance takes on a different character and import. They are no longer casual actions performed without a thought, but become significant inputs into perceptions, feelings, and consequently behaviors. Possession of the power to command deference in these ways is a significant factor in one's

248

perception of one's self as an individual and as a member of the crew.

The Skipper—An Elite Egalitarian

The one position in which all of these manifestations of power appear at once—and where they clash most obviously with the egalitarian ethic—is that of the skipper. The skipper is deferred to in all of the ways mentioned in the last section. People make way for him wherever he may be aboard the boat. His commands or requests always receive compliance. He is rarely challenged verbally on any subject, and his speech takes precedence over anyone else's. People vacate seats when he comes onto the bridge or into the galley, and his every action is treated with general deference.

There are good functional justifications for this deference and respect. The skipper is the official link between the boat and the owners or managers on shore. He is by common understanding responsible for both the safety of the boat and its crew and the success of the trip, no matter what it says on the ship's papers about these being the Master's responsibility. He has complete control over the hiring and firing of everyone on board and over all of the day-to-day movements and activities of the boat. He is also generally considered responsible for maintaining crew harmony, although the extent to which he involves himself in this matter and the methods he uses differ from skipper to skipper. The crewmen on his boat are referred to and refer to themselves as "his" crew.

The skipper's almost total powers of authority, privilege, and personal influence may seem to be at odds with the egalitarianism which the fishermen say exists aboard the boats and which is reflected in the share breakdown, the sanctioning system, and other institutionalized processes aboard the boats, and in many ways they are. Nevertheless, although they possess these comprehensive powers skippers have educational levels in most cases approximately equal to those of the rest of the crew. They are many times consanguinally or affinally related to their crewmen, and they are all, so to speak, in the same boat—away from loved ones and the alternatives of life ashore— for the same amount of time under approximately the same conditions.

Almost every skipper in the fleet has come up through the ranks. Although it is also true that most skippers come from the families of boat owners or of other skippers, kinship is a parameter of opportunity and not of qualification. That is, almost all of the skippers have driven speedboats or cleaned the bilge, worked on the netpile, packed the wells, spliced cable, and performed many of the functions aboard the boat as *regular crewmen*. Being related to an owner's or skipper's family might get you an opportunity to "run a boat" after you have worked in the fleet for a couple of years, but it does nothing to guarantee that you'll remain in that position.

I know personally of two men, close relatives of prominent fishing families, who got the opportunity to run boats during the year I was at sea with the fleet. Both of them, for different reasons, were not successful at catching fish. Both of them "lost" their boats. Connections in high places may have been necessary to get them into the skipper's position, but it certainly was not sufficient to keep them there. Without fishing success even if you don't "lose" the boat you will certainly lose your crew. The high capitalization of the industry on the one hand and the share system on the other put irresistible pressure on the skippers from both the owners or managers of the boat and from their own crew to bring home fish.

Many skippers are somewhat ambivalent about their relationships with the rest of the crew. One night I was standing on the pier in Puntarenas, Costa Rica, with the skipper of my boat while some of the crew were trying to round up others who were still partying in the town. He said that as far as he was concerned everyone was basically the same, but that we react to situations according to our "station." He said he didn't particularly like being the heavy, the one to order everyone back to the boat to head out to sea again, but that that was his "station" and his job. He said that if he weren't the skipper he'd be one of the ones back in town.

He talked about how much you can "give" a crew. He described an occasion when he was a new skipper and had been in that same port and had all of the crew back aboard except for one fellow. He let another fellow talk him into going back to look for the first. Then another to look for the two. Then another, until he had five men ashore. He ended up ashore at three in the morning pulling everybody out himself.

He said you can be too hard on a crew. He cited examples of what he called "mutinies" (the crew "calling the skipper down" and telling him to "take the boat in," things that I know happened during the year I was with the fleet), fights, and whole crews walking off the boat after a trip—all of these incidents being caused by a skipper being overzealous in his pursuit of the tuna or lacking an understanding of the needs of his crewmen, or both.

He said, however, that it was harder for a skipper who empathized with the crew. He said that if he were running an "operation" he would want someone who hadn't been "in the ranks" making the decisions. He said he thought that skippers should maintain a certain distance from the crew. He said that no matter how the trip goes there is always going to be griping, even from otherwise good crewmen. He mentioned what old Sicilians used to call the "saw"—a man who relays all the crew's comments to the skipper. He maintained that "saws" only make unnecessary trouble for the whole crew, that all it does for the skipper personally is to add potential worry, and that the kind of comments "saws" make shouldn't affect the skipper's decisions anyway. He said that he didn't especially like being in the "station" as the impersonal decision-maker, but that someone had to be.

Each skipper has his own way of handling his "station." Each thinks differently of how much one has to "give" the crew and the best way to preserve order and catch fish and still keep the crew (themselves included) relatively happy. Each reflects a different degree of egalitarianism in his behaviors.

There are several general areas within which the skippers can modify their behavior to try and achieve this "best way."

One of them is the extent to which a skipper exerts his authority, his power to directly influence the behaviors of his crew. The vigor and tone of his direction in the sets, the amount of criticism or instruction he gives outside of the set, the character of his communications with the crew in general—all of these things affect the "social condition" of the crew and the concomitant effects of the interactions aboard the boat on each individual's mental and physical condition.

Some skippers, like the one mentioned in an earlier chapter, believe that one ought to "keep off" the men except during the set itself. The general theory behind this seems to be that to apply pressure where it is not immediately needed is to subject the crew to unnecessary harassment without which they will get along better. Others, a small minority, insist on maintaining some instructional and authoritative input at all times. They reason that mistakes should be corrected as well and as soon as possible and that the skipper's continued authoritative presence will give him better control in the end. The general level of skill versus error aboard the boats seems to permit most skippers to follow closer to the former course. It is a fact that skippers who do so have less crew turnover, and I would venture to say generally equivalent fishing records.

A second input into the "best way" to relate to one's crew lies in the amount of information-sharing or consultation a skipper does with his crew. Some say that a skipper ought to give his men as much information as he can without compromising privileged communication or "giving away" fish through the crew's conversations with crewmen from other boats in port or through their radio calls home. Others say that avoiding these compromises and information losses is impossible, and that in any case the crewmen do not "need" to know about what is going into a skipper's decisions about where and when to fish. Others go so far as to say that too much information-sharing or consultation shows weakness on the part of the skipper which will lose him the confidence of the crew and may very possibly mean that he doesn't know what he's doing anyway.

The general continuum exhibited in these comments is the one between "people feel happier if they know how the decisions which affect their lives are being made," and "people will tend to compare their opinions with the skipper's and their boat's fishing success with that of other boats and end up feeling discontented and relatively deprived." There seems to be a fairly normal distribution of skippers' opinions and behaviors between these two extremes.

A third determinant of the "best way" to relate to one's crew is that of the "best" interpersonal distance. Some skippers, for example, make an obvious attempt to spend time interacting with the rest of the crew. They say that this develops a feeling of camaraderie which makes the crew work together more smoothly and try harder as individuals to do well in their separate tasks. Other skippers purposely spend most of their time on the bridge or in their cabins, partially because they say that this is the only way they can do a proper job of collecting all the information they need and adequately contemplate their decisions. Some add that maintaining this interpersonal distance helps them to maintain the control they desire—the familiarity-breeds-contempt argument. Others, like the man I mentioned a moment ago, do not want their personal feelings to enter into their decisions about the fishing process and see physical separation as a way of avoiding that problem.

As with the previous point, most skippers seem to balance these two extremes against one another. Most make a deliberate decision about the levels of their interaction with and their isolation from the rest of the crew.

Personalities in the Structure

The term "interpersonal distance," however, has several connotations. One is structural: the amount of hierarchical or task-related status separation one desires to put between oneself and others. A second is social distance: the impressions one wishes to convey to others about one's social attributes—one's personal qualities which are reflected in the groups in which one

253

claims membership. A third kind of interpersonal distance is psychological. It involves the personal relationship each crewman has with each of the other crewmen.

Interpersonal distance in all three of these senses is controlled and manipulated not only by the skippers, but by each and every crewman. It is manipulated not only because the fishing and navigation processes require coordinated interaction to accomplish their ends, but because the crewmen share with all of us the need to adjust our perceptions of ourselves and others to fit both the "real world" distribution of skills, attributes, statuses, and relationships and at the same time the unique requirements of our own personalities.

Part of the resources the crewmen use to affect this control are the various "powers" discussed at the beginning of this chapter—authority, privilege and personal influence. The way these powers and other behaviors are used to obtain this "fit" and the effects of their use on the total set of interactions among the crewmen at sea are the subject of the next chapter.

10 Interpersonal Relations

Some Parameters of Interaction

BEFORE ONE CAN understand the nature of the interaction on board the boats, it is necessary to recall who is working on them and the nature of the work itself. The fleet is owned and the key man positions staffed by Portuguese and Italians. These men have tended to hire their friends and relatives to work on their boats in the manner described in Chapter Six. With the growth of the fleet in recent years and the movement of the registry base south of the border, however, the number of Mexican and South and Central American crewmen on the boats has risen greatly. The exact proportions of various ethnicities and nationalities within the fleet is unknown, there having been no one either willing or able to collect these figures.

The head of the largest union in San Diego, which despite being the largest accounts for only about a third of the men on the boats, told me that his membership was 30 percent Portuguese (he himself is Portuguese), 20 percent Italian (his number two assistant is Italian), 40 percent Mexican and the rest gringo, Slav, and other mixed ethnicities. The second largest union, and virtually the only other union with a significant membership, is predominately Portuguese with a minority of Italians and a very small minority of mixed ethnicities. These two together, however, account for only about half of the men in the fleet, the other half being "down-south" crewmen, Mexicans, and a good number of San Diego men who simply do not belong to the unions.

Within these categories of ethnicity the number who do not speak English, or the number of English-speakers who also speak Spanish, Portuguese, or Italian is also unknown. These latter three languages are fairly similar in structure and even in vocabulary, and the particular brand of each that is spoken on the boats has been tempered over the years by the fact that speakers of one have had to communicate with speakers of another, resulting in many recognizable linguistic changes. Although these changes have worked to improve verbal communication between these linguistic groups, when combined with ethnic and cultural characteristics the linguistic differences still arise as a significant actor in interaction.

Because my own first-hand experience with interaction aboard the boats was with a particular mix of these ethnicities and languages, I will present them as the sample from which many of my generalizations are drawn. All these generalizations are made after collecting corroborative data from crewmen on other boats. My impression, however, is that the men with whom I spent five months at sea represent fairly closely the ethnic and linguistic distribution in the fleet as a whole.

On my first boat, nine of the fourteen crewmen were Portuguese. Of these, five were first-generation, born in Portugal, and four were second-generation, born in the U.S. of foreign-born parents. There was one Costa Rican, one Mexican, and three gringos. The skipper and all of the key men except the Mate were Portuguese. All of the crewmen lived in San Diego. Four of the Portuguese men spoke no English. All of the English speakers except four, however, spoke either Spanish or Portuguese, the skipper and his paper Master both speaking the latter. The boat was fairly representative of a "Portuguese boat" in terms of the mix of ethnicities; mostly Portuguese with a few positions (Chief Engineer, cook, Mate, skiff driver/mechanic) filled by non-Portuguese. Many of the "Italian boats" in the fleet have crew lists much like this but with "Italian" substituted for "Portuguese."

On my second boat, the skipper was Italian, as were three other members of the crew. All three of these Italian crewmen were first-generation. There were four Mexicans, three Peruvians, two Costa Ricans, two Portuguese, and two gringos. Only eight of the seventeen lived in San Diego. Seven of the crewmen did not speak English. Only one of the English-speakers, the

Mate, did not speak either Spanish, Portuguese, or Italian. The skipper spoke English, Spanish, and Italian. This boat was fairly representative of a "down-south" boat: the skipper and the key men were of the same ethnicity and with one or two exceptions all lived in San Diego, and the remainder of the crew was filled with men from either Mexico or Central or South America. The total first-hand sample, then, divides as in the accompanying table.

Besides variations in ethnicity and language, the crewmen's positions in the various processes of the boat must be taken into account to understand the nature of their interaction. The most general division is between the deck and the engine-room crews. Because the great majority of the time at sea is spent looking for the fish, during which time mostly routine maintenance is done, the general category of maintenance to which one is assigned becomes very important. The deck crew spend most of their time on the working deck or on the netpile, while the engine-room crew spends a lot of time on the well deck or in the upper or lower engine room or shaft alley. There are many activities, of course, in which the "watch" to which one is assigned plays no part (for example, making net or salting the wells), but most general maintenance such as painting, greasing,

The Ethnicities of the Men with Whom I Fished

Ethnicity	1st Generation	2nd Generation	Living in San Diego	English	Other Language	Total
Portuguese	6	5	11	7	10	11
Italian	3	1	3	2	4	4
Mexican	5	0	0	4	5	5
Costa Rican	3	0	1	1	3	3
Peruvian	3	0	1	1	3	3
Gringo	0	0	5	5	1	5
Totals	20	6	21	20	26	31

1st generation—Foreign-born.
2nd generation—Born in the U.S. of foreign-born parents.
Other language—Portuguese, Spanish, Italian.

and cleaning is divided into either deck or engine-room work and determines with whom one spends most of the working day.

The division between deck and engine room is also important in terms of the watches a crewman takes. Watches are exactly what the name implies—a time to watch for things that might affect the actual progress of the boat or the state of its cargo. Very little, if any, work is done "on watch." The deck crew have watches on the bridge for at least four hours each day, while the engine-room watch has almost no occasion to go above the main deck. This means that the deck crew has much more contact with the Master, Skipper, and Mate, at least two of whom spend most of their time on the bridge, than does the engine-room crew. The engine-room crew has much more contact with the Chief and the Assistant, who are almost never seen on the bridge but spend most of their time below decks.

A secondary division is that of one's job in the set itself. People who perform the same function or who work in groups of three or more—for example, the speedboat drivers, the brailers, or the bow or working deck crews—often have the opportunity to interact more often with each other than with other individuals in the crew.

Besides these factors—ethnic and cultural differences, linguistic differences, differences in physical proximity and different jobs—each individual crewman's personality has an effect upon patterns of interaction. An individual's personality determines not only with whom he prefers to interact, but also how he behaves under the stresses and constraints of the fishing life; the notion of a "bad apple" and his effects on the rest of the crew are very familiar, at least in myth, to the fishermen.

Conflicts, Cleavages, Segments, and Cliques

There are three potential arenas for conflict, clashes between individual or group protestations of power, aboard the boats. A conflict may exhibit characteristics of or stem from one or a combination of the three.

The first is work-oriented activities. These may be disagreements about the order in which work ought to be per-

258

formed, a particular decision made during a set, or in general any allocation of effort made in the running of the boat's physical processes. Conflicts here generally express perceptions of hierarchical distances within the crew.

The second is social activities involving some or all of the crew: entertainment during evening hours, watch schedules in port, berth assignments, or the sanctioning of an individual or group which transgresses some social norm. Conflicts in these matters often are expressions of social distance.

The third is personal conflict between individuals. This directly affects and is affected by interpersonal distance. It may result from many of the same phenomena as the first two arenas of conflict, but is different in character and resolution in a way which will be described later.

Conflict in these three arenas tends to take place between groups and individuals which form along the lines of the parameters set out in the preceding section. The most common types of resultant stratification, segmentation, and cross-cutting ties are as follows.

There are only two real cleavages which form aboard the boats. These cleavages are orthogonal to one another. Cleavages are divisions which cut completely across the crew either vertically or horizontally.

Calling the skipper and Master the "top" and the general deck and engine-room crew the "bottom," the possession of authority in the sense described at the beginning of the last chapter creates a horizontal cleavage with the key men on top and the rest of the crew on the bottom. On many boats there is also a cleavage into groups which include men related to or possessing a common ethnicity or place of residence with the skipper. On each of my boats, for example, there were men from the very lowest to the very highest positions on the boat who possessed a common ethnicity (Portuguese on one boat and Italian on the other) which gave them an identity and a claim to certain kinds of status and power. Each member of either of these kinds of division may claim certain powers by virtue of his connection with authority, authority which the "key man" group officially

259

shares but which the skipper-and-friends group "officially" does not.

Both within and cross-cutting these divisions are groups of crewmen who form segments. A segment is a portion of the crew which shares an attribute that induces a feeling of commonality, and at least a nominal preference for interaction with that segment.

Language is an important factor in segmentation. The men who spoke only one language formed segments which interacted almost exclusively internally when not actually involved in the fishing process. The Portuguese-speakers and the English-speakers on my first boat and the Italian-speakers and the Spanish-speakers on my second are examples of this kind of segment. Men with common ethnicity and nationality also form segments. The gringos on my first boat interacted as a sub-segment of the English-speakers, while the Costa Ricans and Mexicans inter-acted as sub-segments of the Spanish-speakers on the second.

Segments emphasize patterns of preferred interaction. The gringos, for example, on both of my boats readily accepted me into their segmental interactions, as did the speedboat driver segments, while I had to make an effort to be included in the interactions of the other segments. My attributes and skills did not "automatically" place me in these other segments.

These segments both cross-cut and divide other groups. The skipper, for example, may not be included in much of the segmental interaction of the regular crewmen of his ethnicity. The deck crew and engine-room crew segments may divide the larger group of those who do not have authority. On each of my boats, the gringo segments cross-cut the authority and non-authority categories. Segmentalization within a stratum may reduce one's ability to claim power from both strata.[1] The same thing applies to multiple-segment membership, which occurs when one or more individuals have attributes of or connections

1. Hierarchical, social, and interpersonal distance may also juxtapose within the segments and strata. Two men may be hierarchically and socially very distant but interpersonally very close, and so on with all the various combinations of these three kinds of distance.

to more than one other segment of the crew. Such persons may be in the position to claim power from each segment, but at the same time they may lose their ability to operate as full claimants in any one group because of their multiple membership.

Friendship sometimes causes people to align in cliques with people outside their normal interactional group on a particular issue or in a particular situation. When men of different ethnicities work together in small tasks such as refueling the speedboats, washing the mast, or throwing seal bombs; when men from different work segments follow one another on watch, where they have a regular chance to talk alone together; when men in conversation find common experiences ashore—these are times when friendship and personality enter into the character of the interactions among the crew. Friendship may mean a Portuguese using his personal influence to stick up for a gringo amid some mild form of harrassment by the other Portuguese. It may mean a Chief using his authority to give one of the engine-room crew an easy job time after time; it may mean the leaders of two segments getting together and averting possible conflict between their two segments, or simply inducing more interaction between the segments. Cliques need not cause separation; they may also produce unity.

Friendship aboard the boats, however, is not friendship as we know it ashore—a lasting bond that may develop over long periods of time with no restraint besides the effort the friends themselves make to keep the friendship alive and growing. It is instead a bond of months—renewable, of course, provided the friends make the next trip together or even a trip sometime in the future. But given the movement of crewmen between boats, when a trip ends the crewmen's next meetings are uncertain and so, often, are their friendships.

Personal Interaction

Aside from these socio-political groupings the nature of the personal interaction at sea, whether congenial or otherwise, is affected by several factors. One's international possibilities are severely limited. While we ashore may not interact with more

261

than fourteen other people in a day, we are in surroundings which provide us with a variety of sensory input, much of which is human. We may not engage in face-to-face interaction with its producers, but we know that we could, if we wished, talk or in some way interact with a large number and a great variety of people. At sea it is the exact opposite: one knows for certain that one cannot possibly interact with anyone other than the fourteen men on the boat. One may get on very well with his shipmates, but one is always aware that there is no choice in the matter.

The environment aboard the tunaboats tends to be very intimate. The other fourteen men are eating, sleeping, brushing their teeth, showering, working and exhibiting the effects of their own emotions and personalities right at your elbow around the clock. There is virtually no escape from their company. The seinermen—and seafarers in general—say that a boat is the quickest place to get to know another person in a short time— of necessity.

The entire crew is going through separation and readjustment anxiety for a good portion of the trip. For about a week after the boat leaves San Diego the crewmen exhibit obvious effects of this anxiety. There is a noticeable lack of conversation. Men wander around the decks and spend hours at the rails, looking off into the sky or sea. Jokes are made about what their "people" are going to do while they're gone. Some stay in obvious depression for days, while others grumble that they don't know why they stay in this (blankety-blank) business. There is also a considerable likelihood that there will be more than one new crewman aboard the boat, and this adds to the strangeness and discomfort of the familiar-and-comfortable-yet-isolating surroundings.

Likewise, for about a week before the boat returns to port the crewmen go through a change. They are anxious about what they will find when they return home: what changes have occurred in their families, their friends, and the larger community while they were away? During this period the men tend to withdraw into themselves. They know that there is a real possibility

262

that many of the relationships they have established during the trip will end abruptly when they reach San Diego. In protecting themselves from the effects of this separation and reconciling themselves to what they may find waiting for them ashore, they exhibit much the same kind of behavior as they did at the beginning of the trip—a lack of conversation, solitude, a combination of testiness and bravado in their interactions with other crewmen. There is a name for the anxiety and sleeplessness which this period produces, especially in the last few days of the trip: "channel fever."

These separation and readjustment anxiety periods, which are also evident (but to a much smaller degree) anytime the boat puts into port—because these excursions provide a chance to "escape" from one's fellows—cut significantly into the relatively small amount of time that the men have to get to know each other on their trips to sea. They also serve to remind the fishermen several times a year that he is a man living "between systems."

Personal interaction is continually affected by the crewmen's attempts to exert power over one another. Any use of power—authority, privilege, or personal influence—tends to change interpersonal distance. The exercise of power widens or at least maintains an interpersonal gap. Where several people interact, an exercise of power may widen the gap between two parties and close the gap between others. With many opportunities for the exercise of power and in a situation where the total set of relationships is visible to everyone, the social fabric of the crew is continually being stretched in many different directions.

There is also a considerable amount of peer pressure to maintain the rather hazy social norms, a pressure normally exerted through joking. For example, at some point in the trip two men might be spending a lot of time together in the crow's nest looking for fish, drinking beer in one of their cabins, or in some other activity. This could become the occasion for thinly veiled homosexual jokes, always made at a meal or in the company of several other crewmen in the manner of the sanctioning procedures described earlier. Although the men would seem to take it as a joke, the relationship usually tones down thereafter.

Finally, each man seems to have his own inviolable inner space. Aboard the tunaboats it is obvious when this inner space is being "defended." Men who seem to be becoming the best of friends will suddenly stay away from each other. An act of kindness will be rewarded with a slightly hostile response. A personal confidence will be followed by rough, impersonal verbal treatment from the same man.

As an example of a defense of personal space, another crewman and I had become good friends during one of my trips. He was a man with considerably more power of all three types than myself, but he had never chosen to exercise them over me although he had the opportunity many times. During the fifth week of our trip he hurt his hand while working in the skiff. He developed what turned out to be a serious internal infection, but we could not diagnose the problem aboard the boat and he insisted that he remain on the job.

Along with several other crewmen, this man and I had been working on the speedboats for a day or so. During this particular time we had been working more or less together, progressing well with no noticeable friction. At the end of the day he complained that the pain, which had been progressing steadily since the injury, was getting very bad. We decided that whatever the problem was, it would be better to immobilize his hand. While the rest of the crew, especially the key man, had expressed concern over the injury no one except the skipper had shown any real interest in the problem. My feeling is that this was due more to macho on the part of everyone concerned than it was to a real lack of interest or empathy.

Whatever the reason for the rest of the crew's inactivity in the matter, that night I used the shop to fashion an aluminum brace for his wrist and hand. The next morning we went to the medicine chest and bound his hand to the brace with supplies we found there. He seemed quite pleased, not only with the brace but by the fact that I had bothered to make it for him. He said, "I think it feels better. I don't know if it's the brace or just that somebody paid attention to it." We talked for a few minutes about how it is that things can feel better because of attention, a conversation very uncharacteristic of those aboard the boats, and with a look and a smile of thanks from him we went our separate ways.

The next time we met to work, however, his attitude surprised and confused me. He was not openly hostile, but used his authority to order me about in the work processes in a way he had never done before. For the next few days all of our meetings were short and almost conversationless—very different from those before the brace incident, when he had always been extremely talkative to me on a relatively personal but newsy level. The tenseness of the meetings disappeared after a few days and his talkativeness reappeared, but he never again opened himself to me in the same way as when I made the brace.

One can understand his behavior. The crew knew that I had made the cast for him, and although they said nothing he may have been trying to show the crew that we were not too friendly. The major changes in his behavior, however, were not in those segments of our interaction which occurred in front of the rest of the crew; they were in the interpersonal interaction which took place outside of the larger social arena.

This phenomenon, the desire not to get "too close" to another crewman, has been documented in many other situations of long periods at sea. Statements such as "I can't say why, but it's better for the atmosphere to keep a little distance," and "It's a stress to be in such a small community, one has to defend one's private life," as reported by other researchers, confirm my observation (Herbst, 1972).

These factors—limited interactional possibilities, enforced intimacy, separation and readjustment anxiety, the continual exertion of power, group pressure to maintain social norms, and the desire of each crewman to preserve some part of his "personal space"—work in combination with one another to produce certain consistent behavior patterns. These behavior patterns and their attendant understandings are adaptations to the requirements of the fishing and navigational processes and to the factors in personal interaction described here.

Behavior Patterns

At one level these behavior patterns and common understandings have evolved so that the physical space available to the crewmen can be used in a way which will protect each man's perception of his personal "space" and allow him choice in his personal situation.

The twelve "spaces" described in an earlier chapter—the mast, the bridge, the speedboat deck, the bow, the cabins, the galley, the main working deck, the netpile, the upper engine room, the well deck, the lower engine room, and the shaft alley—take on an added importance in this respect. Even though they are in close proximity to one another, they offer a certain variety and in some cases an opportunity for solitude.

One can go to the galley expecting a bright, clean environment with a good chance of meeting someone at any time throughout the day or night. A man can go back to the netpile and expect to be partially engulfed in darkness but on the edge of the bright lights of the working deck, above the drone of the engines, and have some time in relative solitude to contemplate the areas and equipment which constitute such a great part of his life at sea. He can go forward to the bow area and be away from the noise and vibration of the engines, away from all the lights, surrounded by the noise of the bow wave and the phosphorescent flow of the disturbed sea. He can go to his cabin or bunk and be surrounded by beautiful wood and rich fabrics and comfortable in the company of his stereo, books, or mementoes. He can go onto the bridge and be relatively assured of having only one other companion. He can go up the mast (although this is rarely done, many crewmen considering the mast the domain of certain of the key men and others being simply uncomfortable so far off the deck) and have complete solitude, away from the noise of the boat, the sea, human voices—everything. The different attributes of these "spaces" become very important in providing variety, a certain amount of choice, and a potential for solitude for the individual.

The fishermen pay attention to clues which indicate another's wishes within these different spaces. There are ways a

266

man can indicate that he wants to be left alone without saying so in words. Each man's bunk, for example, is considered his domain and no one will violate that space or disturb the man if his curtain is drawn, even if it is obvious that he is awake. "Signs" of a man's availability for interaction, such as how far he has his curtains drawn or the angle at which the door to his cabin is left open, are commonly recognized aboard the tunaboats, and are also documented among other seafarers (Fricke, 1974). The fact that a man is alone on the netpile or the bow is itself enough to make another approach cautiously, and initial verbal feelers are almost always sent out. If the man seems to break his train of thought and turns toward you, responding with a sentence or two, one may usually assume he is not averse to some form of interaction. If, on the other hand, he does not make eye contact, makes only a perfunctory response to your greeting, and maintains his physical stance it is usual for the "intruder," after a moment, to drift away. The men are good at both transmitting and sensing these kinds of signals, and such very brief "test" meetings are common.

The "random work" described earlier could also be seen as a patterned behavioral response to the circumstances aboard the boats. In allowing the work to take place with a minimum of verbal direction or instruction and allowing the men to move from task to task, the random work pattern both discourages personal confrontation and the exercise of power and permits the crewman to exercise choice both in his task and in his work partners.

Even outside of work tasks themselves, the desire to vary one's companions is evident. Throughout the trip a crewman may be involved in several different interactional dyads and triads, groupings which are constantly forming and dissolving again. One man will "hang around" with one or two other crewmen for a couple of days or a week. Their verbal interaction will revolve around their sharing of some attribute, skill, or commonality of experience. While some of these groups last for long periods, the bulk of them dissolve in favor of new dyads or triads for each member after a relatively short period of time.

This pattern also allows the crewman some variety in personal interaction and a degree of choice in his behavior.

One of the most important activities in the easing of the tensions and anxieties caused by the conditions aboard the boats are the sets themselves. Everyone will tell you that the worst interactional and psychological problems occur during periods of inactivity. The sets provide a catharsis of both activity and emotion. The excitement of the chase, the anticipation of sacking up, the sheer physical exhaustion at the end of a set all distract a man from his thoughts of home and his relationships with other crewmen. The loud, violent, and even abusive character of the activity during the set serve "functions" in this sense. It *feels good* to shove the throttle of the speedboat to full and leap over the crest of a swell; it *feels good* to pull with all your strength on the net; it *feels good* to sweat and heave that 250-pound shark over the side; it *feels good* to curse and yell, the institutionalized mode of behavior in sets.

Even a "skunk" or a bad set helps to alleviate the tension and anxiety which arises from interactional or personal problems or the pressures of uncertainty and risk. The cathartic value of the sets is great. The sets alleviate tension and anxiety, but generally they do so without "solving" any problems or affecting any of the factors which cause them.

The Solution

Very few, if any, of the problems caused by anxiety, tension, or interactional or psychological difficulties are ever solved on board the boats themselves. They are almost all suppressed and either stored or sublimated in some way while aboard the boats. This seems to be the best kind of "solution" for three reasons.

First, there is a definite time to which every "reckoning" may be put off—the end of the trip. A crewman once said to me concerning bad feeling between himself and another crewman, "If he wants trouble *when we get off of the boat,* he'll get it," and went on to relate all the wrongs that had been done him by the other man, most of which were in the form of seemingly minor aspects of the other's personality and behavior which were annoying him. Another who was disturbed about a watch-scheduling problem commented: "This really makes me mad. If we weren't so close to the end of the trip I'd tell (the skipper) off." In the only two direct confrontations I witnessed which in my opinion could possibly have led to fist-fights, the strongest admonitions given were, "If you don't watch it, when we get into port. . . ." These incidents occurred on different boats, between crewmen of varying ethnicities, nationalities, attributes, and abilities.

In fact what happens, and everyone knows it, is that everything is forgotten when the boat reaches port. They often insist that the only things you remember about a trip are the good parts; the dangerous, uncomfortable, frightening, and angry parts tend to be forgotten. There is a good "reason" for this forgetfulness; everyone knows that they are going to go back out there again soon, and no one wants to return to a situation he remembers as bad or to relationships which he did not like. Besides this, when the boat gets to port there are too many things to do, too many places to go, to waste time reconciling a situation which is, as soon as the gangplank is down, part of "an old trip" which fades quickly into the more-or-less distant past.

Secondly, it is the best solution because no "solution" is really possible aboard the boat itself. Ashore, it is easy to have contests with a winner and a loser because the loser doesn't have to stick around and interact with the winner. On the boats, not only would the loser have to stick around, but he would have to remain in an intimate, uncertain, and dangerous environment with the winner, and at several points during the remainder of the trip he might well hold the fate of that "winner" in his hands because of their relationship in the boat's physical processes. Everyone realizes this, and that realization helps to suppress direct confrontations. Some situations are, of course, handled at sea with the sanctioning procedures I discussed in an earlier chapter. These are always indirect and invoked on behalf of the whole crew in the name of a social norm. They never involve a direct confrontation and are generally not used to quiet interpersonal friction between two crew members.

269

Thirdly, there is an institutionalized solution of which everyone is aware and which most fishermen's "mental set" is always ready to entertain: they can change boats when they return to port. There is a certain amount of anxiety in this solution because of the uncertainty of getting another "ride," but most men have been in the fleet long enough to gauge their chances fairly accurately, and in fact they know that in most cases the odds are in their favor.

A more general comment is that men who cannot perform in this manner—who cannot "store" energy, anxiety, or hostility—do not become (or at least do not remain) tuna fishermen. Being a tuna fisherman means accepting the idea that all manner of gratifications can and should be deferred, that kinship and friendship can yield benefits and lead to power, and that everyone around you is in the "same boat" and will be for some time. Above all, it means accepting and believing in the idea that whatever may befall you at sea, you can make up for it when you get back home.

Remember, finally, that these men are individual and independent units in more than their own psychology, attributes, skills, and preferences. They belong to an *occupation* to a much greater degree than they belong to any particular skipper or boat. The way in which crewmen move from boat to boat bears this out. It is true that each man is always dependent on the favor of his present skipper for his job. But it is also true that he is much more dependent for his continued employment in the industry on his reputation with the skippers and men in the fleet as a whole.

The average tuna fisherman has spent many years building the networks he needs to make his living in the fleet, and in the process he has learned how power is acquired and exercised and how to live and get along with others who are all attempting to exercise their individual powers and satisfy their individual needs. The results of this socialization process, more than anything else, explain the patterns of behavior and understanding which exist aboard the tunaboats.

270

11 Community and Self-Image

SEINERMEN, FOR ALL the control they exert over the workings of the boat and the fishing process, are essentially workers on someone else's boat. The crew are dependent for their jobs on the favor of the skipper, and both the skipper and the crew are in most cases dependent on the good graces of the "company" or owner. Though the unions are working to change the situation, there is very little job security for anyone in the fleet.

The general level of education in the fleet is below the average for the community in which the men reside when they are not at sea and to which they would have to turn for employment if they were not "in the fleet." Their skills, while considerable, are not for the most part saleable on shore. The bulk of the seinermen have in the past gone to sea in their middle or late teens—as soon as they have finished high school for those raised in the U.S. (and in many cases, before,) and at the age when they are traditionally considered adults or have completed compulsory military service in the case of those from the old country. Few have had other occupations. For the full-time professional fishermen who comprise the bulk of the seinermen, between one-half and three-fourths of their lives from induction into the occupation in their teens to their retirement at anywhere from age 40 to 60 is spent at sea, in a closed space, in the company of other fishermen.

Many of the seinermen possess ethnic, cultural, and linguistic characteristics which set them apart from the community in which they live ashore, in addtion to those distinctive qualities which stem from the seafaring life itself. Finally—not the least of the generalizable qualities, and one very relevant here—they may, if they work regularly, amass earnings at a level far above the average for shore-side occupations.

Most of these characteristics are common to distant-water fishermen in general. They have profound effects on the fisherman's self-perception and his relationships with his family and his community ashore.

Family and Community

When a fisherman returns from two months at sea aboard a seiner he is coming back from an adventure. He brings with him a wealth of experiences; brushes with injury or death from equipment failures, misjudgment, or clumsiness; conquests of fear and exhibitions of bravery and skill in storms, dangerous crossings, and the general hazards of a fisherman's calling; feelings of camaraderie and friendship from the weeks of confined social interaction under trying circumstances; memories of strange places and strange people. All this he brings home—but finds he cannot share. Families and friends are interested, but interested in the sense of a child being interested in "what Daddy does." They listen, but because they lack the special experience of having been to sea, they generally tire quickly of what to them are "sea stories."

The one audience to whom a fisherman can play without restraint is another fisherman. He tends to congregate with people who accept and to some extent mirror his own experience, values, behaviors, and preferences, as indeed we all do. This general phenomenon, the formation of casual social interest groups, is not unique—any men "talking shop" at a party or over the fence exhibit it. What makes it different for the fishermen is that the commonality of experience with others in their occupation is coupled with a loss of contact with their community ashore, contact which men in other occupations maintain by simply sharing the same roof with their family. Evidences of this loss of contact are very clear.

For the bulk of the young adult lives of the husband and wife, for example, and more importantly for the pre-teen years of the children, the husband is at sea. The mother, albeit with

272

the help of relatives and friends, is the resident authority, organizer, and emotional object of the household. The effect this has on the lives of the children is a story in itself; my main concern here is its effect on the fishermen. To understand these effects it is necessary to set out the various links which the fisherman at sea have with the community ashore.

While they are at sea, most fishermen keep relatively close communication with their families via high-sea radio calls, telephones in foreign ports, and messages sent with other seiners. There are, however, essentially two separate on-going social processes at work—one at sea and one on the shore.[1]

The men are involved in the social processes of the ship; working out status hierarchies and their attendant behavioral roles, learning the understandings which enable the mechanical and social orders to function smoothly, building and cementing acquaintances and friendships which are often initiated and supported by discoveries of common friends and experiences acquired during their previous periods away from home. These relationships and understandings are constantly changing. Each time a new crewman comes aboard, each time a common friendship, experience, or previously undiscovered skill is brought to light, each time a trying situation confronts the crew, these relationships and understandings develop the potential for change. These potentials for change are realized differently in each man, but all come back from each fishing trip at least slightly different men. Even small differences are accentuated when they are confronted with the changes through which the community has evolved while they were away. For the men at sea these subtle and often latent concerns *are* their world. Relationships are direct, and the immediate environment is, if not under their complete control, open to their complete scrutiny.

In the light of the total nature of the ship itself and the ship as part of the fleet at sea, the community ashore and any communications with it are extraneous inputs. This is not to say

1. I am indebted to Michael MacAlvey for suggesting this concept at a conference on socialization to maritime occupations in Wales in 1974.

that the fishermen do not care about their families and friends ashore. Most think about their loved ones a good part of the time, though mostly to themselves. It is rare for a man to talk much about them to other crewmen. Although there are, of course, exceptions (some men, for example, tape-record diaries to send or carry home to their wives and families), must extend this avoidance-of-thought to pictures and mementoes. One skipper told me that when he clears Point Loma he consciously leaves behind San Diego and all that is in it. He takes no pictures of his family, no wallet save his passport and immunization record; nothing to remind him of home. While he is an extreme case, there is a noticeable absence of memory-jogging paraphernalia aboard the boats. One who dwells on his family or friends ashore is generally chided for being homesick or "whipped." Most make a conscious attempt not to think too much about home, and into the resulting void flow the concerns inherent in dealing with their immediate shipboard environment.

The various strategies which the fishermen use for "calling home" are interesting reflections of these attitudes. The men have four ways of communicating with persons ashore: high-seas radio, VHF radio, long-distance telephone from telephones in foreign ports, and letters and packages sent out with other tunaboats.

Calls over high-seas radio have certain disadvantages. The caller must filter his conversation to avoid giving out information useful to rival fishermen. Anyone is privy to the calls, and skippers sometimes urge their crewmen, who are listening for a chance to put in their own call, to watch out for any "leads" they might hear concerning another boat's whereabouts or fishing successes. Anyone listening may readily identify the calling boat, the crewman calling, and often the approximate position of the boat—making these calls a potential source of good information. Skippers will sometimes ask a crewman to hold off for a few days on making his call to avoid giving away their position. These calls in general lack privacy and this may bother the crewmen or their wives. It is also relatively expensive—

roughly five dollars for three minutes from the areas of the Pacific where most of the fishing is done.

The VHF calls, while considerably cheaper, are subject to the same lack of privacy and have severe range limitations. They are generally used when the boat is less than a day out of port on the way home.

Shore-side telephone calls eliminate the need to filter information and afford privacy. They are, however, expensive—approximately the same as high-seas calls from the Eastern Pacific but considerably more expensive from Puerto Rico where many of the boats unload—and if the machinery runs well and the fishing proceeds normally, one may never get ashore to use them.

Letters and packages sent via other boats are slow and relatively unreliable means of communication—one boat may not see the other for quite some time—and the information they carry tends to be out-of-date by the time it arrives, although it may be very valuable personally.

There are four general strategies which the men use in calling home by radio or telephone. One is the once-or-twice-to-hear-your-voice-and-make-sure-everything's-all-right strategy. This controls the expense while maintaining contact, but the interval between calls is hard to calculate when you have no idea how long the trip may last. A second strategy is the when-we're-half-full-and-when-we're-two-days-from-port theory. This also controls the expense while timing the calls to reflect how the fishing is going and raising expectations only when it is legitimate to raise them. The third is the it's-worth-it-to-spend-the-money-and-it's-nice-to-talk-once-a-week theory. If limited to short calls this method need not be expensive, although 200-dollar-per-trip phone bills, especially in the ranks of the skippers and other full share men, are not uncommon.

The fourth strategy is that of no call home at all. This is surprisingly common, and the reasoning behind it is as follows. If I get good news, I can't celebrate or share my happiness; if I get bad news I can't do anything about it; in either case you're

275

frustrated and depressed because you're in the middle of the ocean thousands of miles away from whatever it is that's happening ashore. While this strategy is common, there are interesting reactions to it from other fishermen. A skipper-owner and an ex-navigator with whom I discussed this point both very vehemently asserted that the men who do not call home are "chicken," and that they behave in this way because they are afraid to face up to their responsibilities at home while they are at sea. The same thinking applies to the carrying of mementoes—that those who "leave the world behind" do so because they can't "handle" the fishing life with all of its attendant features.

The feeling of isolation reflected in this last strategy is no small matter. Some men grow obviously irritable and moody after calls. Others exhibit excitement and anticipation before the call which may extend through the call itself and even last for a short period after the call. There are good calls, and there are bad calls. Even a "high" from a good call is sometimes followed by a mild depression when you once again realize where you are, for how long, and what you're missing. This later concept, that of "missing" life ashore and its companion, that of "making up for the time I was gone" are common among seafarers.

Besides these immediate effects, the isolation has other long-term effects on the lives of the fishermen and their families. News of most of the significant events in a person's life—births, deaths, accidents, friends' and family's accomplishments and successes, significant political or economic happenings—is received at sea. I remember hearing a conversation one night in which a man was told that his father had died an accidental death two days earlier. Relatives had not been able to get through to the boat over high-seas radio, and from where the boat was when the man received the news there was no possible way—even if the boat headed for the closest port at full speed and the man took the first and fastest available transportation to San Diego—for the man to get home for his father's funeral, which was scheduled for three days after the day of the call. I also remember hearing a young woman tell her husband that she had miscarried

276

two weeks earlier and lost their anticipated first child. Calls of this nature are not rare events.

This kind of call is particularly excruciating because after the call, which in itself is trying enough, the man is left to think, "This happened—days ago. I was driving a speedboat. I didn't even *know*." But even if one could "know" of these things shortly after they occurred the lack of control, the inability to help, to fill the role of the man of the house in the traditional sense would still remain.

The feeling of isolation and helplessness which arise from these calls, the simple fact of physical separation, and other factors tend to drive the fishermen deeper into their own shipboard society and make them more dependent on each other. It seems to result in an exaggerated need to feel control, to feel close to some human system, to develop some relationships to which they have access at will.

When the Fleet Comes In

When the fishermen return home this isolation often does not disappear: it merely changes character. While he was at sea, busy with his job and involved with his companions, a parallel but different set of processes was at work ashore. Wives and friends were making new acquaintances and friendships; children were growing; styles and fashions were changing. A fisherman viewing life ashore and a lubber viewing life at sea—if the latter ever gets the chance—are in the same position; the one who was "there," in the system while it was evolving, may be less aware of the changes which have taken place but at the same time may be better able to understand or make sense of the results of those changes when confronted with them. The man returning or the "outsider," on the other hand, even if he can make sense of the changes, has not himself been changed by them in the same way as someone who has evolved with and in many cases has been the cause of those changes.

When the fisherman returns home, all of these factors come into play. Things have changed while he was away, and he himself has been changed by his experiences at sea. While he may

277

share in most of the experiences of his family and friends ashore, albeit from a different perspective, only other fishermen may truly share in his experiences at sea. A fisherman who only goes to sea for one or two trips in a single year, as I did, can only glimpse these effects in microcosm. The effect of this absence is cumulative in the fishermen who remain in the occupation steadily for a number of years.

A point which is obvious but whose effects are hard to visualize properly is that while he has been away the family life has gone on, in most cases smoothly. One man told me of his satisfaction at spending a few months ashore waiting for a new boat to be readied and "really getting to know and do things with" his three-year-old daughter. He said he spent much of his time playing with her and, at her request, showing her how to do things. A year later, after nine months at sea during which time he spent only two weeks at home, the same man told me that his daughter now does not want any help from him, telling him that she can and wants to do things by herself. This may be natural for a child that age. It may be that once he is home for a while (if he has that chance—he was home for two weeks when he related these things to me, and then left for another two to three months), his daughter will come to rely on him again. The point, however, is that he himself thinks that this change in his daughter's attitude was due to his absence. She may not be saying she wants to do things without her father, only that she *can*. Often "want" and "can" tend to mean the same and to be very disturbing to the fishermen.

That the household has been running smoothly also most often implies that it is the mother who has been running it. A comment I heard many, many times from wives in the San Diego fleet, and which is documented in other fleets where the husband is absent for long periods (Tunstall 1962; Anderson 1972; Iñiguez 1973), is that after the initial week or so in port the husband starts "getting in the way." Both husbands and wives are frequently heard to remark that "It's nice to be/have him home, but it's good to be/have him gone again." Each has become used to a lifestyle which out of necessity operates smoothly

278

in the other's absence. It is hard to maintain a stable, continuing relationship between any two individuals—especially an intimate relationship such as that between man and wife—on the basis of three or four months contact per year. With the seinermen, even this contact is broken up into several smaller segments. The men speak of having to get to know their wives again after each trip, much as the man mentioned above had to "get to know" his little girl again. The extreme differences in their environments when separated only accentuates this difficulty.

It is a special difficulty in light of the cultural expectations placed on the men as "heads" of their families. Normatively, they are the father figure—the disciplinarian, the provider, the person in the family with the most knowledge, ability, and control. In practice, however, they are quite peripheral to the day-to-day functioning of the family, and in many cases, they "get in the way" of many routine activities and arrangements.

Their role as disciplinarian is an example. The fathers are normatively the disciplinarians of the family, but even when the mothers threaten the children with statements like "If you don't behave you're really going to get it when your father gets home," the fathers rarely hand out harsh discipline, especially to younger children. A common scene is a father admonishing a young child with a verbal threat or stern face only to be met with a faintly pouting countenance which after a moment breaks into a giggle. That, usually, is the end of that. The father and child then indulge in some kind of play or affectionate teasing. When a man is home with his children, wife, and family for two weeks in the middle of two three-month fishing trips, the last thing he wants to do is come off as the heavy. He wants to be close to his family, to be loved and needed by them. What commonly occurs is that the mother's normally adequate control over the children's behavior falls apart and stays that way until the father goes to sea again. This and other "interfering" aspects of her husband's stay are not especially popular with the wife. She also, of course, needs love and affection from her husband, but that need is soon balanced by the plain inconvenience of his presence.

The fisherman's absence breeds a certain amount of guilt and fear of rejection in his own mind. Because the cultural expectations of his role dictate behaviors he cannot perform while he is at sea and perhaps will not even perform while he is at home, a dissonance is created between his prescribed role and his actual behavior. The fishermen feel bad about this dissonance, and guilty about being in an occupation which creates it.

At the same time they feel unsure about behaving as their role dictates for fear of being rejected by their wives and children. When you see someone only a few times a year you tend to grow unsure of their feelings toward you, especially if you notice other aspects of their thought and behavior changing from visit to visit, as the seinermen certainly do with their children and to some extent with their wives. One is very hesitant to do anything which might have a bad effect on the relationship. This is compounded when it is obvious that your wife is unhappy with your being away so much. Several fishermen told me that on every trip their wife tells them over high-seas radio, "We're going to have to have a long talk when you get home," meaning a talk about the husband's occupation. The men say that the comment always seems to be forgotten when they get back to San Diego, but its effect on the fishermen remains.

This kind of comment is especially common from wives who are not themselves from families involved in fishing or the predominant ethnic systems of the industry, or who do not live in the more spatially bounded neighborhoods of the fishermen. Particularly for the Portuguese and the Italians, the strong ethnic ties and close extended families serve as a support for the wives and children of the fishermen while the latter are at sea. Because these extended families tend to live in close proximity to one another and because boats are in and out of San Diego at different times (with the exception of the first trip of the season), there are usually others, both men and women, on whom a woman can depend and with whom she can interact in the periods of her own man's absence. These "support personnel" are generally not available to women outside the predominant ethnic and kinship systems, especially if they reside any distance from the "fishing neighborhoods."

Any one of the wives may, of course, develop a friendship with other crew wives through introductions at boat departures or arrivals, boat parties, or through the skipper's wife, who is appointed to relay information about the boat's progress to all the wives in the crew in case they do not hear from their husbands for one reason or another. Friendships like this are certainly formed, but the bulk of them occur between women who also have other ethnic, familial, or social ties. As one gringo crewman told me, "If you're not Portuguese or Italian, you and your family have to be loners to get along in this fleet."

The wife's unhappiness with her husband's absence may lead her to conceal the problems he may create in the family when he is in port. More often, however, it leads to stronger guilt feelings for the fisherman and additional conflict between him and his wife when he is at home.

On top of all of this there is a feeling among many of the fishermen that they are "locked in" to the occupation. Partly because of their lack of skills saleable ashore, and partly because of the size of their incomes from the tuna fleet and the high standard of living to which they and their families are accustomed, they feel that they *have* to go fishing. This pressure puts an extra edge on the effects of the uncertainty, danger, and deprivation of their time at sea and their anxiety about their place in their family and community ashore.

I have been discussing married men, who in fact account for the bulk of the fleet. The situation is somewhat different for the single men. The single man has fewer responsibilities to plague him when he comes into port. Unless he has been living with a girlfriend for some time, he probably has a less intimate relationship with a girl or girls with whom he spends his time ashore. In this sense he has less to "re-learn" about another person or persons each time he comes home. He also has fewer structures and systems with which he may be seen as interfering during his stay in port. On the other hand, many

281

single men lament the fact that they have nothing to come home to. Many would like to meet a girl and get married. I met only two confirmed bachelors during the periods of my research.

Meeting women is more difficult for a fisherman than for a man with a job ashore, for three reasons. First, he simply spends less time ashore, time which would normally contain introductions and other encounters with people of the opposite sex. Second, fishing does not conjure up the best image in the minds of prospective partners, either in terms of the relative status of the occupation or the desirability of attaching oneself to a man who is at sea most of the time. Third, when a man returns home he is often "out of it" in terms of the understandings one needs to deal with women, understandings which, depending on the age group, change with fads in dress, interactional styles, preferred social "spots," and many other things. In this he is much like a man who is divorced after many years of marriage; he simply does not know where to start. One of the crewmen on my first boat compared fishermen to men in prison; he said neither knows how to act when he "gets out."

Single men also tend to have more money problems with their girlfriends. All of the crewmen, married men included, joke quite a bit as the boats are a day or two out of port on the way to the fishing grounds, saying things like "Two days, and I'll bet she's got my shares spent already," speaking of their wives or girlfriends. Wives who "take the money and run" are not unknown in the fleet, but single men seem to get caught more often. A wife has some legal commitment to her husband, but a girlfriend has none. One has no real recourse against a woman who has, for example, accepted a car as a present and then used it to make her getaway. In fact, the men to whom this has happened do not seem to make any great attempts to recover the merchandise, but the myth which this kind of female behavior creates does not improve the single fishermen's attitude toward women.

I do not mean to picture fishermen as retiring, guilt-ridden clods with their women and within their families; in fact they are not. They are for the most part excellent providers, and most

282

of their interactions with their wives and families when they are home are warm and loving, perhaps even more so than those in a family with a "normal" breadwinner. The word which epitomizes the feelings and attitudes I have been discussing is timidity, a timidity which clashes with the boldness with which they perform their tasks aboard the boats and many of their other actions ashore.

The fishermen themselves are aware of these situations, and this helps to reconcile them to another trip to sea. On the other hand, they do not think that the situations are desirable, and many often wonder aloud whether "normality" in the sense of average Southern California family structure and interaction might not be better in many ways.

The Fisherman and the Larger Community

The isolation which the fishermen feel from the larger community is perhaps as important as the isolation from the family, but it is harder to illustrate. The most obvious isolating factors are apparent within the ranks of the first-generation ethnic members of the fleet. These are both the older men and women who have lived in San Diego for many years and the new immigrants who have been "sponsored" over from the old country by their relatives with promises of jobs in the fleet. They are generally the Portuguese and the Italians who reside in the communities described in earlier chapters. Many have been here for twenty or thirty years and still do not speak a word of English. There are checkers in the markets, tellers in the banks, and other service personnel in the areas where they live who speak their language. There is always a relative who speaks English and can transact their business when necessary. I have several times done this.[2] The areas in which they live contain outlets for most of their needs within walking distance, hence they do not need

2. Because of the similarities in the languages themselves and the fact that the Spanish, Portuguese, and Italian spoken in the fleet have tended to "borrow" from one another over the years, my knowledge of Spanish supplemented by a few words from the other two languages was sufficient to allow me to communicate with those in the fleet who did not speak English.

283

cars. When I asked some of these men—both Portuguese and Italian—why they never learned the language they answered, "Why should we?"

There are many of these first-generation men and women who have, of course, learned the language and customs of their adopted country very quickly and very well. My landlord in the Portuguese community is an outstanding example. His English is flawless and he prides himself in his vocabulary and the fact that he is trilingual—Portuguese, Spanish, English, and a little Italian. He drives, is active in a local lodge, and at 70 is still a busy carpenter and workman besides fulfilling all his roles in the Socidade Espirito Santo and other ethnic activities of the Portuguese community. There are others like him.

Even these men and women, however, and especially those without a knowledge of English, are outside the mainstream of San Diego's relatively urban lifestyle. They have been socialized under a very different system in a very different milieu (many of the old-country people are from the Azores or Sicily—small, relatively undeveloped island communities), and they spend most of their time once they arrive here at sea, away from the contact which could erode their old traditions and introduce them to new ones.

Other isolating factors apply to fishermen aside from those of ethnicity and language. At sea most of the men are away from news of politics, sports, economics, fashions, and other trends in behavior or thought. To come home months after the publication of the first popular book about wife-swapping; to miss the news of the months prior to a President's resignation; to catch only the tail end of a fight to keep a popular sports franchise in town; to return to a wardrobe out of date with the appearance of bell-bottoms—these are real cultural shocks. These gaps in knowledge or experience are seldom total with respect to any one phenomenon, but taken together over a period of years they add up to a considerable lack of understanding of the events which shape the values and attitudes of the larger community.

There are also subtler, but often just as pervasive phenomenon which affect the returning fisherman. One of these is the sheer speed and confusion of the environment ashore as opposed to that at sea. At sea the external stimuli may be numerous but they are limited, categorizable, usually anticipated, and above all generally susceptible to *direct* control and action. In San Diego, however, the fisherman often finds himself exposed to stimuli that seem overwhelming in number, difficult to fit into his cognitive "map," unexpected, and seemingly beyond his ability to control.

One skipper told me he "can't" drive his car for three or four days upon his return from sea; he is used to fifteen miles per hour, not fifty, and things just happen too fast. Otherwise unargumentative fishermen relate stories of encounters with police, especially over traffic violations, where they were punished for disobeying a rule that as far as they could see in their own particular case was unnecessary and more importantly beyond their power to affect or fight. Standing in lines, minor rules of etiquette such as voice control in terms of volume—fishermen are often described as "loud"—and many other day-to-day situations the lubber has learned to accept are strange and difficult for the fisherman.

All of these factors tend to isolate the fisherman from the larger community, to make him withdraw into the social circle of his fishing friends. The fishermen do, however, have to live in the larger community and on many occasions deal with its representatives and situations. They do this by turning the benefits of their isolation to their advantage.

The Fisherman and His Resources

The most obvious of these benefits is the fact that the fishermen make a lot of money. Full-share men on the boats on which I sailed on during my research grossed $18,000 for the year on the smaller boat and $30,000 on the larger. Averages are hard to work with, especially in the face of the share system of payment and the uncertainty inherent in the venture, but these figures give a general impression of the salaries one might expect to make as a full-time participant in the industry.

This level of earnings gives the fishermen a considerable

amount of freedom and various kinds of power. For some it is the freedom to ignore the larger community. Many of the first-generation fishermen, for example, can live in their own communities and never venture out of them except at their pleasure. They can afford to pay the price to bring what they need into the community and sustain the accoutrements of their social institutions, for example Portuguese Hall. Properly invested—the favorite investment in the Portuguese community seems to be income property—these earnings can sustain them nicely into their retirement.

The money also gives some of them—particularly the younger fishermen—the power to compete with the larger community in the acquisition and display of various status objects. Fancy cars, clothes, houses, furniture, and gifts are all the desired objects of the larger society and those fishermen who desire them certainly have their share. While some of these objects give satisfaction in themselves, others are purchased simply to impress other people, as conspicuous consumption. Upon those who have spent time around the harbor and have seen the styled hair, leather coats, diamond rings, and fancy clothes of some of the fishermen and the big cars, well-dressed children, and furs of the women who come to see their men off on a trip or provide their homecoming, conspicuous consumption certainly makes its mark.

The story is told of the old fisherman who, nicely attired in his golfing clothes, strode up to the businessman's table in a fashionable restaurant, pounded his diamond-dressed hand on the table, and uttered words to the effect of, "You think you're so good because you have an education and make a lot of money. Well I have just as much as you—probably more!" He may or may not have been right, but it is the ability to see himself as "competitive" in this manner that his living as a fisherman has brought him.

Much of the value of their earnings lies in the ability it gives them to sustain the romantic myth of the seafaring fisherman. This myth pictures fishermen as high-rolling, impulsive, honest, able men with the ability to get what they want and take care of their responsibilities. They are very proud of the fact that whether their venture might be a rowdy evening in a local bar or the instant purchase of a car which a wife admired in passing a showroom window, they can be counted on to provide more than adequately. There are stories of bar fights where one of the fishermen involved replaced the broken equipment and furniture out of his own pocket the first thing the next morning; parties where a stained drapery or carpet was replaced by new wares at the expense of one or more of the guests; car purchases where the buyer drove the car away with no payment save his promise to return with the total bill in cash—all carried out with flair befitting men who do as they please and willingly accept the consequences. Most of the fishermen do not break up bars, have wild parties, or buy everything that passes under their noses. Some of them periodically exhibit some of these characteristics, but almost all of them enjoy the *myth* of these behaviors.

Many of these behaviors and their accompanying myths are reactions to their deprivations and isolation at sea and the inadequacies they feel ashore. Their lack of educational status, their relative job insecurity, their loss of understanding through socialization stemming from their frequent and lengthy absences from the shore-side "systems" bring forth reactions in the form of conspicuous consumption, their "myth" and its attendant behaviors, and their strict adherence to the values of direct financial responsibility.

Much of what I have written in this chapter has been in the way of caricature. Many of the families, for example, exhibit very few if any of the characteristics mentioned here. The same is true for the reactions of the fishermen to their shore environment. Traces of all these phenomena, however, exist in all fishermen and their families to some degree; and the main point is that they exist to a degree much greater than that found in nonfishing families. The impressions which most people carry with them of others, and in many cases use as determinants in their own behavior, are in fact myths, albeit tempered by a small

287

amount of first-hand information. This makes it at least as important to understand those myths as it is to record the actual behavior itself.

The Full Circle

When you ask the fishermen why they fish, one of the first things they say is that they do it for the money. Especially when they are at sea, they make a point of grumbling about their situation, and some are heard to swear that if they could get a job ashore that could support them at anywhere near the level fishing does, they would jump at it in a minute.

But, they will also tell you they enjoy the feeling of accomplishment that work in the fleet brings. They leave San Diego with an empty boat, fifteen men, and only their skill and experience to aid them. They return with their living in the holds, wrested "with no help from anyone" from the often dangerous and always seemingly recalcitrant ocean. This thought is worth a lot to them. It is this exhibition of skill, courage, patience, and persistence which generates the pride the fishermen feels in his occupation. Only one who has experienced fishing can understand this pride, and this fact robs the profession of shore-side status and brings into play the reactions set out in this chapter.

Finally, they will tell you that the profession provides a nicely cyclical and varied lifestyle. They feel bad when they leave, but they get over it; there are often opportunities to visit interesting places, places where because of their relative wealth combined with their "visitor" status they can live exactly as their myth of themselves dictates. After a period of the seafaring life they return to family and loved ones and the attendant parties, get-togethers, and intimacies. When they get tired of that, when the strangeness of all the rules and regulations of life ashore and the humdrum of everyday family life close in on them, there is the next fishing trip to once again take them away from it all.

References

ANDERSON, R. 1972. "Hunt and Deceive: Information Management in Newfoundland Deep-sea Trawler Fishing," in *North Atlantic Fishermen: Anthropological Essays on Modern Fishing* (R. Anderson and C. Wadel, eds.). Toronto: University of Toronto Press.

ANDERSON, R., and WADEL, C. 1972. *North Atlantic Fishermen: Anthropological Essays on Modern Fishing.* Toronto: University of Toronto Press.

BACK, K. 1951. Influence through Social Communication. *Journal of Abnormal and Social Psychology,* 46: 9-23.

BARTH, F. 1966. *Models of Social Organization,* Occasional Papers of the Royal Anthropological Association, 23.

COLE, MICHAEL, et al. 1971. *The Cultural Context of Learning and Thinking.* New York: Basic Books, Inc.

DICKIE, L. 1969. "The Strategy of Fishing." Unpublished manuscript. Dartmouth, Nova Scotia.

FIRTH, R. 1966. *Malay Fishermen: Their Peasant Economy.* London: Routledge and Kegan Paul.

FRICKE, P. 1974. Personal communication.

GORDON, H. S. 1954. "The Economic Theory of a Common Property Resource: The Fishery." *Journal of Political Economy* (April), 57: 124-142.

HERBST, P. G. 1968. "Interpersonal Distance Regulation and Affective Control in Merchant Ships." *European Journal of Social Psychology,* 1: 1, 47-58.

INIGUEZ, F., Jr. 1973. Personal communication.

Inter-American Tropical Tuna Commission. 1971. *Publications Issued by the Inter-American Tropical Tuna Commission* (Series). Scripps Institute of Oceanography, La Jolla, California.

LEWIS, T. 1973. "Stochastic Resource Management in Ocean Fisheries." Unpublished manuscript.

LOFGREN, O. 1972. "Resource Management and Family Firms: Swedish West Coast Fishermen," in *North Atlantic Fishermen: Anthro-*

pological Essays on Modern Fishing (R. Anderson and C. Wadel, eds.). Toronto: University of Toronto Press.

MOUSTGAARD, P. 1975. Personal communication.

PACIFIC PACKERS REPORT. 1975. Supplement to *National Fisherman,* Vol. 55, No. 12 (April).

PERRIN, W. 1968. "The Porpoise and the Tuna." *Sea Frontiers,* 14: No. 3 (May–June).

———— 1969. "The Problem of Porpoise Mortality in the U.S. Tropical Tuna Fishery." *Proceedings of the Sixth Annual Conference on Biological Sonar and Diving Mammals.* Stanford Research Institute, Stanford, California.

QUINN, N. 1971. "Mfantse Fishing Crew Composition: A Decision-making Analysis." Ph.D. dissertation, Stanford University.

STILES, G. 1971. "Fishermen, Wives, and Radios: Aspects of Communication in a Newfoundland Fishing Community," in *North Atlantic Fishermen: Anthropological Essays on Modern Fishing* (R. Anderson and C. Wadel, eds.). Toronto: University of Toronto Press.

TUNSTALL, J. 1962. *The Fishermen.* London: MacGibbon and Kee.

WADEL, C. 1971. "Capitalization and Ownership: The Persistence of Fishermen-ownership in the Norwegian Herring Fishery," in *North Atlantic Fishermen: Anthropological Essays on Modern Fishing* (R. Anderson and C. Wadel, eds.). Toronto: University of Toronto Press.

ZOLESSI, J. 1974. Personal communication.

Index

49; picking up the skiff, 65–67; retrieving the net, 46–57; removing porpoise from the seine, 55–57; "rolling net," in, 50–51; setting the net, 36–47; stacking the net, 51–53. *See also* Setting the net

Seniority: and share system, 189–190; as source of power, 247

Set: and bullet fish, 101–102; completion of and preparation for, 67; cruising speed for, 45; decision to, 84, 87–89, 93–94; defined, 28; directions during, 222, 229; mistakes during, 47, 228; "skunk," 87, 88

"Setting on bubbles," 76

Setting the net, 36–47; on porpoise, 93–94, 96–98; and release of anxiety, 268; on school fish not "showing," 81; strain on equipment during, 88

Shaft alley, 17–18, 266

Share system: average salaries in, 285; compared to tonnage system, 187–188; described, 174–176; "earning" the full share, 190–193; pressure from, 250; principles and economics of, 182–185; raises in, 175, 186, 189–190; relative to job and proficiency, 189–193; "split-shares," 170, 172; and switching boats, 177

Sharks: danger of in the backing-down process, 56–57; elimination of from the catch, 60; as indicators of tuna, 73; and porpoise, 90; in the powerblock, 54–55; in the sack, 59

"Shiners," 85

Sicily, 2

Sideband radios, 106. *See also* Radio Communications

Sightings: categories of, 83–87; evaluation of, 84, 86–87

Signs, in personal interactions, 267

Signs of fish, 82; evaluation of, 84–87; in the search area, 72–75, 78

Skiff: in brailing, 57–58, 61–62; described, 37; driver of, 19, 242–243; picking up of, 65–67; in setting the net, 45–46

Skills: proficiency in, 189–193, 194; required of crew, 219–221, 238, 240–243

Skipjack tuna: compared to yellowfin, 5, 22, 69–70, 98; decision by skipper to fish for, 69–70; as "log" fish, 101; orientation of to floating objects, 73; price of, 69, 70; as a school fish, 98

Skipper(s), 47, 74, 97, 99, 177, 219, 225, 229, 230, 239, 245, 248, 254, 270, 274; cabin of, 20–21; and calling home, 275, 276; change in code group by, 115–116; and cleavages in crew, 259–260; confrontations among, 143, 147; in control of crewmen's shares, 175–176, 185–187; and crew, 146–147, 250–253; decision of to set, 84, 87–89, 93, 103; directions given by, 221–222, 228; as an elite egalitarian, 249–253; ethnicities of, 256–257; evaluation of sightings by, 83–84, 86–87, 103; hiring practices of, 167–172; honesty of, 120, 126–127; "hunch" vs. rational decisions by, 78–80; "hunger" of, 89, 199; individual differences in and information from others used by, 75–78, 102–103; information strategies of, 117–131; and inter-boat rules, 141–145, 147–148, 160–161; language used by, 94; and national boundary claims, 136–139; and "paper" officers, 18–19; radio functions and styles of, 105, 107–109; and releasing information, 110–111; relationship with owners and managers, 163–165, 186; salaries of, 165, 193; shares of, 184–185, 193; selection of the search area by, 68–72, 102–103; in setting the net, 45–47; skills of, 238; and uncertainty, 200–202. *See also* Status: of skippers